BRITISH SPEEDWAY

First published in December 2013 in the UK by
Retro Speedway
Tel: 01708 734 502
www.retro-speedway.com
©Copyright Retro Speedway

Designed by William Clayton
Printed by Henry Ling Ltd
Distributed by Retro Speedway
103 Douglas Road, Hornchurch, Essex, RM11 1AW, England
Distribution email: subs@retro-speedway.com

ISBN 978-0-9559340-8-7

CONTENTS

ACKNOWLEDGEMENTS

Apart from the 200 or so editorial contributors to this book (whose names all appear on p255), we would also like to thank the following for their help and co-operation :

Photographers Ken Carpenter, Alf Weedon, John Hipkiss, Mike Patrick, Mike Clatworthy, Jeff Davies, Eddie Garvey.

John Somerville, Speedway Star.

Front cover pictures (clockwise):

Simon Wigg (England) leading Bobby Schwartz (USA) and Larry Ross (New Zealand) at King's Lynn, 1984 World Team Cup qualifier (Ken Carpenter).

Peter Collins inside Michael Lee at White City, 1977 Inter-Continental Final (Mike Patrick).

Ove Fundin leading Peter Craven (Alf Weedon).

INTRODUCTION

By Tony McDonald

FOR most of us, memories are all we have left. But as none of us are planning to rush off from this planet anytime soon, no matter how much we might get down about our great sport, I thought it might be a good idea to share our favourite speedway recollections, anecdotes and opinions and then gather them all together in one handy place of reference.

During the 2013 season we at Retro Speedway distributed a questionnaire asking 10 questions and invited supporters, ex-riders, promoters, team managers, announcers, PROs, track staff and journalists to respond. We're happy to say that around 200 of you did and over the next 250-plus pages I hope you enjoy discovering some shared experiences and general reminiscing among kindred spirits.

The bad news is, I get to go first, so please indulge me as I enter a world of nostalgia and take you back to the start of the 70s . . .

FIRST TIME

Tell us about the first speedway meeting you remember attending and what or who led you to go?

I blame it all on Joanne Bond for starting a childhood obsession that became my career. Chasing after long-legged girls with blonde hair and beautiful blue eyes can get a man into an awful lot of trouble, but in this case it was all very innocent fun. You see Joanne was just eight-years-old and I was 10 – two school years above her at Chadwell Heath Primary – when we first met some time in 1970.

Her parents, Brian and Maureen, and youngest sister Denise moved in just across the road from us in Fauna Close, so our families became friends. As kids, we bounced around the quiet cul-de-sac on our orange Spacehoppers and it was when I visited her house that I discovered her father was an avid speedway supporter.

There was always a copy of *Speedway Star* on display in the living room and when Brian had finished reading it I'd pick it up to see what he found so interesting. It soon became clear that the Bonds were all mad-keen on this sport that I knew nothing about and all four of them would regularly attend several meetings a week, at West Ham, Hackney and sometimes Rayleigh and Wimbledon, on the evenings the girls weren't attending swimming lessons.

Like me, Brian also supported the same football team, West Ham United, so we hit it off straight away. I was soon invited to join them on their speedway travels and Brian would also take me along to Upton Park on Saturdays.

My father, Terry, took me to West Ham Speedway once or twice in the mid-60s, when I was about five or six. I vaguely remember us being at Custom House the night Dave Wills was

The programme that marked West Ham's sad demise in 1972.

killed in 1965, although I have no clear recollection of the meeting itself or that tragic accident.

The first meeting I recall seeing was the individual Mike Letch Trophy event at Rye House on Sunday, October 16, 1970, in the days when the little Hertfordshire venue operated on an open licence basis and staged only a handful of meetings each season. Mike Letch was a 21-year-old Aussie trying to make his way in the sport when he cruelly suffered career-ending spinal injuries in a crash at Rye a couple of months earlier and this meeting was to raise money for the lad from Melbourne who would never walk again.

Ipswich's John 'Tiger' Louis, the meeting winner, made a big impression on me in his distinctive amber-and-black striped leathers. In those days the pits at Rye House were situated about halfway along the back straight, with only a thin rope separating the riders from the fans walking past. It was fascinating to get up so very close to them and their bikes and there is no doubt that being able to see the riders away from the track, especially in the pits, all helps to fuel a newcomer's enthusiasm for speedway.

Little did I know how Mike Letch would re-enter my life more than 40 years later.

With Simmo at Rye House for his book signing in 2006.

I was eager to see more and just two nights later Brian drove us to West Ham for the Hammers' final meeting of the season against King's Lynn Stars, who were spearheaded by Terry Betts and Malcolm Simmons. How could I possibly know then how Mike Letch and Simmo would re-enter my life in much different circumstances some 35-40 years later.

In 2012, an appeal through our two magazines raised £1,500 for Mike to buy a new lightweight wheelchair to make his life a little more comfortable. I admired how he made the most of his life by being so active and becoming a deep sea diving instructor back home in Melbourne and it was a sad day when he died of kidney failure in November 2013.

I 'ghosted' Simmo's column in *Speedway Mail* when he signed for Hackney in 1986 and 20 years later we published his controversial book, *Simmo: The Whole Truth*, followed in 2009 by his story on DVD. Malcolm also became our first star name columnist in *Backtrack*.

Although my first taste of speedway had been all too brief before the curtain came down on the 1970 season, I was well and truly hooked and took every opportunity from then on to keep tabs on the sport via Brian Bond's copy of *Speedway Star*, reading every issue from cover to cover and studying every picture in great detail. From the start of the 1971 season, speedway virtually took over my life.

My passion for the sport continued after the Bonds moved further out in Essex and we lost contact for many years. Then, out of the blue, Brian phoned the Retro Speedway office one day to take out a subscription to *Backtrack* magazine. By then, he knew what he'd started!

TEAMS & TRACKS
Where did/do you watch speedway most regularly?

As I said, I was taken regularly to West Ham, Hackney, Romford, Wimbledon, Rayleigh and Rye House from the start of the 1971 season – we were spoilt for choice in London and the south-east in those days, although the demise of Romford and West Ham within the space of seven months in 1971-72 was a terrible double blow. At the last ever meeting at Custom House (where the Bombers had set up temporary home for seven weeks before they, too, were evicted), I remember getting all the home riders to sign a team photograph I'd bought that night and then scouring the floor of the pits picking up discarded visors. When the crowd had virtually all left for the last time, I think me and my school mates even ran a lap of that famous, old track before we said our own 'goodbyes' to the place and, months later, the bulldozers arrived to do their dirty deed.

At Hackney, we were part of a regular crowd, including our very vocal good friend Tony Lee, who stood in front of the main stand at the entrance to the first bend. My dad, Terry, also joined us most Fridays. I wore a kids' replica Hackney racejacket bought from the track shop and would run up and down, or ride around our close on my pushbike, pretending I was Bengt Jansson or Garry Middleton.

I attended my first Hackney away match in 1973, aged 13. It was a different world back then. Parents thought nothing of letting their kids travel around on public transport and one Saturday I booked myself on to the Hackney supporters' club coach for an adventure to Cradley Heath. To make the evening even more memorable, the Hawks claimed a rare and fully deserved away win.

That night was also my first experience of dodgy promoters trying to pull a flanker. With Hackney coasting to inevitable victory, the home management suddenly decided it would be a good idea to hold the weekly raffle draw after Heat 11, just after the heavens opened and rain was falling. It was farcical. The draw seemed to go on forever and I can still hear the musical strains of Leo Sayer singing 'Oh, look at it rain' – a line from his hit record *One Man Band* that was playing over the tannoy as the wet stuff continued to lash down.

Fortunately, this crude and cynical ploy by the Cradley promotion to try and get the meeting abandoned failed miserably. The last two heats of the match were completed just in time for our boys to complete a handsome 49-29 win.

It was a memorable night for others reasons, though. As I soon discovered, Sampson's coaches (sorry, Pete, for dragging this up!) Hackney SSC used for away transport had a nasty habit of breaking down and on this occasion we were still stranded in the car park at Dudley Wood Stadium until around midnight before they finally got the thing going.

The problem was, I'd arranged for my mum, Jean, to meet me back at Hackney Stadium at around the same time we left the Black Country. Obviously, in those days long before mobiles and no phone box in sight, I was unable to make contact with her to warn her of the delay. She was still waiting patiently at the wheel of her green Ford Escort – festooned with speedway stickers that I'd plastered on every available inch of the rear and side windows – when the coach eventually limped into Waterden Road at something like three o'clock on the Sunday morning. It was nearly daylight by the time she drove us home to Chadwell Heath.

By this time I'd long since given up early childhood dreams of following Dad and becoming a professional footballer. He'd played in the same late-50s West Ham United youth team as Bobby Moore and John Lyall, who would go on to become England's iconic World Cup-winning captain of 1966 and the Hammers' longest-serving manager respectively. After Dad left West Ham to join their East London neighbours Leyton Orient, he scored their famous winner against Manchester United in 1962. O's fans still talk about his goal and the club's only season in the top flight when Dad – a nippy and tricky left-winger in his day – and I go there to watch games now. So how could I possibly follow that?

I didn't have a clue what I wanted to do before or after leaving school – other than dream of becoming a top speedway rider. At the age of around 11, I rode a 24-inch cycle with a red 'glitter' frame that I stripped down to make it look more like a speedway bike. I shortened the mudguards and fitted cowhorn handlebars with red and white twist grips. I'd cycle up to the disused Hawbush Hammers cycle speedway track near the main Eastern Avenue at Goodmayes and spend hours riding around, sometimes with friends but often alone. I'd change my 'style' for every 'race' and imagine I was different riders.

At home we had an L-shaped kitchen with a slippery tiled floor – perfect for me to come running down the hallway and broadside in my socks while attempting to turn left at the correct moment, which was roughly the midway point of the kitchen. The room was probably shaped a bit like the first bend at Newport's Somerton Park. It was great fun trying to judge precisely how to avoid the fridge but my antics drove Mum mad as she was trying to prepare dinner.

When I wasn't belting through our kitchen at the speed of light and pulling perfectly timed 'lockers', more often than not I'd be playing the speedway game Mum made especially for me. She was a school teacher, quite artistic and the piece of cardboard on which she painted a perfectly symmetrical shale-coloured oval around a green centre and white inside line, plus a white safety fence and even crowd faces around the edge, was better than anything Picasso ever knocked up as far as I was concerned. My 'riders' were those Britains die-cast speedway models, which came in packs of two – one rider in red helmet, the other in white, but a spot of blue and yellow paint soon sorted out that problem.

After a few years, I'd worn my 'track' out to such an extent that both bends were cutting up quite badly, so Mum had to design me a new one. I think she even widened the bends and lengthened the straights with the Mark II version and I still have it in the shed. See, who needs Len Silver, Colin Meredith or Ole Olsen?

Mayfield Boys secondary school did nothing to improve my academic education but I learned everything I possibly could about speedway throughout my time there. I'd pick up *Speedway Star* magazine from the local newsagent's on Wednesday and the *Speedway Mail* newspaper on Friday and my day was totally ruined if either was not there to collect for whatever reason. I'd take the two weekly publications (as well as the monthly *Speedway Express*) and sit at the back of the class, minding my own business. Unruly pupils would be causing mayhem and running rings round the teacher while

My 'school books' were essential reading and I studied every word and photo.

I'd keep my mouth shut and my head down, looking at the pages on my lap to see if Ivan Mauger had dropped a point in the previous week, or who Garry Middleton was having a go at. I'd be completely absorbed in every word and every picture, studying each one in detail. I was academically thick but I could read and write well enough and would have got a degree in speedway as a schoolboy.

We live in the digital age where the answer to everything is now at the click of a mouse. But back in the 70s, the only way to find out the night's speedway results was to listen to radio stations that bothered to broadcast them, or wait and check the morning papers that carried the match results and one or two top scorers. If the names I. Mauger and O. Olsen weren't showing with 15, 14, 12 or 11 (five rides or four) next to their name, you'd have to wait until *Speedway Star* came out the following Wednesday to find out what had gone wrong.

I didn't care much for girls, drinking or smoking, the things most teenage boys of my age were into at the time. All my mates loved playing and watching football – we were mainly West Ham fans – and we were keen on our music, too. T-Rex, Bowie, Rod Stewart and Pink Floyd were particular favourites – we'd go round each other's houses and play the latest new vinyl single or album. But no-one else in my senior school had any interest in speedway and I guess that is still the case for most young fans today. It's like you are part of some special secret society that no-one knows about. Perhaps for that reason some of the lads at school thought I was a bit nerdy but I always had plenty of mates and I loved football as much as speedway, so that kept me in with the in-crowd.

I sent off for catalogues from Barry Briggs Racing and Rivetts Leathers and started to add up what it would cost to buy a 500cc speedway bike and all the gear I'd need to start racing. I'm absolutely useless at maths (failed the 11-plus exam miserably) but even I quickly worked out that I couldn't afford it on my pocket money and there was no way my parents would agree to help me do something so dangerous. In truth, I would never have had the bottle to be a speedway rider anyway and, to this day, I've never ridden a motorcycle of any kind.

Others among our little group on the Hackney terraces included Barbara and Andy Reeves and their friend Geoff Woolley. By 1975, the two Kent tracks, Canterbury and the newly reopened Crayford, were added to our regular rota. The following year, Andy, Geoff and

Just some of the British fans who travelled to Poland by train for the 1976 World Final.

myself travelled all over the country to watch the Hawks and see many other meetings in the south-east – invariably accompanied by the sound of The Eagles' *Greatest Hits (1971-75)* album (on cassette tape, of course). I'd just left senior school in May, so had plenty of time on my hands before starting a year's electrical engineering course at Redbridge Tech the following September. Electrical engineering? Do me a favour. I even managed to mix up the blue and brown leads when wiring a household plug, so that was another waste of a year. But I didn't care. This was my happiest time watching speedway and we must have attended getting on for a hundred meetings in that sweltering summer of 1976 when hosepipes were banned and there wasn't a rain-off in sight.

I do, however, recall one particularly horrendous late night journey back from The Boulevard, Hull when the weather wasn't too good. There was thick fog all the way down the A1 to Essex and to make matters worse, the windscreen wipers on Reevo's clapped-out Ford Anglia packed up. Perhaps Sampson's Coaches weren't so bad after all.

Despite the late night return from Cradley, Mum always encouraged my love of speedway and in 1976 she paid for me to go to Poland at the age of 16. I travelled to the World Final at Katowice by boat and the Warnersports train tha transported more than 1,000 British speedway fans via West Berlin, 'Checkpoint Charlie' and beyond the iron curtain. It was a different world from what we knew and took for granted. I shared a carriage with a couple of fellow Hackney fans, father and son Tom and Graham Warner, and former Scunthorpe and Boston rider Chris Emery. Tom has since passed on but I still see Graham at the annual Celebration of Speedway event at Paradise Wildlife Park.

Visiting communist Poland at such a young age was a great experience but the Ministry of Defence didn't quite share my enthusiasm for my visit to Eastern Europe when, a year after the '76 World Final, I went for a job interview as a clerical assistant in the Old War Office Building in Whitehall. I somehow got the job but my MoD inquisitors took some convincing that I'd gone to Silesia to see Peter Collins win the world title, not as part of a commie spying mission.

In my one year working in the Army Air Department of the civil service, slaving away and kowtowing to majors and colonels who looked down their noses at us riff-raff civvies, I tried to enlighten them by filling the walls of our adjacent office with full page pictures taken from the covers of *Speedway Star* (I left just enough space for my punk fan colleague to stick up pics of the Sex Pistols and all that rubbish).

Then, mercifully, *Speedway Mail* saved me from a life of boredom. I was staying in a caravan in Dorset – base for a West Country speedway tour of Weymouth, Poole and Bristol with Geoff Woolley – when I phoned home to be given the ecstatic news that I'd passed the interview at the *Mail* and they would be employing me as an 'editorial assistant' from August 1978.

What was/is your favourite away track to visit, and why?

There were so many and for different reasons. Most northern venues seemed so big and fast compared to the majority of the southern tracks I was used to and Belle Vue's Hyde Road had everything. Although the zoological gardens had seen better days and was partially closed by the time of my first visit in the mid-70s, it was still a unique place to watch speedway in Britain. Where else could you enjoy thrilling rides on the adjacent funfair – a section of it towering above the stadium so that you could catch an aerial view of that brilliant racetrack – and be treated to some of the best racing to be found anywhere in the speedway world?

Halifax and Exeter, with their steeply banked tracks and, like Belle Vue, offering a very close-up view of the action, were also different.

Before the M11 was built, journeys to King's Lynn via the A11 and those rural A-roads was also much more scenic compared to the lengthy hauls up the M1 and M6. The racing at Saddlebow Road was rarely short of first class on a well-prepared, ultra-fair track. Martin Rogers always ensured the presentation was top notch and because of his journalistic knowledge of the sport and reputation as a shrewd administrator, he would engage the crowd with a few complimentary and informed words about each of the visiting riders as well as the Lynn team. With the introductions complete, his memorable line as the bikes roared into life (in the days before Health & Safety stopped pre-meeting parades without crash helmets) was: "Ladies and gentleman, boys and girls, welcome one and all to Sunshine Speedway, Saddlebow Road . . . the home of the King's Lynn Staaaaaarrrrs!" I'm not sure if the 'sunshine speedway' bit was still a valid claim on those occasions when a cold chill blew across the fens on Pride of the East night in late October, but it was certainly unforgettable.

My Rayleigh hero Bob Young tries to give me the slip at the entrance to the dressing rooms.

If Hackney were my British League Division One team, then their sister track Rayleigh were my second division favourites – which made Romford an 'away' track, even though, if the wind was blowing in a certain direction, I could hear the noise of the bikes from my bedroom window a few miles away. Remember those blue decimal currency wallets that contained various coins of different denominations that came out in PM Ted Heath's reign early in 1971 and which your mum or your gran bought for you and told you to put away somewhere safe? Well, I wasn't having any of that. The first chance I had, I removed the odd-looking 50 pence and the other coins in the set and that loose change just about covered my child's entrance fee to Brooklands.

Tiger Beech with my rosette of him in 2011.

Sadly, I only saw the Bombers in their final

season there but the Essex rivalry with Rayleigh enlivened many a Thursday meeting and that fearsome, low concrete wall that somehow passed for a 'safety fence' was something else.

FAVOURITES

Name your three most favourite (not necessarily the best) riders, and why you have chosen them?

Sorry, but I'm going to take liberties here and name as many as 17 who meant something special to me as a supporter and then journalist.

Bengt Jansson: My first hero. His last bend swoops at Hackney, where he feigned to go round his opponents on the last bend before checking back and nipping past them on the inside as they approached the finish line, were pure class.

'Banger' had the cool, calculating racing brain of a computer; he could probably have been an international chess player in another life. And as I happily discovered when I got to know him many years later, the quiet Swede is a lovely man, too.

Christer Lofqvist: West Ham might have been our arch East London rivals, but on any visit to Custom House no-one could have failed to be entertained by the little Swede who was the Kelly Moran of the early 70s.

Christer hanging off the back of his two-valve Jawa in those familiar navy blue leathers with yellow stripes, and the sounds of *Sweet Caroline* and *Chirpy Chirpy Cheep Cheep,* are what made Tuesday nights at West Ham memorable for me.

Bob Young: Although never a star in the top flight, tall, slim Bob stood out for me at Rayleigh, where his all-turquois blue leathers caught the eye. It was great for us kids the way we could peer over the pits fence and look down on the riders working on their bikes between races and of, course, shove a programme or photo in their direction and ask them to sign it, which they always did willingly.

Apart from his lean and leggy riding style, what also impressed this 11-year-old about Aussie Bob was that he had this strange accent from a faraway land, in the days when the only 'foreigners' in the second tier were Aussies and Kiwis and before the floodgates opened to every Tomasz, Drazjan and Henning.

Tiger Beech: My other big favourite at Rayleigh was the young man with the Peter Sarstedt dark hair and moustache with yellow-and-black striped football shirt over his leathers. The girls loved him but so did the lads – we all wanted to be him.

In some ways Dave Beech was a throwback to the pre-war Johnnie Hoskins era when all the riders were given nicknames by which they were known – there was 'Kid' this, 'Cyclone' that, a 'Bluey' here and a 'Cowboy' there, and all manner of other monikers promoters felt were essential to give added character and colour to their riding assets.

At Rayleigh, Len Silver had a Geoff, an Allan, a Bob, a Peter, a John, a Nigel, a Terry and a Trevor . . . and our very own 'Tiger'.

He couldn't believe it when I turned up at his place the other year to interview him for our Rayleigh DVD and showed him my rosette of himself.

Barry Thomas: 'Mr Hackney' himself spent 20 years linked to the club from 1970 to 1989 and at a track that delivered thrills on a weekly basis, no-one generated more excitement than 'Thommo'. Thank God he couldn't make a start to save his life.

Dag Lovaas: The stylish Norwegian No.1 spent just the one season with the Hawks, but how imperious he looked for most of 1974. I strangely took to wearing a white shirt with

Zenon Plech before his Hackney debut in 1975 and (below) during our interview in Gdansk in 2012.

'DAG' emblazoned in large letters all over it to Waterden Road, although his 10-plus BL average suggests I wasn't completely mad.

Dag had the delicate throttle control of a surgeon, rarely looked in trouble on track and was the absolute master of wet tracks.

Dave Morton: Few of us knew much about this little northerner we'd signed from second division Crewe until, one night in '74, he blew Ole Olsen away not once, but TWICE in the match.

His fence-scraping style was worth the admission money alone and by the following year he had established himself as our No.1. In 1976 he leapt into the 10-plus bracket and was on the verge of regular England caps.

In 'Mort', we also had a star who performed even better on the northern circuits, where fast engines properly set up for big track conditions were a must, than he did at Waterden Road. He was often the difference between respectability and a bad drubbing. He could be a bit temperamental at times, when his bike occasionally let him down, but he was destined for a big future until he suddenly picked up unexpected grip on the second bend at Hackney in May '77, careered through the fence and badly broke his thigh.

Mort will be the first to admit he was never the same rider after that, although he did go on to enjoy a long career spanning various clubs.

When I visited him at his home near Manchester the other year – to record an interview for his younger brother's DVD – Mort treated me to a 'twang' of his banjo before retiring to his local, where we spent a lovely afternoon discussing our shared passion for real ale and drank to the 'good old days' at Hackney. The Hawks race-jacket he kindly gave me will remain one of my most treasured possessions.

Zenon Plech: This is fast turning into a Hackney who's who but how can I possibly leave out the former Poland No.1? From the moment he burst on the international scene in 1973, most saw him as a world champion in the making. He did finish third in the World Final that year and again in 1979 but he could have gone right to the top if only he'd been given clearance from the Polish authorities to race in the British League much earlier than he eventually did, and on better machinery too.

I'll never forget his heart-stopping, long-awaited Hackney debut shortly before the end of the 1975 season, when he appeared in his all-white Stal Gorzow leathers and spent his first four laps bouncing off the safety fence. He was utterly fearless – except when it came to receiving treatment for injuries. If an arm or leg was hanging off, he'd rather battle on than go to hospital.

Zenon is such a smiling, laid-back and very likeable character. When Hackney were up at Belle Vue in 1976 I cadged a lift to Manchester with Zenon's dope and oil man, Ivan 'Jack' Jackson, who also helped Len Silver prepare the Waterden Road track. We were in the front of the car while Zenon slept all the way there curled up on the back seat. When we arrived at Hyde Road, he awoke, headed straight for the funfair, had a spin on the dodgems and then rode in the meeting. Not exactly the Ivan Mauger method!

It was almost 40 years after I first saw him ride that I finally interviewed 'Plechy' at length for *Backtrack* in 2012. He collected me from Gdansk airport and drove me in his car on a guided tour of his home town, followed by a meal in one of his favourite restaurants in the historic coastal city.

The next day he introduced me to all his friends at the local speedway track, where he is still a legend, and after proudly showing me the junior track he had built behind the main stadium and where we did the interview, he made us both a cup of coffee before we watched a league match with around 8,000 fanatical Poles. Everyone we passed on our way from the car park to the pits stopped Zenon and shook him enthusiastically by the hand.

In Poland they rave about Tomasz Gollob, who has been great to watch and managed to win the world title that eluded Zenon, but for me there will always be only one Polish hero – Zenon Plech.

Vic Harding: In June 1979, a year after joining the *Mail*, I had to write my first obituary for the paper. It is never a pleasant task but this time it was much more disturbing because, at

SPEEDWAY ACE IS KILLED IN CRASH

Reporting on the death of a friend was tough.

that point, Vic was the one speedway rider I'd got to know better than any other. In '77, Vic's regular mechanic Tony Arthurs couldn't make it to Hackney for a couple of weeks so, knowing my passion for the sport and the Hawks in particular, he suggested that I could help Vic out with the most simple tasks of doping and oiling and squirting chain lubricant in the right places after each of his races.

From that point I followed Vic's progress with even keener interest and it was absolutely awful to be there, some two years later, and witness his tragic accident with Eastbourne's Steve Weatherley that left Steve in a wheelchair at 21 and cost the unlucky Vic his life a month short of his 27th birthday.

Peter Collins: How can anyone who watched speedway in the 70s fail to admire one of the most thrilling and spectacular racers ever to sit on a bike? The fact that PC was one of the poorest gaters among the world elite made him even more unmissable when Belle Vue

John Louis after showing the young ones the way round Hyde Road in 1979.

were in town or he was appearing in a Test match or international meeting.

He was particularly brilliant in the period 1975-77 and possibly never better than when he romped to the Inter-Continental title at London White City in '77, just before the disastrous leg injury that wrecked his hopes of retaining the world crown in Sweden.

How the Aces' fans at Hyde Road were spoilt watching PC and his old pal Chris Morton splicing the opposition to pieces race after race, always in the most breathtaking style from the back.

Malcolm Simmons: Although it is no consolation to Malc, his winning the silver medal at Katowice in '76 was the icing on the cake for us Brits in the crowd of around 100,000. He really was 'Super Simmo' that year, ever the supreme stylist who made everything look so effortless. There weren't many riders wearing white leathers until Simmo strolled out wearing his in '76 – the man just oozed quality.

In recent years, since publishing his autobiography, we have become good friends and it's a measure of his honest take on speedway past and present that I still always look forward to calling him up each time for the words to go in his *Backtrack* column.

Michael Lee: We all knew from the start, as a 16-year-old on debut at King's Lynn in 1975, what a great rider he would be. The only disappointment is, like Peter Collins, he didn't add to his one individual world title but I don't go along with the common misconception that he totally wasted his racing career.

He had at least eight brilliant years in the sport and a few less memorable ones when he let himself and others down.

Most of those seasons were spent at the highest level and he achieved the ultimate. He had nothing left to prove on a speedway bike, so he went off and did his own thing and experienced a completely different side of life that few of us will ever understand. I don't knock him for that. His choice.

Many of the problems he has had at various times in his life, on and off the track, have been self-inflicted – we all know it and he has fully admitted it – but it's still impossible to stop liking this fundamentally decent person who was always popular with his peers – if not officialdom, who were definitely out to nail him once and for all.

How the SCB got away with banning him for a year (reduced from five on appeal) for what he did at King's Lynn in 1984 remains one of the most outrageous punishments ever meted out in sporting circles.

I, like many, always prefer to remember Michael as one of the most naturally talented and successful riders the sport has ever seen.

Kenny Carter: We're really getting into controversial territory now, but whatever you thought of him, as arguably the best British rider in his prime he was pure box office in the early 80s, when England were a fading force. Certainly, England has never replaced him since his tragic death in 1986 and neither has British speedway as a whole recovered from his loss.

Bruce Penhall: The American and his nemesis Kenny Carter will always be intrinsically linked whenever people talk about the superstars of the 80s. Bruce copped a lot of unwarranted stick from British fans when he helped his fellow countrymen to qualify from the Overseas Final at White City in 1982 – all he did was what countless English, Polish and Swedish riders have done for their mates since time immemorial.

He had to fend off more criticism for deciding to retire on the rostrum moments after retaining his world title at LA in '82? But why? It was his choice to make, he owed speedway nothing. He had been one of British speedway's finest for five years and the sport certainly missed its most charismatic superstar when he left it at the very top. What a way to bow out.

Kelly & Shawn Moran: The diminutive Californian brothers never scaled the greatest heights their natural talent warranted but they were both great for speedway in the 80s; great entertainers and great people. To watch them team-riding in Test matches, side by side while cheekily waving to their jubilant American buddies in the pits, was poetry in motion.

I don't go along with those who reckon the Morans and Mike Lee wasted their talent. All three enjoyed great success on track and off it, they lived life to the full. Would they have traded places with the ultimate professional, Ivan Mauger? No way! It was very sad to see Kelly's premature demise in 2010 at the age of 49 but he definitely didn't die wondering and there's a lot to be said for that.

Six years earlier, he helped us launch *Backtrack* from our stand at a show in Coventry. We didn't ask him to do anything but he picked up a copy of the mag and started waving it about to drum up business and awareness. It was typical of a lovely bloke who cared more about others than he ever did himself.

Ivan Mauger: Without hesitation, I'd say he is the greatest speedway rider ever. We all know Tony Rickardsson also won six individual world championships and the Swede was, of course, also a brilliant performer. But only the first of Tony's titles were won in the pressure-cooker situation of the one-off World Final era, a year before the Grand Prix series was introduced in 1995 and one bad race, or even a sub-standard meeting or two, could still be overcome.

Ivan believes he (and Ove Fundin and Barry Briggs) would have added to his record-breaking tally of world titles had the GP format applied in his day and it's very difficult to argue against it. What sets him above Rickardsson in my book is not just what he did at international level – who else could have dragged a very ordinary New Zealand team to World Team Cup glory at the expense of England, USA and Denmark, as Ivan did in 1979? – but his immense leadership qualities that brought unprecedented success to his British League clubs, Belle Vue, Exeter and Hull. How many times did he slow a race down to crawling pace to team-ride and nurture home a much less talented team-mate? And then there is the knowledge, mechanical know-how and experience he passed on to those same colleagues, to make them perform better.

I wore a Mauger rosette to the 1975 World Final and regularly had to defend the great man from terrace criticism. So it was ironic that after I began working for *Speedway Mail*, he was the first and only rider to ever refuse me an interview. It was my fault as much as his, though. I was too insensitive. We were in the pits at White City, where Ivan had just been eliminated from the 1981 World Championship – the first time he'd failed to reach the final in 16 years – and, not being in the clique of national hacks he knew well and trusted, he didn't take kindly to me asking for a few quotes.

A few years later, with our brief and frosty exchange long forgotten, he phoned the *Mail's* office seeking publicity for his big farewell meeting at Belle Vue and we have got on very well ever since.

In fact, Ivan has been a very strong ally for Retro Speedway, offering to track down former riders to interview and putting us in touch with the right people. Until he was suddenly hit by ill health in 2012, he was usually the first to send an email or get on the phone from his Gold Coast home to order almost everything we produced. That's another thing I really like about him: the way he has always valued and respected speedway's history.

CLASSICS

Of all the meetings you have been to, do you have one memorable classic that stands out from all the rest?

Plenty of others in this book will understandably nominate the 1981 World Final at Wembley but, apart from those two great duels involving Bruce Penhall, Ole Olsen and Tommy Knudsen, the racing was nothing special. It was the sense of occasion that made it such a memorable occasion and the fact that no other speedway meeting has been held there since. This final has got better with the passage of time, because of what it stands for.

There are others that stand out. The first England v USA Test at Wimbledon in 1980, which ended in a pulsating 54-54 draw, will take some beating. The Californians had brought welcome colour and razzmatazz to the British League and this South London thriller – the start of their 3-1 series victory – confirmed their arrival as serious world class performers.

Can you single out one particularly great race that will live longest in your memory?

Having been brought up at Hackney, there were a million and one fine races that are impossible to recall in detail. We could devote a whole chapter to the wondrous feats of Barry Thomas, the most notable of his many brave bursts from the back coming in 1977, when he denied Exeter the league title (nominated later in the book). Unfortunately, the 'internet' in those days was a curtain for indoors and the TV cameras were not present to capture Thommo at his best.

And that's the point: every match at The Wick in the 70s invariably produced a few really good races that sent you home happy regardless of whether your team won, drew or lost.

Again, leaving others to recall the two epic encounters at Wembley in '81, I'll look elsewhere. Let's start with the 1975 British Final at Coventry. In those days this meeting actually meant a lot – not only in terms of national pride, but because it was a very tough and important stepping stone towards the World Final. Only the top four Brits would qualify for Wembley and on a steamy hot Wednesday night at Brandon, with around 20,000 packed in, the competition was intense – far superior in depth of quality compared to what today's British Final has to offer.

Winner John Louis (Ipswich) and runner-up Peter Collins (Belle Vue) demonstrated the power of the new Weslake engine that made its bow that season, although Malcolm Simmons (Poole) showed that the two-valve Jawa wasn't quite yet obsolete by taking the third rostrum place. It was between Ray Wilson and Martin Ashby who would join them and a run-off was needed to separate the No.1s of Leicester and Swindon respectively.

Thankfully, ITV's *World of Sport* cameras were there to capture all the magic of this wheel-to-wheel thriller that lasted the full four laps, with 'Wllly' forcing 'Crash' just wide enough on the last turn, without actually fencing him, to snatch a momentous win on the line. Maybe Martin will look back and think he should have been harder on Ray. But it was the sportsmanship and mutual respect they showed for each other that added to its magnitude.

Bruce Penhall had established himself as the new darling of British, if not world speedway, well before the 1979 British League Riders' Championship at Belle Vue, so it was a major shock when he was pipped for the title by 39-year-old veteran John Louis. The Ipswich legend dealt with everything the Cradley Heath man could throw at him, almost pinning him to the fence around the pits turn when they met in Heat 18 to hold on for a breathtaking victory.

I had taken a break from speedway when Mark Loram was pulling off outrageous manoeuvres from the back at the highest level but at least we can now all re-live many of his superb highlights thanks to video, YouTube and the DVD we produced on his career. You'd have to go a very long way to see a more engrossing battle than his hard-earned victory over his great mate Chris Louis in their run-off to decide the 1994 British Final at Coventry.

THEN AND NOW

What do you miss most about speedway in the past?

Where do we start – this could become another book in itself.

Crowds: The most obvious contender to be top of everyone's wish list. Five-figure crowds at the BLRC and Internationale were common place in the 60s and 70s. The GP organisers are delighted to see 40,000-plus at Cardiff each year but nearly the same number turned out to watch England v Sweden at Wembley in 1973. As for attendances at domestic meetings, it would bring tears to a glass eye to even begin comparing them with today's meagre turn-outs.

Routine and continuity: The season used to begin in March or early April and run to the end of October – 30-plus meetings a season run weekly on a regular race night, so fans wouldn't get out of the habit of going.

Defunct tracks: Every time another track closed in the 80s, thousands more supporters were lost to the sport forever.

Well prepared tracks: The days when the genuine racers got value from a track and were encouraged to risk their necks to make a pass on tyres and engines that were suited to track conditions.

Individuality: It's not just speedway that is lacking in characters today – the same can be said of most sports where money has eroded old values and spirit and 'professionalism' has gone too far – but the loss of riders' individual identity is something our sport has brought on itself. The uniformed race suits that were introduced in the mid-90s definitely made teams look more the part, but there has been a price to pay. Riders used to be distinguishable by their different multi-coloured leathers and, as a kid, I recall wondering in eager anticipation what my heroes would be wearing at the start of every new season, and what other new designs they would introduce during the course of the campaign. If race suits had been invented in the 60s, there would never have been a 'Little Boy Blue' or 'Red Devil'.

What, if anything, would you like to see reintroduced to speedway today?

Without repeating most of the above, it should be abundantly obvious to everyone associated with the sport that British speedway is paying out more than it can afford to riders and engine tuners, so anything that reduces running costs is the first starting point towards survival and hopefully recovery. The introduction of four-valve engines in the mid-70s was the start of the slippery slope – they should have been nipped in the bud and banned from Day One. Costs spiralled overnight, causing the retirement of a number of British riders who, though not stars, were solid team men. Speedway became too expensive from 1975 and has been struggling to make ends meet ever since. And how can the BSPA expect to persuade young Brits to try speedway when the entry costs and ongoing expenses are so ridiculously high and unsustainable? The amazing thing is, even ordinary riders are taking too much out of the sport in the UK and the riders don't even have a meaningful union to fight their corner. The SRA has never been as toothless at is it today but the riders – who, in turn, feel they have to spend heavily on their bikes and therefore line the pockets of tuners – are still bleeding the sport dry. The figures just don't stack up, so the BSPA either has to get tough with its employees or face oblivion.

A return to two-valve engines might be problematic in the short-term but drastic situations call for drastic measures. Maybe the new Formula 2 bikes trumpeted by Pete Seaton could be a big step in the right direction? It has to be fully explored.

Briggo at his Surrey home before pizza was served in 2008.

The promoters have to recognise that what they are offering now for £15 or so per adult is not value for money – effectively it costs £1 per minute to watch 15 minutes of often mind-numbing league 'action', strung out over two-to-three hours, on slick tracks that are not conducive for good racing.

Costs and the general apathy of riders were the reasons why the old second-halves were chopped from the programme but the BSPA has to come up with a way to add extra entertainment to what is currently an inadequate but costly package.

MOMENTS TO TREASURE
What is your favourite memory you take from speedway?

Impossible for me to answer without taking up many more pages, so I'll try and keep this one as brief as possible. Then again . . .

The next best thing to taking part in any professional sport is to write about it, so I consider myself very lucky and privileged to have been able to meet and interview all my old heroes and so many others in speedway since 1978. Without wishing it to sound like gratuitous name-dropping, there are some personal experiences I will never forget:

*To delight in seeing Ivan Mauger at his imperious best and winning World Finals and then, years later, interviewing him for a few hours in the White Lion pub at Wimbledon, just across the road from where his career in England began almost 50 years earlier, was poignant and special.

*Eating pizza with Barry Briggs at his and Jan's Surrey home and helping Briggo in some very minor way with his recent autobiography.

*The invaluable insight I gained about speedway from being a passenger in Colin Pratt's Citroen estate each Saturday of the 1983 season as he drove us to and from Norfolk to perform his team manager's duties for the Stars. Blimey, I thought I could moan about speedway! Seriously, if every promoter cared about speedway as much as Pratty does and they were all as straight as him, the sport would be in much better shape.

*Being invited by an initially reluctant Ole Olsen into his trophy room cum office at his Haderslev home . . . and spending hours listening to him put forward a plethora of typically radical views on the sport. He might still be talking to today if I hadn't had a flight to catch.

*On another trip to Denmark, enjoying a meal out with Erik Gundersen and then some late night brandies back at his farmhouse as my favourite Dane spoke from the heart about

Peter Collins proudly showing off his 1930s Eric Langton JAP in 2010.

that crash and how he fought for his 'second life'.

*Anders Michanek taking me to lunch from aboard his little fishing boa after we'd finished the interview in the grounds of his beautiful 50-acre farmhouse on the tiny island of Singo, just up the coast from Stockholm. Standing there in disbelief as the 1974 World Champion clambered up into the loft of his barn to find his speedway racejackets, before throwing them down to the ground amid clouds of dust and then saying, in all sincerity: "I really don't know which one I wore at Ullevi that night."

*Peter Collins collecting me from his local railway station before showing me his impressive collection of vintage bikes and then filming him at his home for our *World Finals of the 70s* DVD.

*Enjoying many hours spent in the company of Malcolm Simmons. I've always preferred those who tell it like it really is and no-one offers a more candid public opinion on speedway past or present than Simmo, who has also admitted his own past misdemeanours.

*Getting to really know John Berry, surely one of the most complex characters the sport has ever seen, in the nine years he wrote for *Backtrack*, during which time we published his three books and could probably have put out a few more if we'd printed the endless emails we exchanged between here and his home in Perth, Western Australia. To many he appeared to be or was aloof, arrogant, surly, enigmatic, intolerant and impossible – and sometimes all of those things on one day. But for all his faults he was an honest, intelligent man who must rank as the best promoter of my time.

JB became a good friend, advisor and confidant and Susie and I saw a compassionate side to him that only his small but trusted circle of friends ever really knew.

*Working closely with Michael Lee and Mark Loram on books and DVDs, while at the same time getting to know them as people, reaffirmed what very likeable, down to earth blokes they are. They don't tell anyone what they achieved – their records speak for them.

Both have endured personal nightmares in recent times for one reason or another but the character, strength and resilience that made them worthy past world champions will, I'm sure, also get them through their bad days and hopefully enjoy the future they deserve.

*Some people are 'on the radar' for a long time before you actually arrange to meet and get to sit down and chew the fat with them. So you can imagine how very fortunate and honoured I felt to interview that very humble double World Champion Freddie Williams at his Berkshire cottage just eight weeks before he died from a stroke in December 2012.

Freddie's sudden death shocked us all, because he looked so good and fit for his 86 years.

*The circumstances were much different when I dialled the number of a California hospice to interview the terminally ill Kelly Moran less than two months before he died of lung and liver failure in April 2010, aged 49. Typically, he picked up the phone and before I could speak he quipped: "Hi-ya, Kelly Moran's office!"

*We always remember the last time we spoke to certain people in our lives. There was the phone call at the office, in May 1986, from Kenny Carter, his usual bumptious, self-important self, whining about us putting Peter Collins on the front of the *Mail*. I liked Kenny and always got on well with him, though. A week or two later he got his wish, but this time he was front page news again for all the worst possible reasons.

*Although he was never involved in speedway directly, Alan Carter – Kenny's younger brother and former part-time mechanic, under-age chauffeur and general dogsbody – is a character known to many and I am pleased to have met and got to know this special man. What Kenny did by shooting dead his wife Pam and orphaning their two kids was unforgivable but spare a thought for the people left behind to try and pick up the pieces in the wake of that terrible tragedy. Alan has been to hell and back in the past 25-plus years. To see him so happy with a smile as wide as The Pennines on the day we launched his book at the 2011 Cardiff GP, a brief respite on a long journey of personal torture, was one of my most rewarding moments in publishing.

*We published Simon Wigg's story, too, but that was in 2005, some five years after he'd been taken from us due to a brain tumour at the age of 40 – the same illness that claimed my Mum at 59. Being out of speedway circles from 1992 until 2003 while working on other sports publications, I'd lost touch with Wiggy in the years leading up to his sad death but I will never forget the occasion when he starred at the 1985 World Final weekend we organised for *Speedway Mail* readers. The FIM had banned Simon from the speedway World Championship for a year for his part in the sensational *Sunday People* race-fixing allegations but the sport's loss was our gain as we got him to be our VIP guest at a supporters' forum at a hotel in Leeds, hosted by Terry Hardaker, before going on to the final at Odsal the next afternoon. As charismatic and forthright as ever, Wiggy had them eating out of his hand.

*With speedway, as in life itself, there are always ups and downs and the lows don't come any worse than witnessing the death of a rider, but that's sadly what happened twice in just three years at Hackney with the loss of Vic Harding and Denny Pyeatt. I was also at King's Lynn the night Leif Wahlmann was killed. Knowing Vic's family at the time of his accident, and then meeting them again in the last year or so, makes you realise some of the pain they have been through and served as another solemn reminder of the risks all riders take to entertain us.

*Some of the best fun times were spent with friends such as Martin Neal and Colin and Marilyn Gear on the National League northern tours in the 80s, although I still refute Martin Goodwin's accusation that I taught him how to drink when Arena-Essex were up in Scotland.

*I do like a beer or six, though, and, I'm glad to say, so too does *Speedway Star* editor Richard Clark. Many people might have assumed us to be rivals when we first met as editors of the respective weeklies in the early 80s but we never were. Clarkie and I have enjoyed many a long and memorable (and not so memorable) session – along with Britain's former top ref Graham Brodie and others – putting the speedway world to rights and still do. The day the powers that be finally take any notice of us is the day we stop ordering the next round, which is probably not good news for our respective livers.

I could go on forever recalling many other personal memorable moments but I've taken up too much space already, so let's press on.

WHY SPEEDWAY IS SPECIAL
Whether you used to attend speedway meetings or still do so today, describe what makes speedway so special to you?

Aside from all the pleasure it has given me and all the wonderful people I've been lucky to meet through speedway, the ingredients of what first attracted me to the sport are still fundamentally there. Obviously, most of my waffle here is routed in the past, because the 70s and 80s, in particular, was my favourite time and this period is at the heart of what we do at Retro Speedway today.

But that doesn't stop me appreciating what speedway still has to offer in the modern era, even though we'd all like to see its best qualities on show more often. Whether we favour the once traditional one-off World Final or the Grand Prix format introduced in 1995, it has to be said that the GPs have produced some of the best racing you will have ever seen anywhere. To watch the likes of Darcy Ward, Chris Holder, Emil Sayfutdinov, Tomasz Gollob and Mark Loram strut their stuff on the world stage in recent years, performing the seemingly impossible at the highest possible speed, is entertainment and spectacle as good as anything I've seen any sport deliver. Four honest riders going at it hammer and tongs for four laps on a well prepared track, courageously pushing each other to the absolute limit but never beyond, all in the blur of 60 seconds . . . well, no other sport can match that for pure adrenalin-fuelled entertainment.

The fundamental basics of speedway are often still very good. Those of us who follow it closely can become so negative about all the bad elements – and I include myself here – that we easily lose sight of the fact that there are plenty of other sports out there, some generating millions of pounds more in TV revenue and guaranteed massive media interest, which could also be much better run and are prone to attract the same cynicism and ridicule that occasionally blights our sport in its worst moments. Football, cricket, rugby – their highly rewarded administrators and rule-makers mess up every bit as much as the BSPA do. The FA have been a laughing stock for years; the ECB and RFU are equally derelict in their duty to their national game at times. OK, so many of us couldn't care less about other sports and the reason we continue to gripe is that we care about speedway and become very frustrated every time it shoots itself in the foot.

When speedway gets it right, there is nothing to touch it. It's all the other important stuff around the actual racing that our sport needs to improve on: long-term planning, organisation, promotion, marketing, administration, a much simplified rule-book, track preparation, a structured nationwide youth policy . . . and the appointment of the independent governing body British speedway so desperately needs but will probably never get.

Anyway, that's more than enough from me. Now let's read about your memories and opinions . . .

1 FIRST TIME

Tell us about the first speedway meeting you can remember attending and what led you to go?

Bert Loader: My first speedway meeting was in 1930 as a four-year-old in Birmingham – not the Perry Barr track but the one opposite. I also went to Coventry around the same period. The person who took me was a boyfriend of my cousin. I lived near Malvern and was staying with my uncle in Birmingham during the school holidays.

Maurice Plowright: In the summer of 1932, at Arlington (Eastbourne), where my brother helped water the track.

Eric Marchment: Wimbledon in 1935, aged six. Memories of being in a large, enthusiastic crowd pressed against the fence; the lights above the track swaying; the smell; the noise of the bikes as they flashed past. I had been introduced to a life-long obsession. A family move to the country and the Second World War prevented me attending any more meetings until

Wembley Lions legends Bill Kitchen, Tommy Price and George Wilks.

Wembley in late 1946, which was an absolutely mind-blowing experience. Approaching the stadium were hundreds of cars, motorcycles, cyclists, buses and pedestrians. The atmosphere was electric inside – 90,000-plus supporters with club scarves, rosettes, badges and most memorable and noisy of all, many fans sporting surplus wartime wooden rattles.

The two biggest Wembley stars were Bill Kitchen and Tommy Price. Tommy soon became my first favourite: immaculate equipment, immaculate in appearance, a hard but fair rider.

My other memory from 1946 is Rye House – a Sunday track, a mere nothing when you consider the five big London tracks in close proximity, but it was a good Sunday afternoon out. Late 1946 – I can't remember the actual meeting – but the memory that does remain is the guest of honour who was the famous pre-war Australian rider Ron Johnson, who was still a great rider at the time. He was dressed like a star in a well-tailored suit and long overcoat.

The other event which occurred that day, which I have never experienced before or since, was the local vicar conducting a short service on the centre green before the meeting began.

Mick Brown: My first meeting was when I was 18-months-old, in 1932. I was taken to West Ham by my father. The Hammers' captain was Tiger Stephenson. I didn't go again until after the Second World War ended. By then, in 1946, the West Ham team was: Eric Chitty (captain), Colin Watson, Malcolm Craven, Buck Whitby, Dick Geary, George Gower and Frank Lawrence.

John Hyam: The opening meeting of the season at New Cross in April 1946. I was persuaded to attend with a schoolboy friend and his mother. I knew so little about the sport – I thought the riders were racing when they were actually only cruising the track before moving to the tapes. I was astounded when they did start and roared into a first bend dash.

New Cross beat The Rest 46-37 in a challenge match and the first race I saw was a 5-1 for the Rangers. Ron Johnson and Phil Bishop led from Ron Clarke while Jack Parker had engine failure. The time for the four laps of the 262-yard track was 61.8 seconds.

Tiger Stephenson, West Ham's famous pre-war captain.

Mick Bird: At Wembley in 1946, when I was seven and didn't appreciate teams, riders, etc. I just enjoyed the bikes going after knowing nothing but bombs.

I soon recalled Bill Kitchen, Tommy Price and George Wilks as the Wembley stars and remembered visiting riders like Jack and Norman Parker, Alec Statham, Ron Johnson and Eric Langton, to name just a few.

Cedric Read: It was 1946 and things were getting back to normal after the war. I was 15 and one day my elder brother John said: "According to the newspaper, speedway is starting at Perry Barr on Saturday, May 5, Birmingham v Norwich, would you like to go?"

"Ok," I replied, "is it bikes or cars?"

"I don't know, but it sounds fun."

And fun it turned out to be. Standing on a cinder bank between the third and fourth bends, we watched as the tapes went up on Heat 1 and

Ron Johnson led New Cross to a home victory against The Rest in 1946.

Bert Spencer, the Norwich captain (blue helmet!), raced off, to be chased for four laps by the Birmingham captain Tiger Hart. He set up a track record of 76 and 2/5, which held for two years until the cinders were replaced by granite chippings. Straight away we were hooked into a life-long passion. Birmingham won a close meeting 56-48 and we went happily home to relive the evening by filling in the programme in ink (ball pens didn't exist and at the meeting you used pencil).

Twelve months later and by now ardent Brummie supporters, Les Marshall, the Birmingham promoter, appealed for fans to support the opening of his second track at Cradley Heath on a Saturday afternoon – June 21, 1947. I was 16 and working in the centre of Birmingham. It meant going directly from work at 12.00pm and catching two buses to be there for the 2.30pm start. I remember the stadium looked very bare and new, with soil piled up in the centre 'green'. Cradley beat Wombwell 46-36, with Les Beaumont, Geoff Bennett and Eric Irons scoring nine each. Alan Hunt, who was to have a highly successful but tragically brief career, scored three at reserve. The meeting finished about 5.00pm, too late for me to get to Perry Barr that evening (6.30pm start). I had taken sandwiches from home, so I can't comment on whether the famous Cradley pork sandwiches were on sale!

Ken Wrench: I was taken to Belle Vue when I was 14, in 1946, by friends who I was staying with in Knutsford. They had previously gone pre-war. I lived in Gloucestershire at the time. It was Belle Vue v West Ham, with Jack Parker captaining the Aces and the Canadian Eric Chitty leading the Hammers. I was hooked by the first meeting. Hyde Road looked immaculate with the solid white fence, black cinder track, green centre and large crowd. There was a dramatic feel about it with Parker, resplendent with a white scarf round his neck, walking from the pits with Chitty to toss the coin at the start line. There was a feeling of pure theatre about the presentation.

Ken Carpenter: I was too young to know the date (probably 1946 or 1947) but I do know that my dad used to take me to Wembley to see the Lions every Thursday night as soon as it

The Cradley Heath team at the track's opening meeting in June 1947.

restarted after the war. The night began with a fanfare, which would make the hairs stand up on the back of my neck. Then the riders entered one by one to be introduced to the massive crowd just like a World Final. My heroes in those days were Tommy Price and Bill Kitchen, whom I met and photographed many years later at Belle Vue's Kirky Lane.

As a small boy the highlight of the evening was the interval entertainment when a man set fire to himself and dived from a great height into a tank of water which briefly exploded into flames. I later learned, from the clerk of the course at Belle Vue, that this chap was a captain somebody and only had one leg. I've searched the internet but can find no reference to him anywhere. I'd love to see a film of this if one survives. I wonder if Alf Weedon has a snap of it?

The other big attraction was the counter marching of the guards' bands while the track rakers, probably ex-servicemen, would rake the track in unison with their white-painted rakes marching in line like soldiers on parade. What a spectacle.

The film *Once a Jolly Swagman*, starring Dirk Bogarde, Bill Owen and Sid James, gives a good impression of how speedway looked during its heyday. They raced on deep, ash tracks in those days. The ashes were supplied by a local firm in Wembley, which later became Biffa Waste Services. You always knew who had been to speedway because everyone going home on the tube or the bus would look like they had been made up for *The Black and White Minstrel Show* with white teeth and eye balls.

Ron Byford: My first experience of speedway was as an 11-year-old. My dad was a fan of Stamford Bridge before the Second World War. In April 1946, he took me to Plough Lane, Wimbledon.

John Chaplin: My first encounter with speedway was in the second great boom period when, after six years of mortal conflict, the sporting public was able once more to assemble in large numbers.

With the resumption of full-time league racing, a total of 1,211,355 people paid to see speedway at Wembley alone – four times as many as attended meetings at the Empire Stadium in 1939.

Jack Parker, with his familiar white scarf, and Australian ace Jack Young.

In a *Daily Mail* poll, speedway was placed fourth ahead of horse racing, rugby, tennis and golf. Football topped the poll followed by cricket and boxing.

And in the *Sporting Record's* Sportsman of the Year voting, England and Belle Vue captain Jack Parker came fourth ahead of Stanley (later Sir Stanley) Matthews (football), Gordon (later Sir Gordon) Richards (horse racing), Bill Edrich (cricket) and Bruce Woodcock (boxing). Denis Compton (cricket) was top, followed by Reg Harris (cycling) and Tommy Lawton (football).

Speedway and I became acquainted that same year, 1946, at Birmingham. I was 12-years-old. And the sheer thrill of the spectacle, the packed crowd, the colour, the glamour and the utterly intoxicating aroma of burned racing fuel captivated me completely – and has done ever since.

Birmingham's opponents on that momentous day were Sheffield. It was Saturday, July 6 and the teams were – Birmingham: Phil 'Tiger' Hart 10, Roy Dook and Bob Lovell 9, Laurie Packer 8, Stan Dell 6, Ernie Appleby 4, Cyril Page 2, Charlie Appleby 1. Sheffield: Tommy Allott 15, Jack Bibby 11, Tommy Bateman 10, Alf Elliott and Dick Geary 3, Stan Williams and J.D. White 2, Reg Lambourne 1.

The match report recorded that 'Birmingham won a really magnificent ACU Cup match against Sheffield by 49 points to 47. A dry and difficult track did nothing to detract from the merit of the racing in which team-riding was well in evidence.

'The result was in doubt right up until the final lap of the final heat . . . the lead changed hands with bewildering rapidity (and then) Packer, Ernie Appleby, Williams and White lined up for the all-important 16th heat.

'Williams shot into the lead with the Birmingham pair close behind, but Packer drove inside . . . to take the lead. White fell at the start of the second lap, leaving Williams requiring to win to save the match for Sheffield.

'But Appleby chased and caught Williams, after which the second position changed hands several times each lap until Williams came through on the last bend. By this time it was much too late to interfere with the flying Packer and Birmingham won the match.'

Well, it couldn't have been scripted better – the narrowest of wins for the home side. There could have been no finer introduction to speedway, so thank you Sheffield. And my first words to my parents were: "Can we come back next week?"

Dave Banks: It was one summer evening back in 1946 (aged seven) that I went with my parents to my first-ever meeting at Odsal. I thought it was absolutely brilliant and got hooked straight away.

We went to every home meeting for some years to come and enjoyed watching great racing with top riders of that era, like Vic Duggan, Jack Parker, Tommy Price and Bill Kitchen, plus good riders from the Odsal team such as Oliver Hart, Max Grosskreutz, Jack Biggs and great memories of the one and only Joe Abbott (The Iron Man). At times, after he had been in a collision and probably was not feeling too good, the first thing he would do was put a cigarette in his mouth. Then they would put him on a stretcher and the St John's Ambulance attendants would carry him through a gate on the third bend and up some steps, through the crowd to a small hospital at the back of the stadium. But 20 minutes or so later, he would walk back down, making his way to the pits to the applause and cheers of the crowd.

I remember when West Ham visited Odsal and we would be entertained by Howdy Byford giving us a song during the interval. I can also remember one lady standing by the fence on the pits bend who would put chewing gum on Ron Clarke's saddle on his bike, her intention

Leg-trailer Oliver Hart was popular at Odsal.

being that he would not fall off!

But the person who made it all happen was the great man himself, promoter Johnnie Hoskins, who was a brilliant showman. After the team line-ups and tossing of the coin for positions at the starting gate, he would throw a coin into the main stand (which I believe was a half-crown, 2/6d).

As a seven-year-old, my favourite rider was Max Grosskreutz. At the interval, I used to walk around the stadium looking for 'Turf' cigarette packets, as they had cards in each packet of sports stars, including speedway riders. Once, I was walking past the main stand towards the pits when I saw Max Grosskreutz walking slowly up towards the changing rooms so, like you do, I asked him for his autograph. He turned me down, saying: "Beat it, kid." I was kind of upset, but still classed him as a great rider.

Some time later, he was involved in a bad smash and broke his pelvis. When he had recovered, he decided to retire from speedway. At his last meeting when he said his goodbyes to the fans, I remember they played *Now is the Hour* by Gracie Fields, which I found to be quite sad.

I still have my old Odsal badge from 1946 (with Boomerang year bars) to keep the memories alive.

Cecil Rockey: In 1946 at Alphington, Exeter, on cinders and it was very exciting to see Jack Parker, Bill Kitchen, Eric Chitty and others.

Mrs Pamela Birtles: Relatives came up from rural Oxfordshire and wanted to sample the 'delights of a big city', so they dragged my mother and I to Belle Vue Speedway. I have been going ever since. The occasion was a war-time afternoon meeting. Oliver Hart? Wow, what a rider!

Mrs Lucy Burton: At West Ham on Good Friday 1947. I was 14-years-old and I went with two of my friends.

Dennis Hoppe: As a 16-year-old boy fresh from school, an uncle, with whom I was lodging in Bexleyheath, took me to my first meeting at Custom House to see West Ham. That was in June 1947, when I was a smitten teenager.

Glynn Shailes: At Bristol on July 18, 1947 when they raced against Wigan in a British Speedway Cup match. I sang in our local church choir and the organist had an opportunity to meet the organist at Bristol Cathedral and have a 'guided' tour. Afterwards, they were all going to Bristol Speedway, where the famous Laurel and Hardy would be making an appearance. I jumped at the chance and travelled to Bristol in the sidecar of his motorbike. I enjoyed looking around the cathedral and upon my arrival at Knowle Stadium, I was amazed at the huge car park that was rapidly filling up. I really had never seen anything like it before.

Keith Walker: It was summer 1947. One Saturday, a school mate said: "My dad is going to Odsal tonight, would you like to come?"

The boom days when crowds filled the terraces at Odsal.

Employing my best grammar school intellect, I said: "What's Odsal?"

"It's Bradford Speedway," retorted my friend.

I agreed to go, despite not knowing what speedway was. My friend's father was employed as a chauffeur to a wealthy old lady who lived in the leafy suburbs of Harrogate and she allowed him to have the car for his own use on occasions. I don't know how many people went to speedway in a Rolls-Royce in those days – probably not even Johnnie Hoskins – but I was impressed. Unfortunately, I can recall nothing of the actual meeting but I was hooked.

Subsequent visits to Odsal meant an hour's trip on a number 53 bus and a twopenny tram ride to Odsal Top from the centre of Bradford, followed by a mad dash down the precipitous slope of the Odsal bowl to grab a place hanging over the safety fence next to the pits. Happy, innocent, cinder-showered days!

Tony Emmott: My parents took me with neighbours living in Frizinghall to Odsal, Bradford when I would have been about five or six-years-old (1947-48). I do not remember anything about it – I think I found it boring!

I recall a big crowd at the stadium where, at that time, the terracing was comprised of old railway sleepers on black shale/cinders and I finished up filthy. We stood at the second bend.

The other memory I have of the day is catching an old tram from Bradford city centre to Odsal when the trams were just about to be phased out. I don't recall riding on a tram after that.

When we moved house to Wyke (south Bradford, near to Odsal) in 1950, I recall my elder brother riding cycle speedway, which was very popular at that time (I also rode up to the early 60s) and all his mates went to see the Odsal Tudors (renamed after the name Boomerangs was ditched) on Saturday nights.

I enjoyed going, as did all my own mates and other lads at Belle Vue Grammar School, so my heyday was about 1952-60. When Odsal closed, the team rode for two or three seasons at Greenfield Stadium, Dudley Hill, Bradford (demolished and now a Morrisons supermarket distribution centre).

Wally Loak: Tommy (Arnold) Tye, my young neighbour from childhood days in Rothwell, Northants, got me to go on the local, private coach service of Buckbys one Friday night to Blackbird Road stadium, home of the then Leicester Hunters, in 1949. It was the sight of Harwood Pike coming off into the fence and getting back up as though nothing had happened that led me to go again and again. Great stuff. I thought, these 'gladiators of the shaleways', this sport is for me, and it still is at just 82 years young!

Oliver Chapman: My dad took me as a five-year-old to Blackbird Road when Leicester re-opened in 1949. We continued on a weekly basis until I was about 10 and Dad had a word with a friendly 'Browns Blue' bus driver who ran a special Friday night bus to the speedway. He looked after me, providing I collected the bus fares for him.

Keith Barraclough: Speedway opened at The Shay in Halifax in 1949, and continued for only two more seasons - 1950 and 1951. I was only four years of age when the first meeting against Yarmouth took place but I can't remember which was the first meeting I attended. My father took a keen interest, so much so that I have in my possession every home programme for those three seasons. In fact, my mother used to say that I learned to read by reading the heat results in those programmes.

I have a photograph of my father holding me up on the first and second bends at The Shay at the meeting v Oxford on June 1, 1949, so I'm going to say this could have been my first attendance. Halifax won 66-18. However, my main recollections of that occasion are of the noisy lads standing in front of us leaning over the fence.

Stanley Harris: I was just eight-years-old and went to Wembley in 1949.

Peter Jackson: The Harringay Trophy meeting on October 14, 1949. We all went – my mum, sister, brother and I. Dad was the starting marshal at Harringay from 1947 to 1950, so he got the family seats in the stand. As a lad of five, the whole experience was mind-boggling . . . a huge crowd, the roar of the bikes, the stadium lights going out (apart from the track lights) for each race.

There was a massive queue for trolley buses to get home and I fell asleep. It was hard work for my mum to get three kids back home through the milling crowd. I seem to remember my first bag of peanuts too!

Ken Taylor: At Brough Park in Newcastle, which is my home town. I would have been about 11-years-old but I'm not sure what prompted me to go. I do know I loved it all from the very start and would go on a regular basis for the next seven years or so.

Until the end of the 1950 season, I would go to Brough straight from school on Monday nights. I had an uncle who lived near my school and I remember calling there and having tea with him, but even so I would be there before the track opened.

John Skinner: My earliest memory of going to speedway is Wembley on a vintage Bedford coach and stopping on the journey for bacon rolls. At Wembley every Thursday, the atmosphere was great with plenty of banter between rival supporters.

My favourite track was Norwich, which holds many memories for me. My claim to fame was that I think I was the first supporter to have a 'mechanical hooter', not a rattle, and when Wembley rode at Norwich I was mentioned as 'Captain Hornblower' in the programme. That was about 1954-55.

Roy Blanchflower: Norwich v Cradley Heath in 1950, and as a small boy I was so excited to see the leg-trailers like Bert Spencer. The reason I was there is that my father Harry prepared the track at Norwich, until just before it closed in 1964.

Michael Mayo: My late father took me to see Wembley v West Ham at the end of August 1951.

Tim Templeton: At the now defunct Banister Court in Southampton in 1951.

I cannot remember who was there rider-wise, but that night I was bitten by the speedway bug and it has never left me. My father took my elder brother and myself. I was just four at the time.

Malcolm Jealous: Taken to Walthamstow by my parents in 1951. I was seven and I didn't like the noise! Jack Young (Edinburgh) and Reg Reeves were the stars at that meeting.

David Walker: It would have been in 1952, at the age of seven, when I went to Brandon Stadium for the first time. My aunt was the receptionist for the track doctor, Dr. Harry Kenyon, who served the Bees for many years and was followed by his son in the same role. The spin-off to this was complimentary grandstand tickets, via my aunt and uncle, so I had a flying start.

My father actually reckoned he had been at the very first meeting at Brandon, in the late 20s, and could point out the tree he'd climbed up to see the racing, being only a kid and having no money to pay to get in.

Getting there in those days was quite a performance, as there were far less cars, so it was 1s 41/2d return on the bus (no half fares) from Wheatley Street. After the meeting, there would be up to a dozen buses in special queuing lanes in the Brandon car park.

Those early matches were in the old Third Division and I remember us riding against teams like Motherwell, Ipswich and Cradley Heath. Names from those days were Vic Emms, Johnny (the Cream Bun Kid) and Peter Reason (who lived near my grandmother), Peter Brough, Derek 'Dabber' Tailby, Charlie New, Bob Mark, Jack Wright, Stan Williams and John Yates, most of them wearing black and yellow hooped jumpers over their black leathers.

Tony Webb: The first meeting I went to was snowed-off! That was the grand opening of Ipswich Speedway on Easter Monday 1951. My father's construction company had built the track and all the workers were guests of honour. One of the workers, Rod Laudrum, was in

Coventry trio Derek Tailby, Johnny Reason and Reg Duval.

the Ipswich team. All I remember is thousands of cars and buses trying to get off Foxhall Heath. We finished up with Smiths crisps and Vimto in the local pub.

Later that year, around school holidays, my aunt and uncle, who lived near Southend, took me to Rayleigh. The match was against Long Eaton. Two names stuck out – Pedlar Palmer and Tom O'Connor. What caught my imagination more was the presents, chocolates and adulation that were bestowed on the riders, the smell of Castrol R and the flower-decked starter's box. From that day on, I dreamed of being a speedway rider. My relatives were dyed-in-the-wool Rockets fans, but my heart was always with Ipswich.

Barry Scowen: Foxhall Stadium in 1953, to see Ipswich v Exeter. I remember Goog Hoskins in his white boots, but don't ask me why this has stuck in my mind as I was only six at the time.

John Cross: The year was 1953 and, as a young boy living in a Leicestershire village, I often passed advertising billboards. One, in particular, always caught my eye – an advert for Leicester Speedway depicting a person on a motorcycle and stating the following week's visiting team.

Of course, as a boy of 11, I didn't expect to travel into Leicester and visit the Blackbird Road Stadium, as it was not normal for a family to own a car in those days. Quite unexpectedly, on Easter Monday, my friends invited me to join them to go to the speedway. A coach passed through the villages picking up passengers on a return trip to the speedway. I was given half a crown (12.5p), which covered the cost of the bus fare, entrance to the stadium and a programme.

My friends explained the programme to me and that the Leicester riders wore red and blue helmet colours and the Motherwell Eagles' riders wore white and yellow/black. The stadium was packed all around as four riders rode round to the starting area. The engine noise increased until suddenly the starting tapes rose and the four riders dashed forwards and around the first bends on the loose shale surface with no brakes. I was amazed because they were so close together. Even at my young age, I felt total respect for what I had just witnessed and, to this day, I still feel total respect for anyone who becomes a speedway rider.

I've never forgotten the result of that race: Gordon McGregor was the winner for the Eagles followed by Len Williams of the Hunters. Third was Noel Watson for the Eagles while the Hunters' Joe Bowkis fell. The scores were close all the way through but, to our relief, the result was a 43-41 win for Leicester.

Colin Gear: I lived with an aunt in Queniborough, which was part of Greater Leicester, during 1953. Uncle Roy, a very strict disciplinarian, asked me and his son, my cousin John, if we would like to go to speedway. We were both nine-years-old. Of course, things were very different in those days and any trip out was more than welcome.

He took us to Blackbird Road, the home of Leicester Hunters. We both immediately fell in love with speedway but had to behave ourselves more than usual, otherwise he wouldn't take us again.

A few of the names I remember from that meeting are captain Len Williams, Jack Geran, Charlie Barsby and Ivor Brown.

Around this time, Ken McKinlay was only doing the second-half scratch races but he was proving to be a very good rider. If I remember correctly, Len Williams broke his leg and the club contracted McKinlay. The rest, as they say, is history.

I did go on to have a few very awkward conversations with Ken whilst I was managing the Speedway Riders' Association because he was still one of my boyhood heroes.

Richard Bott: It was at Leicester's Blackbird Road at Easter sometime in the early 50s. It was the school holidays and I was staying with my uncle and aunt. They had never been to speedway but I persuaded them to take me and remember it was a challenge match between Leicester and Bradford. I loved the noise, the smell, the excitement and the pop music between the races.

Mike King: I first saw speedway when my dad took me to Exeter's County Ground on a hot and sunny Bank Holiday Monday in the early 50s. How well I remember sitting atop his shoulders and watching spellbound as the riders roared around the steeply banked circuit. The roar of the un-silenced engines echoing back off the whitewashed steel safety fence and clouds of acrid blue smoke drifting over us, bringing with it the intoxicating smell of Castrol R racing oil.

I don't recall who the opponents were but I do remember shouting very enthusiastically for a Falcon of the day by the name of Goog Hoskin.

Tony Lethbridge: I have vague memories of being taken to speedway at the County Ground by an aunt and watching pudding basin-helmeted riders on the fourth bend from the Greyhound Bar. My dad was watching from his favourite spot by the pits.

But the first meeting I clearly remember was on August Bank Holiday 1953, when the Falcons beat Plymouth 51-33. The track was pretty dusty and Johnny Applegate broke his ankle and was taken off on a stretcher. He told me many years later that his team-mate Jack Geran had knocked him off. When I asked Jack about this, he replied with a grin: "Of course I did!"

James Easter: It was at Caister Road, Great Yarmouth. We were on holiday at a nearby caravan site. It was August 1954 and I could recall hearing the noise when we were on holiday the previous year. The huge crowd, the smell, the noise . . . it was, at that time, the most exciting thing I had ever seen and it remains a superb sport when run correctly.

Edward Jinkerson: My first meeting was at Yarmouth 63 years ago. My mate's father took me in an old milk van.

Philip Dalling: I was taken to a Long Eaton v Exeter match at Station Road, which was close to my home. This was in the early 50s when an uncle and aunt from North Devon were on holiday in Derbyshire. I was barely five-years-old and can only remember the noise and what seemed to me at the time to be a very big crowd. I also recall being faintly embarrassed by the fact that my uncle was shouting very loudly for Exeter.

In August 1962, the situation was reversed and I was on holiday in North Devon. A local farmer invited me to go with him to the County Ground to see the local round of the Provincial League Riders' Championship, won by Len Silver with Pete Lansdale in second place. I can remember the exact spot where we stood on the terrace below the grandstand and I was hooked for life!

Paul Hiscock: I used to go to West Ham, where my hero was Jack Young. He was quite brilliant around Custom House and it was rare to see him get beaten.

I recall one year in particular when he partnered Alan Smith and 'Youngie' would often team-ride him around – when that initiative was quite a common practice – only to roar past

Provincial League star Len Silver of Exeter leading at Wolverhampton.

his partner off the final bends. But sometimes Smith would manage to turn a cert 5-1 into a 4-2 or a 3-3, even at that late stage of the race.

I can remember Keith Gurtner who had blue leathers, coloured leathers being quite unusual in those far-off days, and I remember the Hammers signing Gerry Hussey and a Norwegian called Basse Hveem, who didn't stay long but looked good. I think he had to return home for National Service. Split Waterman was another character.

Local derbies were also eagerly anticipated and to beat Wimbledon or Harringay seemed to add to the occasion.

Of course, the actual stadium itself helped to create an atmosphere as well, the grand ambience of Custom House contrasting greatly to what appears to be a council tip at Arena-Essex!

I do think that promoters went out of their way to entertain more in those far off days. There would often be an interval attraction (high-wire performers, for example) or some guy diving into a tank of lit fuel.

Punters did get value for money. A Britannia Shield match would span 18 heats and there would still be a second-half.

Also, Custom House would be the venue for the Golden Helmet match-race deciders, always a special occasion, and the two riders would ride in the second-half as well.

It was never quite the same when the club re-opened its doors in the 60s but was still a fine night, with a good atmosphere in a terrific stadium.

I lived in Ilford at the time and my mum would take me to the speedway because my dad worked there part-time on Tuesday race-nights. We'd get the bus from Ilford to Barking and then another to the Green Gate before getting the trolley bus to the stadium. On the way home, regular as clockwork, we'd stop at the chippy at the Green Gate for a bag of chips to eat on the bus home, while I worked my way through the *Speedway News*. Nostalgia is just not the same these days!

Eric Howard: My dad took me to Norwich when I was seven-years-old and I've been a speedway fan ever since. I can remember one meeting at Norwich when Jack Chignell came off on the second bend right in front of me. His bike picked up and sped off across the centre green, missing members of the track staff before hitting the safety fence near the pits, breaking the wooden fence. I can't remember if anyone was injured but in those days we used to stand against the fence to touch the riders' hands after a race. I used to like it when the riders pulled their handkerchiefs and goggles off, so we could see their faces.

I will always remember the rakers, the St John's and the track staff marching out to start the meeting to the tune of *Old Comrades*.

Bert Harkins: It was back in the mid-50s when my dad took me to Glasgow White City to see the Tigers. He was a Glasgow fireman and we lived in the Fire Station at Govan, within earshot of the un-silenced JAPs on a Wednesday night. If Dad was on the night shift, one of the other firemen would take me to White City.

Paul Ackroyd: It would have been at Odsal, Bradford, around 1956. My father took me there, apparently, from the age of one in 1952. He had attended the early dirt-track racing at Elland Road, Leeds before the Second World War. He then went to every single meeting at Odsal following the end of the War until they closed in the late-50s.

His friend was the 'pusher-offer' in the yellow jersey who kindly took me as a five-year-old

West Ham's Aussie Keith Gurtner wore distinctive blue leathers.

onto the track and into the pits prior to the start of a meeting. I can remember sitting on Arthur Forrest's bike and talking to him, and also meeting the rest of the Odsal team.

Prior to becoming a referee in 1980, I attended most of Bradford's meetings in the Provincial League, at both the Odsal and Greenfield stadiums, then Halifax from their first meeting in 1965 through to 1979.

Rob McColl: I first went to see the Rockets in the mid-to-late 50s when I was about 10-years-old. We would walk from where I lived in Hart Road in Thundersley down through Thundersley Common and up Claydons Lane to the track. On a quiet night, I could hear the racing from my house.

I used to follow the Rockets whenever I could afford to go and watch them but then I got a job at a local printing firm where we used to print the bookies' cards for the greyhounds, which introduced me to Tom Stanley.

I managed to get a stadium pass from him to give me admission to the track for meetings and practice sessions. This got me a job at the speedway, working track-side, and my first season was as a grader at The Weir (roundabout) end of the track, raking the surface back after each race and getting as close to the action as I could ever have dreamed of.

My second season saw me working in the pits, getting the bikes ready for the next race and then pushing the riders to start them. There were four of us, we worked as two teams and we swapped home team and away team each meeting.

I remember once pushing the bikes out onto the grass in front of the main stand for the presentation. I was pushing Sandy McGillivray's bike out when I jumped onto the saddle and dropped the clutch! My own motorbike was a pig to start and I often had to bump-start it, which I did by habit. Fortunately, I realised what I was doing and grabbed the clutch before the engine could fire. I never did it again!

Another job I had was after the racing had finished. If there was a greyhound meeting scheduled, it was my job to go round the track with a broom and clear all the dirt off the hare rail so that it could perform correctly. This earned me an extra £1 on top of my wages for the speedway meeting.

Richard Tyrrell: At Oxford on Good Friday in 1957, Oxford v Leicester Hunters. I've still got the programme. At the time, I was spending some hours at a local cycle speedway track, when the big boys weren't around, behind the air raid shelters opposite my primary school – much to my father's disgust, as I'd come home with buckled wheels, bent forks, etc, not to mention grazes and skin burns.

Easter was coming round and the boys were getting excited about going to speedway. My father wouldn't let me go with them so I begged him to take me. He'd already been a couple of times with his brother to the old Knowle Stadium in Bristol so, in the end, he relented. We cycled to the stadium and locked our bikes outside the turnstiles. We were late and rushed up the steps on the fourth bend just in time as the riders came out for Heat 1. They made their way on the cackley-sounding bikes away from us to the start. There was a roar and they were off, away from us round the top bend before coming down the back straight. I was amazed because they seemed to be going so fast. I was quite scared that they would all crash into the fence but, no, the back wheels came out, big plumes of shale and round the bend in front of us. I was immediately captivated in that moment by something I have followed ever since, giving me a lifetime of pleasure and interest.

Chris Birtles: My parents took me from being only a few months old. The first meeting I remember was Belle Vue v Swindon in 1958 and Mike Broadbank's distinctive red leathers. I was five at the time and with it being at Belle Vue, with all its entertainment, it made a big impression.

David Gordon: My cousins Gordon and Carol Boon took me to Belle Vue in 1959. I think it was Belle Vue v Coventry and I remember an exciting young rider called Tink Maynard. I

Rayleigh trio Jack Unstead, Tom O'Connor and Sandy McGillivray.

thought, 'how fantastic to be named Tink' but he was actually called Derek! Sadly, he was killed in a tragic track crash at Norwich the next year.

Stephen Jinkerson: I was taken by my parents. The first meeting I have vague memories of was at the age of two, Norwich v Swindon, about 1959. I think it was the last meeting of that season and I remember being frightened of people setting off fireworks on the terraces. I can remember seeing Mike 'Spider' Broadbank in his red leathers.

Roly Clarke: At Swindon in around 1959-60, when my family went to support our local grass-track hero Ron Taylor.

John Pharaoh: It was New Cross, in either 1959 or '60. I went with some other

Mike Broadbank - The Red Devil of Swindon.

local kids, Johnnie Smith and his sister Barbara, 'little' Jimmy Whitmore and 'Porky' Rowlands. I was either nine or 10-years-old.

I remember being told I'd been on television (we didn't have one then) when an outside broadcast of speedway at New Cross was featured on *Sportsview* with Eric Dimmock.

Martin Rogers: I was a 16-year-old cub reporter with Reg Hayter's sports reporting agency in London in 1960, dreaming of becoming a famous cricket writer. At the same time, I was also covering a variety of other sports for all the daily and regional papers.

One day, I was told that that evening I would be going to Wimbledon to report on their match against Swindon – and had to ask 'what is speedway?' because I really only had the faintest knowledge of its existence, still less its many nuances.

Fortunately, some ultra-friendly scribes such as Eric Linden and Len Steed of the Press Association gave me an on-the-spot briefing and that was the start of an involvement with the sport which developed enormously over the next few years and kept me fully engaged for three decades.

Even now, I can still picture the scene at Plough Lane, the colour, the noise and of course, the smell. Ronnie Moore was in his pomp, the Dons were the Manchester United of the day, and the cheery, character-crammed Robins were easy to admire, too.

Phil Rice: Somewhere in my psyche, speedway must have always been there. When I was very young, I had Subbuteo Table Speedway as a toy where you sent metal balls down a tube, which hit the toy rider, propelling him forward – hopefully! Then I saw an advert on a hoarding near to where I lived advertising speedway at Stanley Stadium. I had to give it a go.

My first meeting was Liverpool v Stoke in the Provincial League on Easter Monday 1960. Brian Craven got a maximum for his losing Pirates whilst Ray Harris top scored for the Potters. This was the first Liverpool meeting of the 1960 season.

The Pirates were generally a poor side and finished above Bradford and I think only beat

Bradford at home that season. On reflection, it was probably no surprise when the side did not see out the season, closing in September.

The Pirates gradually strengthened up with old-timer Wal Morton, Kiwi Bryce Subritsky and Dave Dodd joining and a late season showing from one Garry Lindsey who I think turned out to be Belle Vue manager Ken Sharples, who rode for Newcastle the following season. But all the other sides were getting stronger, with Reg Fearman and Trevor Redmond making mid-season comebacks.

John Brownhill: The opening meeting at Sheffield's Owlerton Stadium on Thursday, April 21, 1960, when Frank Varey re-introduced the sport at the beginning of the Provincial League. The Sheffield team was made up mainly of older riders, who had virtually retired in the 50s, and a younger element from second-halvers at Belle Vue. They raced against a Belle Vue second team and were well beaten but Varey signed on several of the Belle Vue youngsters, such as Tony Robinson and Jack Kitchen.

The publicity surrounding the reopening in 1960 was quite extensive and the local evening newspaper, the *Sheffield Star*, produced a speedway special edition for some time. This publicity was what firstly attracted me to visit the track and I, along with crowds estimated at seven or eight thousand, shouted for the Tigers. The team was strengthened over the first season and the crowds really looked forward to their Thursday night's speedway. Every Thursday, there was a meeting. I did not visit any other track that season but did so in later years, when able to travel to Hyde Road, Manchester for the special meetings there.

In late 1961, the team manager was Ernest Palmer, who had ridden speedway himself, and

Wimbledon's Ronnie Moore presenting the prizes to the finalists of a supporters' Subbuteo Table Speedway event.

he convinced Frank Varey to sign a rider who had been mainly involved in second-half racing at Norwich. Clive Featherby was to prove a sensation and a great crowd favourite at Owlerton. His hard and determined racing often brought the crowd to their feet, especially his dives down the inside of opponents on his favourite third bend at Owlerton.

To tell people now that you would go home hoarse from shouting following Thursday nights at Owlerton is something *today*'s supporters will find hard to believe. There is so little in *today*'s speedway to get excited about.

Clive soon became my first speedway favourite and, during his best years in the sport at Sheffield, certainly was not far from controversy on many occasions. We still keep in contact.

Doug Wyer: I first went to a speedway meeting with a school friend. His father was a supporter and we went with him. I remember Len Williams riding, so if it was early in the 1960 season, I would have been 12-years-old. He won many of his races that night and I remember black leathers, chrome bikes and the rider in the red helmet colour winning most races. I know now that these riders were the heat leaders and the best riders.

I found out later that Len Williams lived in the next village to me and he also worked in a factory next to where I worked. As time went on, he didn't like going to away matches because he had to have time off work, something that I got the sack for in 1970 when I had a week off work because Frank Varey asked me to go on a southern tour to stand in for an injured rider.

We raced at Swindon on the Saturday, stayed at the Middleditchs', raced on Monday at Exeter, back to the Middleditchs', Poole on Wednesday and then Sheffield on Thursday.

I didn't go to work on Friday and was sacked on the Monday morning. They asked me why

Clive Featherby was always hard and determined.

I had taken the week off and then I was told to decide if I wanted to be a speedway rider or a centre lathe turner in the company. When I said I wanted to be a rider, I was told I was mad and that I should write out my notice, so I worked a week's notice and then I was out of a good job and not in a team! But later in the year, Frank put me out on loan to Berwick so I could earn some money and get some valuable experience. The rest is history.

Jeff Davies: I've been going to speedway since I was born (1950) but I don't remember the early years. I remember 'Peo' Soderman, who rode for Coventry in the mid-50s, but the first meeting I recall well is when Henryk Zyto, who rode for the Bees, won the Midland Riders' Championship in 1960. It was a big meeting in those days and I remember him being mobbed by all the female fans after the meeting.

John Somerville: My uncle took me to Edinburgh in 1960. I'm sure it was a bit of a journey, involving two buses and a train from

Fife. I was about 16 at the time and he just about fainted when Dick Campbell was riding because he remembered him from the 1948-54 era (Dick looked older than he was because of his premature balding). I had seen speedway on BBC TV in the 50s and loved it.

Andrew Edwards: A match at Cradley Heath in 1960, the first year of the great Provincial League. Best speedway ever in 1960-61. Amazingly, I cannot remember why I went!

Harry Ward: Real childhood memory stuff here. It involved getting on a bus in Prince Regent Lane, Custom House – yes, the home of the Hammers. I would have been five-years-old or so. We then got a train to Whitechapel (which I was convinced was called White Apple). From there, another train to New Cross and somewhere around 1960, we were going to my first taste of speedway. I distinctly remember lots of people crowding around a man in a white coat selling little star-shaped orange badges with riders' pictured on them. I can remember riders such as Stan Stevens, Barry Briggs, Reg and Eddie Reeves. Sadly, I remember nothing about the racing but instead the smell, dust and my cheese spread sandwiches. It was a long way home but the start of a long love affair with speedway that has seen me watch racing not only all over the country, but also the world.

Alan Jones: Recollections of my first speedway meeting are hazy, to say the least. I was probably around the age of six or seven when my parents took me to watch Leicester Hunters at Blackbird Road. I don't remember the exact meeting but what I do recall is Ken McKinlay taking his hands off his handlebars halfway down the back straight to adjust his gloves every time he came out to race. As a young boy, it is the silliest of things you recall above the racing.

The highlight for me every week was a bottle of Vimto and a Wagon Wheel purchased from the stall at the bottom of the terracing halfway along the back straight.

In those days, I was not allowed to attend meetings every week with my parents, particularly during the early and late weeks of the season when it was really chilly. So on race-nights, my parents put me to bed without saying a word to me about the fact that they were leaving the house to watch the Hunters race. My grandmother baby sat and so as not to alert me to the fact that they had left the house, my parents sneaked out and pushed the car down the road far enough for me not to hear the engine start.

Another thing was the end-of-season donkey derby race and gigantic fireworks display, which I was eagerly looking forward to. To my dismay, I missed it because I slept all the way through it and was only woken when it was time to go home.

To get to the point of answering the question, it was the 1960 World Final at Wembley that I remember with any detail. The walk up Wembley Way wearing a Ken McKinlay rosette in the red and yellow colours of the Hunters pinned to my coat and the sight of the stadium has stuck in my mind. The excitement of cheering on three Leicester riders – McKinlay, Bryan Elliott and Stefan Kwoczala – and the added bonus of seeing former Hunters riders Rune Sormander and Marian Kaiser race again was a night to remember. Then, of course, to top it all, the three-man run-off between Ove Fundin, Ronnie Moore and Peter Craven for the title. A magic day out for a seven-year-old.

Dennis Lindo: My first meeting was in 1961 at Cleveland Park, Middlesbrough, who were then in the Provincial League. I think the visiting team may have been Wolverhampton with Graham Warren riding for the Wolves. I was taken by my 'uncle' Tom, who was sports mad. My brothers and I called him uncle but he was actually Dad's cousin. He announced he had a surprise for me in a few weeks' time (a lifetime for a nine-year-old) but didn't tell me what it was, and I could go with him provided I had behaved myself and Dad gave the thumbs up.

New Cross Rangers of 1960. Left to right: Jimmy Gooch, Eric Williams, Leo McAuliffe, Reg Luckhurst, Barry Briggs, Tommy Sweetman, Derek Timms. On bike: Split Waterman.

When he visited, he would ask Dad: 'How's the thumbs?' and he also warned me that the surprise would only go ahead if the weather was fine.

When the day arrived, there was some rain and I assumed the surprise was cancelled but it wasn't and Tom went by himself. He then offered to take me the following week. This time, I would be at his house at 6.00pm whatever the weather. When Thursday arrived, we took the bus from Thornaby to Middlesbrough – the bus stop was right outside Cleveland Park.

Having entered the stadium, we walked past the pits and I remember there was a lot of people standing around the pits watching the riders prepare their bikes. At this time, I still had no idea what to expect. As we took up our position on the back straight, I heard for the first time the sound of a speedway engine as the riders began warming up their machines. Soon the bikes were wheeled out onto the track and lined up on the home straight. Then the pop music being played over the public address system gave way to the *Entry of the Gladiators* march and the riders and track staff marched from the pits towards the waiting bikes. Following the introductions and the playing of the national anthem, the bikes were fired up and the riders completed a lap of the track waving to the crowd, all in black leathers and their respective race-jackets. They didn't have to wear crash helmets on parade in those days. I was hooked from that moment, it seemed to be such a spectacle and I hadn't even seen my first race. When the first race took place, I was simply amazed at what I was seeing.

Stephen Quinsey: Although I had been taken to speedway at an earlier date, my first memory was when a school friend introduced me and that was May 22, 1961 at Wimbledon. The Dons won but I can't remember who the away team was. All it took was for the riders to leave the tapes and hit the first bend. From then on I was hooked on the sport.

At the time of that first meeting, I was 10-years-old and have followed speedway ever since. I have my friend to thank for getting me interested to start with.

Andy Wilkinson: The father of a school friend and neighbour used to take us to Wimbledon once in a while on a Monday night. This was a couple of years before the formation of the British League and my memories of those visits are a bit hazy.

I do remember hanging around the riders in the pits after the meeting while they loaded their bikes into, onto or behind their cars, more often than not hanging out of the boot. Ron How was the rider I remember from that era.

My first real memories are from the start of the British League when I was persuaded to go with some friends from school and my girlfriend (now wife). It was then that I started taking notice of what was going on. Ron How had moved on but the Dons had put together a solid team

Leicester's Ken McKinlay holding his favoured inside line.

of Nygren, Hedge, Luckhurst, Tebby, Dugard, Edwards and Coomber or Hughes.

Paul Jeffries: I was aged 14, it was March 1962, Northern Cup, Sheffield 59 Newcastle 19. At that time, there were lots of advertising posters around the city, blue and yellow, with a sketch of a rider in action, and each week near the bottom of the poster they would paste an overlay detailing the next meeting. I'd begun noticing these the previous summer, and when they started reappearing for the new season, me and a friend worked out that we had enough pocket money to give it a try. There were special buses from the city centre, crowds were five or six thousand, and despite the runaway score we were captivated by the atmosphere, the black leathers, the chrome machines under the lights, the roar of the engines (long before silencers), the delicious smell of the Castrol R. I bought *Speedway Star* at the track to find out more – I still have it – and I have every issue from that day to this, lovingly filed in the attic.

Rod Haynes: I went to Sheffield during early May 1962 when I was 11. I was taken along by my elder brother Tony and a friend of his.

Having moved from Salisbury aged 13, where I had supported Southampton football team, I noticed in the local paper that Southampton Saints speedway team were top of the National League in 1962. That, and the fact that Swindon tracked a Swedish rider in Arne Carlsson was interesting, something soccer did not offer then. So I finally made my debut at the last Swindon home match of 1962 against Wimbledon.

I wasn't hooked that night, but my second visit featuring a last race decider made me a regular and the arrival of Barry Briggs at Swindon sealed it.

Geoff Tillotson: My first time was in 1962 at Greenfield Stadium in Bradford. An uncle took me to see it when I was around 11-years-old.

Dave Ede: I believe the first meeting I ever heard was the 1962 World Final (Peter Craven's last win) when I sat outside Wembley Stadium with fellow 13-year-olds. I think it was the sound of the bikes and the crowd reaction that originally got me hooked.

Malcolm Salter: I was about seven-years-old and my dad took me to Exeter one Monday

Wimbledon trio Johnny Edwards, Mike Coomber and Trevor Hedge.

night. I can remember hiding behind the fence when the riders broadsided into the third bend where we were and getting a covering of shale. Also, the smell of methanol and Castrol R.

Glen Norton: It would be Norwich Speedway back in 1961. I can't remember too much about it, but they were great days at the Firs Stadium.

Paul Kerry: I was born and raised in Halifax and remember my dad talking about "going t' dirt-track" at The Shay before I was born and also watching it "up Thrum Hall", the Halifax RLFC ground, before the War.

One spring evening in 1962, when I was in the top class at primary school, he bundled me and a pal into his Ford Anglia and took us to Greenfield Stadium in Bradford, about six or seven miles down the road, to watch Bradford Panthers v Sheffield Tigers. I didn't know what to expect really but, as soon as the tapes went up, I was hooked forever. I couldn't believe the speed, colour, noise and smell of the racing. I can't recall the score but I know Bradford lost, as they did most times that year. Someone told us about *Speedway Star* and I ordered it every week and devoured everything about speedway.

David Hoggart: I can remember my father taking me to Cleveland Park in the Provincial League days, not every week because he was on call and had to be at home every other week in the evenings. I clearly remember Kevin Torpie, Dave Younghusband, Eric Boothroyd, a very young Eric Boocock, Clive Hitch, Brian McKeown, Slant Payling, Alan Butterfield and Johnny Fitzpatrick, to name a few who represented the Bears then.

It seemed like you had five regulars and a couple who were in or out for whatever reason. Ivor Brown was one of the visitors booed the most and when Cradley were in town, it seemed like everyone was talking about it from Monday morning to Thursday night. The *Middlesbrough Evening Gazette* used to do a Speedway Special every week, a broadsheet wrap-around with eight pages. Just imagine a full page broadsheet preview of 'tonight's match' and a full page match report on the last home meeting.

I can't remember a specific meeting but what I do remember is the smell and the atmosphere. The stadium used to erupt when the tapes went up and it was all holler for four laps.

Richard Mason: As a child in the 60s, our annual holiday was a week up to relatives in Stockton-on-Tees. Along with visits to the local seaside resorts, it also meant the once-a-year Thursday night trip to speedway at Cleveland Park, Middlesbrough.

My earliest memories are of the silver machines being pushed out and lined up along the track and then the riders parading out, all in black apart from the basic team body colours on their chests.

When the racing started, the distinctive helmet colours were the only way I could tell the riders apart, although the rest of the crowd seemed to know every rider. Then there was the magazine seller who paraded round the terraces. The earliest programme I have from this period, although I can't remember the actual event (I was only five), was the Battle of Britain Trophy in September 1964, won with a 15-point maximum by a certain Ivan Mauger.

Steve Casey: My first-ever visit was to Belle Vue's Hyde Road, the playground of the north! I was seven and taken by my friend and his mum and dad who were big Aces fans. I remember being terrified as I watched from the stand in the middle of the back straight. I couldn't believe the speed, the noise and the smell. I don't remember who it was against, but I do remember a tiny rider with red hair and a green scarf being pushed off from the pits. It was Peter Craven, so it must have been fairly early in the 1963 season and he was the reigning World Champion at the time. I wished I had paid more attention to things now, though.

Peter Oakes: The first meeting I can vividly remember was a Test match at Belle Vue between Great Britain and Sweden. It was pouring with rain and the majority of riders wore waterproofs over their leathers but Soren Sjosten was absolutely brilliant in the wet. I'd been to quite a few meetings before that one, dating back to my first visit to hometown club Liverpool in the 50s, but this one meeting stands out in my mind. How the meeting ever went on, I am not sure.

Young Eric Boocock surrounded by a group of admiring fans at Middlesbrough.

Howard Murphy: My first meeting was around 1963 at Belle Vue when my dad took me – he had been a massive fan of speedway in the 40s and 50s. All the riders were in plain black leathers and the noise and exciting racing were brilliant to a young lad at that time.

Richard Lambert: Cradley Heath v Exeter at the back end of 1963. Rained-off! I went with school friends and we still meet up at the Cardiff GP each year.

Robert Rogers: My parents took me to West Ham on April 7, 1964, when the sport returned there, for the opening meeting v Wimbledon. Bjorn Knutson scored an unbeaten 12 as Hammers won the challenge match 46-38. The eight-man West Ham team was: Knutson, Stan Stevens, Barry Briggs (guest), Ron Brett, Norman Hunter, Reg Luckhurst, Alf Hagon and Bob Dugard, while the Dons had: Sverre Harrfeldt, Roy Trigg, Leo McAuliffe, Pete Jarman, Olle Nygren (who dropped his only point in five rides to fellow Swede 'Knutty'), Gerald Jackson, Jim Tebby and Ernie Baker.

Paul Goodwin: Near the end of the 1965 season, I think I saw West Ham v Swindon and Exeter. At the time, I worked with Dave Erskine, who later became Hackney team manager, and he got me interested. I worked for a small trade magazine publishers in Farringdon Street in the advertisement department. It was in the mid-60s. I loved the smell, the atmosphere and the involvement as well as the programmes and the friendliness of the other fans.

Steve Wilks: Unfortunately, I remember very little about my first speedway meeting. I was taken to West Ham when I was about six by my next door neighbour. I don't really remember anything about those first few meetings but I recall the names Hunter and McKinlay and the fact they seemed to win a lot.

It was at my local track Sunderland (Boldon, actually). I had seen the advertisement for it in a shop. I'd seen speedway on the television, but never live. I went along with a friend and we were both unsure of what to expect but it was Sunderland v Newcastle, a derby for our first-ever meeting. It didn't get much better than that.

Sunderland Saints' team consisted of Maury McDermott, Dave Collins, Graham Coombs, Gordon Guasco, Vic Ridgeon, Jim Airey and Ray Day. Newcastle Diamonds tracked two riders who were to play a big part in our future speedway enjoyment throughout the next 10 years – Ivan Mauger, who, on that first night, was unbeaten, and Russ Dent, who would go on to captain Sunderland when the sport returned to Boldon in 1971.

Once the meeting got underway, I was captivated immediately. The sight of four riders hurtling around a track was scary (and I was only watching), thrilling and enjoyable. The noise and the smell of Castrol R was something else.

The Saints lost by 32-44 but somehow that didn't seem to matter that much as we felt we had had a terrific night out. Suffice to say, I attended all of the nine meetings staged before Messrs. Parker and Bridgett closed us down in order to reinforce both Newcastle and Wolverhampton with Sunderland riders. I was that annoyed and angry that I stopped going to speedway – in fact, I swore that I would never go to another meeting in my life. I had not attended any away meetings in 1964.

But in 1971, speedway was revived at Sunderland under Len Silver and Allied Presentations. My vows were forgotten and I duly turned up at the first meeting.

For four years, I was in my element. I met a lot of people who became friends, some no longer with us. We worked on the track (for free) and paid to get in to try to keep costs down (nothing changes). After changing hands a number of times, the track closed in 1974 and has never re-opened for speedway.

Doug Nicolson: May 1964, Glasgow 53 Newcastle 25. Maury Mattingley became the first rider to beat Ivan Mauger in the Northern League that night. A classmate at school had been to all the Tigers' meetings and did a great job selling it to the rest of us. He changed my life.

Robert Wiles: The first speedway meeting I ever attended was Great Britain v USSR at Wembley in 1964. My parents used to watch speedway at Harringay in the early 50s so were familiar with the sport and they decided to take my sister and I to this meeting.

I would have been seven at the time and had never heard of, or seen, speedway. The things that stick in my mind to this day are the noise, the glittering chrome on the GB team's bikes

Norman Hunter and Ken McKinlay were big stars at West Ham in the mid-60s.

and the spits of blue flame from the exhausts. Plus how big Wembley Stadium was, especially to a seven-year-old.

The sport sort of faded from my mind after that and I didn't get to attend another meeting until a friend's parents invited me along to watch Canterbury in 1969. That was the first time I fully experienced the addictive smell of methanol and Castrol R fumes. Although I didn't know what it was then, I became hooked.

Ken Burnett: I first went to speedway in the 60s. I can remember the smell of the bikes in the pits and my brother telling me the tapes were there because the riders had to jump them. I was very young and believed him!

Geoff Theobald: I was on holiday in Bournemouth and was taken along to Poole. It was August 25, 1965. My mother had been to Belle Vue when my dad was stationed up there just after the War and I have a couple of Hyde Road programmes she passed on to me – the Daily Mail National Trophy semi-final v Wimbledon being one, plus a Harringay London v Australia match from the same year.

What I remember about that first visit to Poole was sitting on the terrace steps, where now the big glass grandstand is, and being very excited when Pete Smith fell, picked himself up, and almost caught the rider in front as the fans roared him on. I reckon I was hooked from then on.

Dave Stallworthy: My brother John used to race speedway and grasstrack and took me to Swindon v Exeter on May 29, 1965.

David Beresford: My first meeting was a challenge match between Belle Vue and West

Ham at Hyde Road in 1965. The track was saturated and it rained throughout. If it had been a league match, it probably would not have gone ahead. I went with a friend called Nigel Roylance, whom my mum badgered into taking me because she was fed up of me being bored. That night changed my life; I was hooked!

Paul Watson: The third meeting ever held at King's Lynn in 1965. I recall standing on the dog-track fence to be able to see.

Ray Griffiths: Mine was West Ham in 1965 when I was five. I can't remember much other than the noise and the backs of people's legs. My dad Vic was born in East Ham and so liked to visit his old stomping ground.

Karl Fiala: At Rye House in about 1965. I went on an expedition on the train with some friends and immediately became hooked.

Clive Inwood: An early season match, Oxford v Long Eaton, in 1966. Jimmy Gooch had just come back from injury. I lived near Henley-on-Thames and was interested in the speedway results and because Ron How was virtually always the only Oxford scorer shown (as now, only the top scorers were in the paper), I became a fan of him. Sadly, I never saw him ride but I became interested in speedway and persuaded my father to take me to a match. I was hooked from that moment on. My father later told me he used to go to New Cross in his younger days and Cordy Milne was his favourite rider.

Carol Stock: It was July 4, 1967, West Ham v Hackney, and Hammers lost 37-41. My parents Frank and Doris went to West Ham before they were married and Dad later got a job on the turnstiles there.

Mum decided to take my brother Keith and I "just once" to see where Dad worked part-time. That was 46 years ago and Mum and I are still going to speedway.

Tony Barnard: It was at Halifax in the first week of May 1967, Dukes v Belle Vue.

Martin Jackson: In 1967 at The Shay but I cannot remember who the Dukes rode against. Mum and Dad took me as they were speedway fans.

Jimmy Gooch on a winning night at Oxford.

John Farr: The Wills Internationale at Wimbledon in 1967. As I was only 11 at the time, I can't remember too much about the meeting, except the heady smell of racing oil. It reminded me of my first passion, motorcycle road-racing, which I saw at Brands Hatch. A family friend – an avid Wimbledon supporter – took me to see my first speedway meeting. I didn't go again until the start of the 1969 season, this time at Hackney.

Mike Keir: The 1968 Wills Internationale at Wimbledon. It was Whit Monday, so I probably didn't have school the next day. I was taken by my elder cousin (he had a car) and his girlfriend. I was weeks short of my ninth birthday. The stadium was packed, the atmosphere electric. I remember the bikes went round the opposite way to what I had expected. But the stand-out thing was the exotic names of the riders: Odd Fossengen, Torbjorn Harryson, Ivan Mauger (how can that possibly be pronounced 'Major'?), Sverre Harrfeldt, the alliterative Barry Briggs, and one called 'rider' (Reidar Eide). Even the English riders had peculiar names – Boocock for heaven's sake? I was enchanted before a wheel was turned in combat.

Chris Gosling: King's Lynn in 1968, aged five. It was scarily noisy, thanks to the JAPs and their open exhausts. I can't remember who the opposing team were but I remember the smell of Castrol R and the chrome and shiny black leathers. My father had always gone to Norwich but when King's Lynn opened, we went there frequently

Fans look down on the steeply banked, fast Shay track at Halifax in the mid-60s.

Ray Walters: King's Lynn in the late 60s, I think, when my sister was Miss Ipswich Speedway!

Ian Glover: Canterbury v Belle Vue 'Babes' on May 18, 1968. It finished 38-39 after a last heat decider. As a nine-year-old, my dad took me along to see this 'new sport' at Kingsmead. What a thrill, crowds the like of which I had never witnessed – and dust!

Greg Unwin: At the end of the 1967-68 football season, my football team, Plymouth Argyle, were relegated from the old second division. The team had suffered a really terrible season, winning only five matches at home, and they were relegated by Easter Monday.

I was so depressed about it all and, as a 16-year-old at the time, I took the situation very much to heart. In early May 1968, I read in the *Western Evening Herald* that speedway was returning to Plymouth's Pennycross Stadium. A new league was being formed (British League Division Two) and a Plymouth Devils team was to be one of 10 founding members.

I decided to go to the first meeting on May 31 (postponed by one week) against Weymouth and I was instantly hooked. The match was full of incident, which only helped to add to the spectacle. Even better, Plymouth won 41-36 (more later).

"I love this speedway racing," I told a nearby spectator.

"If you think this is good, you want to go to Exeter," he replied. "They go nearly twice as fast as this in Division One."

I decided that before the end of the season, I would visit the home of the Falcons but, in the meantime, I attended every Plymouth home meeting. It did not take me long to work out how to fill in the programme racecard and soon I was discussing tactics and the like with the other trackside pundits.

In July 1968, I did get to Exeter to see the Falcons beat Wimbledon 49-29. The Dons brought a huge following of fans of all ages and both sexes, which surprised me as we never saw any away supporters at Pennycross.

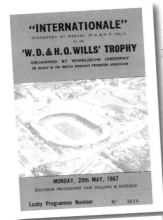

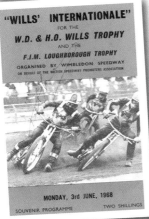

Both the Falcons and the Devils went through the 1968 season with 100 per cent home records, which was a remarkable achievement for promoters Pete Lansdale and Wally Mawdsley. As Exeter's development team, the Devils had achieved their goal of providing riders for the Exeter side, with four of the Devils appearing for the Falcons that year.

Steve Johnston: I believe I was first taken to speedway at the age of eight by my father. It was the Great Britain v Russia World League match at West Ham on June 29, 1968. I recall it being a Saturday evening and having to be carried on his back part of the way home, as it was a long walk from North Woolwich through the Connaught Bridge (docks) and down Prince Regent Lane to the stadium. Although I can recall hardly anything of the actual meeting (GB won 52-26), I do know I was hooked and began to go regularly not long afterwards, right through to the sad end at Custom House in 1972.

I still have my first speedway badge from that night - a West Ham badge.

And I must add this: watching Retro Speedway's *50s and 60s DVD*, there it was, footage from the above meeting! Thank you very much – after all these years, I never knew it even existed.

Kay Walker: I first went to speedway at Hackney. It was the last match of either the 1968 or 1969 season, Hawks v West Ham. One match and I was hooked.

Richard Clark: Wimbledon v Newcastle, around September-time, 1968. The old man was working on the milk in those days and had been assigned to a Wimbledon depot for a couple of weeks to help in relief. He got friendly with a bloke there, Alan, who told him about speedway, and invited the old man and old dear along. They went to, I think, Wimbledon v Wolverhampton and came home saying how much they'd enjoyed it and how I should go with them the next week.

I was more into football at the time, but agreed to give it a whirl. I thought it was OK, and did go a couple more times that year, but the turning point was having a school mate, Tony Hitchin, go along with me in the early weeks of the 1969 season. He got into it and we became pretty avid fans. Inevitably, being speedway, after his first meeting he decided Terry Betts was his favourite rider, so I had to explain to him they had this weird system called 'guests' and Bettsy wasn't actually a Wimbledon rider but rode for King's Lynn at the time. I still can't really explain it very well to this day!

Bryan Newbold: Leicester v King's Lynn on April 1, 1969. I'd never heard of speedway before but my dad, who used to go to Leicester Super many years before, asked me if I'd like to go. We'd moved up to Leicester from Bromley in the previous September and my only experience of live motorsport prior to this was one visit to Crayford to watch stock cars.

Before the first lap had been completed that evening, I was completely hooked and had a new sporting hero in Ray Wilson. I knew from that first lap that all I wanted to be was a speedway rider. I was completely captivated by the smell, speed and sight of the chrome-plated bikes under the floodlights.

Mark Wilkinson: Leicester v Belle Vue on July 29, 1969. The Lions won 43-35, despite

Plymouth Devils in 1968. Left to right: Tony George, Ian Gills, Frank Payne, Mike Gimlett, Phil Woodcock, Chris Roynon, Dave Whittaker. On bike: Mike Cake.

providing only five heat winners. Ivan Mauger won the opening heat from Norman Storer, Ray Wilson and Chris Pusey before going on to complete a 12-point maximum. Leicester's match-winner was young starlet Graham Plant with 10 from reserve. I lived only a few minutes from Blackbird Road and it was a school friend who asked me to go.

Alan Johns: The first meeting I went to with my mum, dad and brothers Roger and Peter was at Wimbledon in 1969. We'd been invited along by a couple of families we met at junior grass-track racing in Kent on Sunday afternoons. The Dad's name, I remember, was Alan Rowney and his son John raced against Roger on 200cc Triumph Tiger cubs. Luckily, Wimbledon was our nearest track so after that first visit, as a family, we were hooked.

Bill Halliwell: I first went to Belle Vue in 1969 when I was six-years-old. My parents used to go in the 50s and I think the reporter on the old local paper had free tickets, so my dad took me. From the first race, I was hooked on the noise, the speed and then the smell. I almost never missed a home meeting until Hyde Road closed in 1987.

Steve Smith: My father took me to my first meeting. As I recall, it was Belle Vue v Coventry in 1969.

Pete Rout: It was when Ipswich reopened at Foxhall Heath on April 17, 1969 against Rochester Bombers. My dad used to go to Foxhall in the 50s and my cousins asked if I'd like to go. In the Rochester team that day was Frank Wendon, who now rides with us in the 'Blast

Ray Wilson in 1969 with actress Carol Dilworth, the hostess on TV's *Golden Shot*.

from the Past' vintage races.

Dick Partridge: At Foxhall Heath in 1969, but I can't remember the opposition. I went following reports from my elder brother that it was a spectacle to behold. I was not disappointed and became a keen track raker for a few years before acquiring a JAP from Poole's Geoff Mudge.

John Vine: I was always keen on spectating at scrambles and grass-track racing, so when my father-in-law suggested going to Poole Speedway in 1969, I jumped at the suggestion. The Pirates thrashed Cradley Heath and I will always remember the cheering throughout the racing, not just at the end. Even now, I can remember the announcer Jack Knott saying "hello everybody" before giving the result. From memory, the top riders were Pete Smith, Geoff Mudge, Odd Fossengen and Ross Gilbertson.

Robert Gray: As an eight-year-old and taken to The Shay to see the Coventry Bees with my younger brother John in 1969.

Pete Butler: My first meeting was as a schoolboy at Reading's Tilehurst track in late 1969 or early 1970. I had a school mate who lived in our road and his older sister's boyfriend and his mates used to go. I was told they used to race their cars back to the village (about eight miles), so when he asked if I wanted to visit the track, it sounded like an exciting evening out, though I think it was the car trip home that appealed more as I don't recall knowing what speedway was!

John Perry: The reopening of the Wembley Lions in 1970. My dad had been an avid Lions supporter until they closed in the 50s and after that first match against Hackney Hawks, I was totally hooked.

Peter Lush: Wembley Lions v Sheffield Tigers on June 6, 1970. I lived in Cricklewood, a bus ride from Wembley, was 15-years-old and a friend took me. I don't think I had even heard of speedway, football and cricket were the main sports I watched. But it was a good outing on a Saturday night. It was the Lions' second home meeting. Ove Fundin top scored with 11, but Sheffield won 39-38.

Kevin Ashcroft: Belle Vue v Wimbledon, 1970. I went with my father, mother and brother and hardly ever missed a home meeting after that for many years, apart from holidays. I went to Belle Vue almost every Saturday night for years and, 44 years later, I still go as much as I can.

Steve Ridgway: Belle Vue v Poole on July 11, 1970. I'd originally wanted to go and see the stock cars and had never considered speedway at all. My dad put it off a few times and eventually took me to watch "this speedway thingy" instead. I wanted to go every week after that.

Rob Scrutton: Young England v Young Sweden at Foxhall in 1970. My parents were supporters in their courting days and went to Norwich by motorbike every Saturday before there was a track at Ipswich. They then followed the sport at both venues until around 1956, when my sister was born. She was followed by me and my brother over the next five years, so speedway pretty much stopped for my parents.

When Ipswich reopened in 1969, there was good coverage in the local newspapers so I asked all sorts of questions to find out what it was all about and was told lots of stories about the likes of Ove Fundin, Sid Clarke and others of that period. Mum and Dad took their three kids to the England v Sweden match, which was a total surprise to us, but I think we all experienced the 'wow' factor.

The second meeting was Young England v Young Sweden in 1971 and we then went to all of the remaining home fixtures in that season. Of course, 1972 in Division One followed and we were all hooked. We didn't realise how lucky we were when John Berry was in charge. We didn't find out until he wasn't there anymore.

John Baxter: I first went to Boston when they raced on Wednesdays in 1970. My uncle and auntie loved motorbike racing and used to go to Norwich Speedway, so when speedway started locally, we went with them.

Kevin Fall: It was at Leicester for the East Midlands Open on September 1, 1970. I was 12-years-old and a sports fanatic. I was particularly football crazy and wanted to go to every Leicester City home match with my friends, but my father was horrified by the growing tide of hooliganism and violence associated with the game, so he wouldn't let me go. I moaned and moaned about how unfair it was, so one Tuesday evening, he told me he was taking me

The 1969 Poole Pirates who won the British League championship. Here the Pirates are pictured at Exeter (left to right): Arnold Haley (guest), Pete Smith, Odd Fossengen, Ted Laessing, Frank Shuter, Gordon Guasco and Bruce Cribb.

Paul Tadman: At Romford on May 29, 1969, the Bombers v Crewe Kings. I had no idea what speedway was, just that they were going to have racing at the home of Romford FC, about 20 yards from my house in Brooklands Road, number 54, where I lived with my parents Peggy and Paddy. My neighbour opposite, who I called 'uncle Bunny' although his real name was Bernard, had been an avid speedway fan in the past and as a 12-year-old I was asked if I wanted to go with him and see what all the fuss was about. If I'm honest, I can't really remember a lot about that first meeting. I did, though, take an instant shine to the sport.

One problem at the almost ready-made track was the pits entrance onto the track, because it prohibited supporters from gaining access to the first bend. After a couple of meetings, a wooden bridge was erected and it was a great viewing area to look into the pits.

The area by the turnstiles was a busy place on a Thursday night. The old programme shop and the Romford Bombers Speedway Supporters' Club were situated in huts here and people would gain entry into the main grandstand. Of course, the man selling the programmes would stand around this area as you walked in via the turnstiles. Programmes were a shilling each and to this day I can remember him shouting:

Tapes up on the first-ever race at Romford's Brooklands Stadium on May 29, 1969 – the night the Bombers met Crewe. From the outside, the historic first four to ride the Essex track were Pete Saunders, Ross Gilbertson, Dave Parry and Frank Wendon.

"You can have two programmes for two shillings", as if you were getting a bargain!

The supporters' club boasted around 1,000 members in 1969, which was one of the biggest of the day. The signing of Des Lukehurst really turned things around mid-season and the Bombers went so close to winning Division Two in their first year.

Unfortunately, 1970-71 didn't quite live up to that 1969 season. The captain of the Bombers was my favourite rider, Scotsman Ross Gilbertson.

Romford Speedway was forced to close down at the end of the 1971 season following complaints from local residents about the noise, but I have many lasting memories from there. A glimmer of hope of building a new track within the borough soon faded and the Bombers moved to Custom House for the 1972 season. There was talk of the team moving to the Arena-Essex Raceway (now home of the Lakeside Hammers) but nothing came of that. West Ham had been given notice to quit their stadium for redevelopment the year before and unfortunately the Bombers only lasted a handful of meetings there before moving up to Barrow. That, I thought, would be the end of my speedway association.

Bengt Jansson (left) and Reidar Eide lead out Hackney and Wembley on the night league racing returned to the Empire Stadium in 1970. Allan Emmett and Garry Middleton are the two Hawks immediately behind 'Banger', whilst Norwegian Eide is followed next by Des Lukehurst, Ove Fundin and Lions' team manager Freddie Williams.

WEMBLEY SPEEDWAY

Saturday 30th May, 1970   7.30 p.m.
BRITISH LEAGUE – DIVISION ONE
WEMBLEY LIONS v. HACKNEY HAWKS
Official Programme Two Shillings

to the speedway at Blackbird Road and if I enjoyed it, he would let me go on my own because there was never any trouble at speedway.

Basically, I loved it, the noise, the smell of the fuel, the excitement and, of course, the non-threatening atmosphere.

Garry Robinson: The 1970 Knockout Cup Final at Hyde Road between Belle Vue and Wimbledon. I was 10-years-old and awestruck at the noise, smells and atmosphere.

Arnie Gibbons: It all started due to Pauline Rowe's altruism. She attended Tilehurst as a St. John's Ambulance Brigade volunteer and her son (and my friend) Andrew dragged me along to watch the speedway in October 1970 – a challenge match between Reading and Eastbourne.

The Eagles won the first race I ever saw with a 5-0 to Dave Jessup and Laurie Sims after Mike Vernam and John Hammond both failed to finish for the Racers. Richard May scored a 12-point maximum as Reading recovered to win 44-33. As a wide-eyed 10-year-old, I was hooked and couldn't wait for the start of the next season.

Martin Neal: I'm still not entirely sure of the first meeting I ever went to because I was so young, but it was definitely at Rayleigh in about 1970 or 1971. I pretty soon developed a 'healthy interest' in programmes that remains today and the earliest one I have in my neatly filed, logged and not-at-all-obsessive collection is Rayleigh v Peterborough (August 8, 1972). But I'm pretty certain that, at the grand old age of eight, I'd been to a few meetings by then and that somehow I'd manage to mislay the programmes at some point over the years (my mum had her loft done out a few years ago and I insisted she threw nothing out until I'd been through it looking for the missing programmes. I was gutted not to find them, although I did unearth a couple of Rayleigh Speedway posters and a Rye House pennant from 1976).

It was inevitable that I should be a speedway fan, given my dad's love of the sport. In his bachelor days living in London, he was a keen motorcyclist and used to watch Harringay, New Cross, Wembley and the other London teams regularly. Rayleigh was only a few miles away from where we lived in Wickford, so as soon as I was old enough, that was our regular Saturday night entertainment.

Richard May led Reading's fightback against Eastbourne.

Dave Robinson: Sheffield v West Ham at Owlerton in 1971. Most of my friends were going to speedway and they persuaded me to go. The noise was deafening and I was scared! I remember Olle Nygren, with his white boots, Reg Luckhurst and Alan Sage for the Hammers.

Rob Glover: July 6, 1971 at the Peterborough Open and I can remember it as if it was yesterday. I was only eight and remember the ambulance in the last race of the meeting, which was Andy Ross' last speedway race. He broke his leg and never rode again. I can remember Arthur Price and Geoff Bouchard also being in the race and I guess Tony Davey was the other rider, but I would have to get my programme out to check that.

Adrian Stockwell: Wimbledon v King's Lynn in a season-opening challenge match in March 1972. I was 14-years-old and had a school chum called Keith Brown, who was mad about speedway. He chattered endlessly about roaring bikes, daredevil riders, white-knuckle racing, the mighty Wimbledon Dons, the dastardly Hackney Hawks, hero Ronnie Moore, pantomime villain Ivan Mauger, Pirates, Witches, Wolves and Heathens and convinced me to come along and see it for myself.

So it was that the Brown family – elder brothers Norman and Gordon operated the electronic scoreboard and played the records respectively at Plough Lane on race-nights – drove halfway across London to pick me up to take me to my first meeting. Although the Dons lost 36-42, Ronnie Moore was indeed a hero and speedway was everything I'd been told it was, with knobs on!

Stephen Roberts: Oxford v Coventry, 1972. The Rebels lost the match but Garry Middleton defeated Nigel Boocock to claim the Golden Helmet. I used to lay in bed as a youngster and hear the bikes (I lived just around the corner from Sandy Lane) and curiosity got the better of me. Having badgered my father (who attended the very first meeting at Cowley in 1949), I eventually got to see my first meeting.

Steve Wilkes: Ellesmere Port v Sunderland in 1972 (a Division Two fixture, not the opening meeting). I was just nine-years-old. Dad took me and I recall asking him what speedway was, as I'd never heard of it before. My memories of the racing have faded but the track was soaking wet. I also recall Jack Millen riding for Sunderland and disliking the smell of the methanol fumes.

John Murphy: My first live meeting would have been watching Bradford Northern at Odsal in 1972, when I was 14. I can't remember anything about the match but 41 years later, here I am telling you I was there - I was hooked!

The first meeting I remember in detail was Halifax v Belle Vue that same year. We went as a treat, to see first division racing and Ivan Mauger. Funnily enough, I was recently given a batch

Peterborough's Andy Ross flanked by Alan Witt (left) and Richard Greer in 1970.

of programmes and this meeting was amongst them. The match ended 39-all and the Aces were on course to complete their hat-trick of league titles. Eric Boocock was unbeatable on the night but Belle Vue proved their class in bringing away a point. What a top five: Mauger, Soren Sjosten, Peter Collins, Chris Pusey and Alan Wilkinson. I admit, I never cared for the atmosphere at The Shay, which was hostile, but it was a wonderful setting for speedway.

Tim Allan: I was taken to Poole in 1972 when I was six and all I can remember about the first meeting was being splattered with shale on the first turn. I didn't really pay much attention until I was 10 years of age.

Jez Coupland: The first meeting I remember was at New Hammond Beck Road to watch Boston Barracudas in a Four Team Tournament involving Bradford Northern. I can't remember the other two teams. Boston had Arthur Price, Russell Osborne and Jim Ryman riding. My late father took me because in the early 70s there wasn't much else to do on a Sunday night at 6.45.

Derek Barclay: At Canterbury in August 1972, the Crusaders v Long Eaton in British League Division Two. I went along with my best mate and his family. We lived in Orpington in Kent and most of the people on my road (including my own parents) were originally from the Peckham/New Cross area of South London and my mate's dad had watched speedway at New Cross, so he had been a fan and he introduced us to the sport. I remember getting home and my parents were still up and *Match of the Day* was on. My mum knew I was a massive football fan and she asked in jest: "Was it better than football, then?" I immediately replied: "Yes!"

John Davidson: I have vague recollections of my brother taking me to our home track, Belle Vue, in 1972. But my first specific memory is of going to Wembley to see the 1972

Boston Barracudas in 1972. Left to right Ray Bales, Vic Cross, Lyndsay Davies, Carl Glover, Tony Featherstone, Cyril Crane (promoter) and Russ Osbourne. On bike: Arthur Price.

World Final. My dad didn't have a ticket for me, only for himself and my brother, but since I was just a little kid, he stuck me under his arm and slipped the man at the turnstiles 50p to allow me inside.

I remember the run-off between Ivan Mauger and Bernie Persson, how the crowd rose to its collective feet when the race started – but I was too small to see anything. Dad offered me a running commentary as best as he could until finally he said: "He's done it. Ivan's won!"

After the meeting, we slept in the back of Dad's van and awoke to an eerily deserted Wembley car park.

David Golley: Exeter v Poole, 1973 Easter Trophy and the Falcons debut of Ivan Mauger. I twisted my dad's arm into taking me to see the man with the gold bike after he had appeared with it on *Blue Peter*.

Andrew Skeels: Being born and bred in Scunthorpe, it was Scunny v Hull in a challenge at Quibell Park in April 1973 when I was nine. I was forced into going by my dad! He'd always been into motorcycles and used to go to speedway as well as the Isle of Man TT in the early 60s. Speedway started up at Scunny in 1971 and I have no idea why it took Dad a couple of years before he decided to go. He dragged my brother and I along and I remember not being enthusiastic at all about going in the first place. My brother didn't like it and I don't think he ever went again, but I loved it.

Paul Rickett: Thursday, August 2, 1973. Sheffield Tigers 45 Leicester Lions 33 . . . and so began decades of love, hurt, pain, anguish, mediocrity, delight and a myriad of other cheesy adjectives.

Back in the day, as they say, speedway was well publicised and around the whole of the city and beyond there were great big seven-foot colour hoardings advertising speedway, which even had a box underneath. A little man would drive around every week and slap on who that Thursday's opponents would be.

One week, having met a girl on holidays in Yarmouth who was a big Lions fan, I noticed the little man had pasted that Leicester were that week's opponents. I had to go. So off I went on the bus, on my own, and at the stadium the noise was astonishing (none of those girly silencers back then), the smell was intoxicating and when Bengt Larsson smacked one of the Lions riders on the nose after a race, I was hooked for life.

Andy Povey: I can't remember the opposition but it would have been a 1973 Reading home meeting at Tilehurst. We lived (and still do) only about a five-minute walk from the old stadium and as my dad was a regular down there, I finally persuaded him to take me one night. I loved it and from then on I went there regularly with my parents.

Mark Sawbridge: My dad had a 'thing' about live sport and when I was seven-years-old, he decided to pass it onto me. We tried football, although he wouldn't take me to league games at Wolverhampton Wanderers because of the crowd trouble at the time, so I watched reserve and testimonial games instead. He also ingratiated me into the worlds of greyhound and horse racing. However, as the fun in those activities was limited to gambling, it really didn't appeal to me.

At the time, lots of people in Wolverhampton were talking about some guy called Ole Olsen. There was 'Ole, Ole, Ole' graffiti on various railway bridges which I saw every time I came into town. His name would appear on the back page of the *Express and Star* as many times as that of John Richards or Derek Dougan. So Dad decided that we would go to watch the speedway at Monmore Green.

He knew the racing started at 7.30 every Friday night, and I still remember the frisson of excitement I felt on August 10, 1973 as he parked the car by the East Park and we walked to the turnstiles on what was then the cheaper 'popular' enclosure. We paid our money, bought our programme and looked forward to seeing the famous Olsen and his Wolves team in action.

However, in a stroke of bad luck that has stalked my speedway-following career from that day to this, we discovered that Wolves were actually 120 miles south, riding in a league meeting at Hackney. However, promoter Bill Bridgett believed in running speedway on every Friday night. He had therefore arranged a challenge meeting between two select sides – Billy's Boys and Booey's Bombers. The riders on show that evening read like a Who's Who of 1970s speedway: Nigel Boocock, Alan Wilkinson, Soren Sjosten, Dag Lovaas, Dave Jessup, Bert Harkins, Garry Middleton . . .

I was hooked by the smell, the noise, the racing and the atmosphere. I remember filling the programme in by resting it on my knee. Dad promised that he would make me a proper programme board in his workshop and when we went back the following Friday, it was tucked under my arm. Forty years later, I still take that same programme board to Monmore Green each week.

Craig Saul: At Poole in 1974. My mother had been a West Ham supporter in the late 40s and early 50s – I will always remember that her favourite rider was Lloyd Goffe – and nudged me to go along with a school friend.

It was a British League match between the Pirates and Newport, and it finished with the perfect score. Yes, happiness was indeed 40-38.

I've been fortunate to be involved with the sport 'from the inside' for the last 21 years. It

Seconds before his first race after signing for Exeter in 1973, Ivan Mauger lines up at the tapes alongside Poole's Geoff Mudge at the County Ground.

began when I approached Peterborough co-promoter Peter Oakes with a number of presentation ideas, which led directly to a number of match night 'theatrics' and then on into a roving mike spot. So I have had two 'lives' with the sport.

Eddie Garvey: The first meeting I ever saw live was the 1974 World Pairs Final at Belle Vue, although the first speedway I remember seeing was the ITV coverage of the 1973 Daily Mirror International Tournament from Wembley. I can't remember with whom, or exactly how, I came to attend that pairs final but what I do know is that it changed my sporting life forever.

The old Hyde Road stadium was a 20-minute walk through Gorton for me and part of the attraction that night was the knowledge that after the racing was over, you could gain free entry to the funfair next door. I recall going into the old stadium through the entrance that was situated on the corner of Hyde Road and Hunters Lane and once inside I was immediately taken by the number of people that seemed to spill from every corner of those wooden stands.

The second thing I remember was seeing the photo booth that was adjacent to turn two – that old wooden box filled with black and white 6x4s and 10x8s gave me so much pleasure down the years and ultimately led me to a career as a professional photographer.

In my ignorance that night, I had no idea of the standing the meeting had on the international calendar, but it didn't take me long to find out that England were being represented by Peter Collins and Dave Jessup, the added bonus being that this bloke Collins actually rode for Belle Vue.

I have to admit that my memories of the actual meeting itself are scarce but I was taken by the noise and smell, it was like nothing I had ever witnessed before. Then there was PC, a 20-year-old leather-clad God, in the most amazing leathers I had ever seen. At a time when almost everyone else was wearing dowdy, dark-coloured offerings, Peter came onto the track in a spectacular red and white suit that was trimmed with red, white and black triangles and his initials in white on his right thigh. A new star was installed in my psyche.

I later learned that England were favourites to win that night but didn't, as Sweden took the crown with another Aces rider, Soren Sjosten, partnering Anders Michanek to victory. Their win meant nothing to me but I left that night with a new sport to follow and, better still, a home grown hero on which to pin my hopes.

Dexter Hockley: Rye House v Newcastle in 1975 with a work mate of my father, who used to go to Hackney and Rye House. I saw him last year for the first time in 20 years and he now supports King's Lynn. When I challenged him about that, he replied: "Well, there's no Hackney now."

Stephen Williams: Cradley v Wolves in the summer of 1975 is the first meeting I remember. Ole Olsen scored a maximum and won the second-half, if my old memory serves me correctly.

My dad used to take me to football on most Saturdays to West Brom. However, as trouble at football matches got worse, my parents decided we needed a safer sport to follow. They had followed Jack Young in the 50s, so it revived the family tradition.

Ian Shelton: As a youngster of 11, my interest in the mainstream sports of football, cricket, etc, was to be extended when I became inquisitive about a sporting stadium just a mile from my home. My parents had no real interest in speedway but after much pestering, my dad persuaded my uncle to take me along to Dudley Wood. My uncle's brother, George Davenport, rode for Crayford and Hull in the early 70s.

The match I watched on that summer June evening in 1975 saw Cradley United, as they were then called, beat Exeter 40-38. The visitors were missing their top two of Ivan Mauger and Scott Autrey and the home side were without No. 1 John Boulger but it mattered nothing to me as Steve Bastable and Bob Humphreys held out John Titman to win the match for

Organised by The Speedway Control Board in association with Trust Houses Forte Leisure Limited

Sunday Mirror World Pairs Final
Belle Vue July 13, 7pm official programme 15

Cradley, even though they had no answer to Falcons' guest Phil Crump who raced to a 15-point maximum.

I fell in love with Cradley Heath Speedway and as I sat on the steps at the interval awaiting the second-half, reading my *Speedway Star* with a photo of Dave Jessup on the cover (I remember that to this day and was delighted to recently find the copy in my collection so I could confirm it to myself), I knew next week could not come quickly enough and there was only one place for me on Saturday nights.

As a postscript, the match I saw was demoted from a Gulf Oil British League match to a challenge fixture due to the make-up of the teams, but did I care?

Nick Nicklin: That was Cradley United v Coventry on July 5, 1975. At the age of nine, I first became aware of having a speedway team on my doorstep as the result of a wet lunchtime at school. Herded into an unused classroom rather than the playground, we were offered the use of a box of aged and well-thumbed comics and magazines. Quite by chance, I was handed a 60s copy of *Speedway Star* with a Cradley team photo on the rear. On asking around within my group of school mates, I quickly learned about Bernie Persson, Johnny Boulger, Bruce Cribb *et al* and the exploits of 'United' on a Saturday night. After pestering my dad for a couple of weeks, I was finally taken on that first Saturday in July 1975 and so began a lifetime's interest in the sport.

As I recall, the meeting was a very one-sided affair as Cradley, quite unusually at the time, as I soon found out, took the visitors apart, running out easy winners by 56-22. Dad, who had been present as a nine-year-old himself when Dudley Wood opened in 1947, was under the impression that the meeting started at 7.45, not 7.30, so we missed the first three heats. The heady smell of Castrol R mixed with cigarette smoke and beefburgers was quite distinctive and the noise, colour and the atmosphere created by that large, local derby crowd will stay with me forever.

Alan Robertson: In our house when I was a lad, TV viewing was generally fashioned by my father's tastes. With just the one set, we four kids found something else to occupy our infantile minds while *Kojak, Starsky & Hutch* or some obscure war film blared out on the box in the corner of our pokey living room and kept 'Pops' miles away in his own little world.

Poverty in the UK 40 years later is maybe the prosperous kind compared to the days of flared trousers, big collared shirts, Bay City Rollers and Showaddywaddy.

In 2013, being underprivileged means not having the latest mobile phone or game console, Sky TV or Blu-ray machine. Just as well, for on many occasions we couldn't even afford a television set to play such facilities on, had they been in existence back then.

Dad, God bless him, was not keen on sport. He would let out a sigh when it came on any of the three channels and resulted in a hasty scramble for whatever else was on. Remote control TV was a few years away, so usually one of us kids was the old fella's alternative.

Perhaps his allergy to anything sport-orientated denied me any knowledge of speedway. I will never know.

We are back in the mid-70s, a time when, I've since discovered, speedway was always on the box, mainly on Saturday afternoon's *World of Sport*.

A youngster from the deprived area of Salford, my life had no focus before speedway jettisoned into it. What occupied my 12 years until then, I don't know.

Another hot summer (they seemed to be the vogue in the 70s) spent idling away time – so warm, you get bored and irritated, when idle hands can go down the mischief route.

I filled part of my Saturday afternoons cleaning a car – a bronze-coloured Vauxhall Victor estate belonging to the corner shop owner, Alec – and gratefully pocketed 70 pence for a 75-minute shift which, to a kid, was a lot of dosh.

Alec's son, Phil, the speedway fan, had clean transport for his evening out later on.

I noticed every week while running my frothy sponge over the rear window a circular sticker proudly proclaiming the words 'Belle Vue Speedway' around an ace of clubs design.

It happened by chance, my first visit to speedway. One particular afternoon, car washed, money burning a hole in my trousers, somehow I had managed an invite later that evening. It would eat up my cash, but I was bored. I went simply for something to do.

Arriving early, about 40 minutes before the start (you had to in those days, to get your usual seat), the pristine car shuddered over a pothole-laden croft opposite the stadium gates on Hyde Road.

The stadium was a hive of activity. Screams carried over from the funfair's terrifying rides and mingled with the popular harmonies blaring from the speedway speakers. There was a sense of anticipation.

Up the steps of A Block, situated in front of the starting tapes, we sat down right at the top of the stand. There was a window behind us allowing a scenic view of some of the hustle and bustle of the fair across the way.

Two nippers appeared on track on mini-motorbikes and proceeded to ride lap upon lap of the circuit. The vast wide-open spaces of the circuit dwarfed the two boys. If this was speedway, what a waste of 70 pence!

The pre-meeting entertainment provided by the two mini-bikes only managed to make the real thing more appealing and bizarre, sort of spine-tingling. I still get that sensation now. The real boys emerged on track and I felt exhilarated at seeing my first-ever speedway race. I can still smell a whiff of warm Skol lager coming from the bar beneath the stand.

The date was Saturday, June 7, 1975. I later discovered Coventry were visitors in the newly-sponsored Gulf Oil British League but, at the time, it meant nothing to me.

Compared to the two nippers, the speedway boys seemed so big. Clad in thick leathers, four men on noisy motorbikes positioned

Cradley's Bernt Persson, Sandor Levai and Bruce Cribb in 1975.

themselves at the tapes – the ace of club design (recognised from the sticker on the car) stood out straight away.

I remember, even five decades on, the shock when the tapes sprung up and the engines roared towards the first turn. It was so noisy, so outrageously fast. I almost jumped out of my seat.

"What the . . ." as the four riders bundled and hustled for the same spot on the first bend, skidding in unison as inches separated each one from brushing the other. Something had to give. I was genuinely concerned for their safety. Surely this was a crazy prank about to go wrong, an accident waiting to happen.

Their actions were doomed to bloodshed, I thought, and was relieved, as much as surprised, when 71.6 seconds later, four madmen returned to the pits unscathed. I was not a kid who delighted on others' misfortune.

Captivated early on, it soon lost its novelty value. I hadn't a clue what was going on, just a continuation of four riders, tapes up, and four laps. There was no meaning to it.

"How many more races to go?" I kept asking. I didn't expect to be attending again. It was OK but my 70 pence would be going on snacks next week.

Belle Vue won 49-29, but speedway was the last thing on my mind as I closed my eyes that night.

Nevertheless, seven days later, car-cleaning money tucked in my patch-pocket trousers, I'm in the back of the 1973 model Vauxhall estate as it again sauntered up Hyde Road towards Belle Vue Speedway.

As we waited in the stands, Phil introduced me to the values of filling in a programme. I purchased my own on the third visit and was confident of this score-filling malarkey. Suddenly I felt all grown up, even if it was in a nerdy sort of way.

That was the defining moment. I liked the feeling of writing down the results and there was no turning back.

Sign of great things to come . . . the entrance behind the main stand at Belle Vue's famous Hyde Road stadium.
Below: The home straight at Hyde Road, looking towards the pits bend.

I used to love the long, summer nights, getting home from Belle Vue, grabbing my pushbike out of the lobby and heading straight to the croft behind Alec's shop, where I claimed one little patch as my own little skidpan.

My sliding prowess created a mushroom-shaped dust cloud resembling what I had just watched on a sun-dried Belle Vue circuit. The downside of my 10 minutes' fun, however, meant part of Sunday was spent repairing punctures.

I was inspired. Not much else was as important. From then on, every spare moment was usually speedway-themed.

Paula Peirce: My parents took me to my first speedway meeting at Coventry, circa 1975. My nan had gone to speedway at Liverpool when speedway started there and my mum went to Coventry when she was 11 (1952). She had about 10 years out and then returned, and we're still going now. My children have been going since they were three-months-old (born out of the season) and six-weeks-old (born in season).

The first meeting I remember well was won by Ole Olsen, who was presented with a brand new car, a Range Rover I think. At my first-ever meeting, although I don't remember much about it, I did get a Mitch Shirra rosette.

Clive Read: My twin brother Jon and I were eight in 1975 and Dad was looking to get us into a sport that we could follow. Football was beset by hooliganism but Dad had been a Brummies fan since the first meeting held after the Second World War at Perry Barr in 1946 and decided we should give speedway a go, even though, with a young family, he'd not been for years.

He wanted to pick a first division team and also one who rode at the weekend. Birmingham were a top class second division outfit at the time but rode on a Monday night – no good when you have school the next day. We went to Brandon for the first time on August 16, 1975 to see the Bees face Wimbledon. We didn't really know what to expect but Dad had talked about the noise, the smell, broadsiding on cinders, the crowds and excitement and we'd also be seeing a four times World Champion in Barry Briggs. From the off, we were hooked, as Nigel Boocock, in his blue leathers, faced Briggo. Four riders controlled their bikes at high speed, team-riding, passing from the back, a blur of coloured leathers, accompanied by the smell of methanol that is still hard to beat today. And the noise! Jon and I winced and put fingers in our ears until we got used to it.

Coventry didn't have the strongest team but we managed to win 40-38 and the racing was close. Bees were a team of hard-trying riders including the immortal Booey, Bob Valentine, John Harrhy, Alan Molyneux, Frank Smith and others, whereas the Dons had a former World Champion, the late, great Tommy Jansson and Edgar Stangeland in their team. We talked incessantly about how exciting it had been and the following week we returned, this time with our elder sister Julia, to watch us draw against King's Lynn.

Julia Wilson: The first meeting I went to was August 23, 1975 at Coventry. I was 11-years-old. My dad, Cedric Read, used to go and watch Birmingham Brummies between 1946-52, with my nanny and Uncle John. Dad decided he wanted to take me and my twin brothers, Jonathan and Clive (see above), to see a speedway meeting. Living in Solihull and wanting a Saturday night track, he had the choice of Coventry or Cradley Heath. He chose Brandon and took the twins to see the Bees on August 16. I said I didn't want to go, as I didn't like bikes and they were for boys!

The twins came back raving about how good it was and I pestered Dad all week to take me too. And so the following week, he took the three of us, leaving Mum at home alone on her wedding anniversary!

I absolutely loved it. I remember the unique smell (that I've often wished I could bottle) and the noise. I remember thinking all the riders were going to fall off as they entered the first bend. And then when they didn't, I wondered what it would look like if one of them did (what a mean thought!). The first rider I saw fall off was Frank Smith and I felt so mean for having wanted someone to fall that I decided to support him in the next race. To be honest, that is all I remember from that first meeting, other than I know all three of us wanted to go again. And that was the start of Mum spending Saturday evenings alone, and many other nights too, between March and October.

Alex Mackenzie: At Wimbledon in 1975 or '76. I had moved to Colliers Wood in 1975, which meant I could walk to Wimbledon Stadium. I was, and still am, a music fan and I was reading a short-lived music magazine called, as far as I can remember, *Strange Days*. The editor must have been a speedway fan and there was an article in the magazine about Belle Vue Speedway and, in particular, Soren Sjosten. I had previously ridden motorcycles and was interested.

Soon after this, I found out that speedway was held at the stadium and decided to take a look. I went on my own and didn't understand everything that was going on but loved it and have been going ever since.

Martin Smith: My dad occasionally attended Ipswich during the 50s and 60s but started going regularly from the early 70s. I think my first meeting was Ipswich v Leicester in 1975 and I can recall pouring rain on the way home and being carried from our garage back into the house by my dad inside his coat. I learnt a simple equation from an early age: speedway + Thursday = rain!

Richard Parsons: At White City when they opened on March 24, 1976. It was a challenge match in which the Rebels beat Wimbledon 40-38. I remember the late Tommy Jansson winning the first race I ever saw and Gordon Kennett twice taking Tommy from the back, in Heats 11 and 13. Tommy won the second-half final as well.

Gordon became my hero and the Rebels my team. All this came about when the *Today* programme with Bill Grundy mentioned White City opening. My sister, who had been to speedway before, asked me if I wanted to go. I'm so pleased I did, as speedway became a very important part of my life.

Richard Gilson: On April 15, 1976 and it was Sheffield v Cradley. My neighbour and his son asked me if I would like to go to the speedway but, to be honest, I had never heard of it. Two hours later, I was on my way home with the speedway bug firmly inside me and it has been there ever since. Sheffield won the meeting 42-35 with Reg Wilson scoring a maximum.

Dean Felton: My family had been taking me to speedway since I was born but the first meeting I can remember was a rain-off in 1976 at Wolves. Because I was only a kid, I didn't really take notice of the racing itself, even though I was always there. I recall Finn Thomsen being my Wolves hero in 1977. I think I joined the St. John's ambulance in 1978-80 and watched meetings from the centre green.

Brian Longman: The Superama at Hackney in 1976. My school friends were enthusing about seeing a motorcycle sport and wearing speedway badges on their blazers. I went along with them and was hooked right away. Dave Jessup won the meeting and after the racing had ended, we went to the pits and collected all the riders' autographs. It was the first time I started going out in the evenings with my friends and felt independent of my parents.

Frank Smith gained a new supporter after he fell off.

Mike Turner: It was during the 1976 season at The Shay, Halifax. My then girlfriend (now wife) took me along. She had been watching the Dukes on and off since the re-start of speedway there in 1965 and convinced me that I would enjoy it. By the first bend of the first race, I was hooked and still am.

My father used to tell me tales of the Fleetwood Flyers, but I had never been to speedway up until that day in 1976. I'm so pleased I went. It started a great family experience which involved our children and travelling hundreds of miles around the UK watching some great stars and meeting up with (and sometimes falling out with) great people, all in an atmosphere of shared experience and without animosity.

Andrew Gallon: My dad was a great sportsman and took me to live stuff from the age of six. I grew up (mostly) near Halifax, where we watched the town's professional football and rugby league teams. Despite Dad having watched speedway at Sheffield, his home town, when he was younger, he wasn't interested in taking me to The Shay to see the sport. A school friend who lived along our road used to go occasionally, so I was aware of speedway's existence and, of course, the track was visible during Halifax Town football games.

Eventually, I persuaded Dad to take me. We saw the Dukes beat visitors Leicester (44-34, I think) on June 12, 1976. I loved it. It was a real wake-up call for the senses. The noise, the smell, the speed, the spectacle of the racing – and I was absolutely fascinated by the practice starts and the endless nervous fidgeting the riders did with their goggles and other equipment.

After I'd done no end of household chores during the week, including bringing him and Mum breakfast in bed every day, Dad took me the following Saturday (v Ivan Mauger's Exeter, 39-39) but that was it. I had to wait another three years until I was deemed old enough, at 14, to go alone (albeit accompanied by my twin sister, worse luck).

Chris Fenn: The 1976 London Riders' Championship at Hackney. I remember Dave Morton having engine trouble and, on one occasion, drop-kicking his crash helmet in frustration. I mainly remember the distinctive leathers and style of the rider who was to become my first hero and then my friend, the one and only Barry Thomas.

Graham Goodwin: My first meeting was a family outing to the National League Pairs Final at Belle Vue in 1977. I think it was my dad's idea as he had followed speedway back in the 50s. We stood halfway up the popular side and got hit by shale. I really wasn't keen.

But the following year, whilst looking for something to do on a Bank Holiday, I saw an advert for speedway in the *Manchester Evening News* and said I wanted to go. Dad was a bit

Top three in the 1976 Hackney Superama – Dave Jessup, John Louis and Ole Olsen.

reluctant as I hadn't particularly enjoyed the last trip, but we still went. The meeting was the 1978 Peter Craven Memorial Trophy, and this time I loved it. I've missed very few Belle Vue meetings since.

Nicholas Foote: My first meeting was back in 1975 at the old Weymouth track. I can't remember who the away team were but the late Simon Wigg was racing for the Wildcats.

My next meeting was at Eastville Stadium in Bristol. For some reason, I didn't go to the first meeting but my dad and my brother went and they remember a bad crash in Heat 13. If I remember rightly, my brother said it involved John Davis of Reading. I went along for the second meeting but, again, I can't remember the away team.

The racing was spot on and I loved it from then on. I remember Dad and my brother standing on the third bend and we saw all the riders walking towards the changing rooms. I remember Phil Crump walking past me – his bag was open and I could see his Bulldogs body colour inside – and the late Tom Leadbitter going by with his dogs. I do miss the old Bulldogs and wish they would return to Bristol.

Gary Moore: As a six-year-old during the summer of 1977 – Friday, July 8 to be precise, which also happened to be the first meeting Glasgow Tigers raced at the Blantyre Sports Stadium. I can't recall if I'd ever heard of speedway, or even seen it on TV, before this date. I was, however, a regular at the greyhound racing with my grandpa and can vividly remember a track being cut out inside the dog track and all the hardcore base being laid down. Curiosity must have got the better of me and my dad took me along to that first meeting. We watched it for free from the top of the old bing (slag heap) which towered over the back straight. In fact, the first few meetings were watched from up there, along with many others it has to be said, before it was flattened and turned into a car park of sorts.

Keith Wiggins: The Sword of Honour at The Groveway, Milton Keynes on Tuesday, March 28, 1978 – the track's first ever meeting. It rained all night but the racing went ahead. My dad took me because he had been to and enjoyed speedway at Harringay, where his hero was Vic Duggan. I remember the racing, lots of programme changes and a rider complaining about the conditions (who I later found to be Mike Sampson, who I think won the meeting).

Chris Rowsell: It was in the 1978 season at Smallmead for the Geoff Curtis Memorial Trophy. It was near the end of the season and I went to the remaining fixtures.

I don't remember too much about the actual racing, but John Davis won comfortably (I looked it up!). The smell, the large crowd, the noise and the whole package was enticing. My cousin had been to a few meetings at Tilehurst in 1972 and '73 and had given me the programmes, but being quite young at that time, apart from looking at the results in the papers occasionally, I didn't really follow the sport that closely, other than watching when it was on ITV.

I didn't give it much thought until my uncle started going in the 1977 season. Halfway through the '78 campaign, he asked if Mum and I would like to go and, from the moment I entered the

stadium, I was hooked for the next 30 years. As was typical of my uncle, he quickly lost interest and had stopped going by the start of the next season, but thankfully a friend of his had also started going and we went with him for a number of years until we could get there under our own steam.

Speedway was not entirely alien to my parents, who had attended meetings in London after the war (Harringay, Wembley and Wimbledon mainly) and then at California

Barry Thomas became London Riders' Champion at Hackney in 1976.

(Berkshire) in the mid-to-late 50s, before bringing up a young family put a stop to it.

Paul Minns: My first meeting was also my first visit to arguably what was the home of British speedway, Wembley Stadium. As a child, I had followed football and watched many Cup finals from that iconic venue. However, I had started to watch the occasional speedway meeting on TV and was really starting to get into it. The football magazine I got every week was dropped and replaced by *Speedway Mail*. However, living 40 miles from the nearest track, and having no car, I had to make do with following speedway via the TV and the *Mail*.

I saw an advert from a local coach company and amongst their excursions was the 1978 World Final. Having an older brother who was already a speedway fan and being only13 myself, I put the idea out there that it would be great to go. To my surprise, a couple of days later, two coach tickets appeared and we were going to Wembley.

The only cloud in the build-up to that meeting was that the rider I had started to avidly follow, Peter Collins, didn't qualify. To this day, based on the form he was in that season, I'm sure he'd have been on the rostrum if he'd made it to Wembley.

However, the day arrived, we boarded the coach and we were off to the capital. Being from Norfolk, our coach was decorated with green and yellow scarves and a large picture of Michael

Home track hero Bob Humphreys with the Sword of Honour he won on the opening night at Milton Keynes in 1978.

Lee in the back window, proclaiming he was going to be the 1978 World Champion. As we made our way to London, the closer we got, we met other coaches all similarly decorated from all parts of the UK – Cradley, Berwick, Poole, etc, they were all represented. Sadly, not a scene you see today.

The atmosphere was everything I had hoped for and imagined. Fans from all over the globe wearing their rider's colours. Stalls everywhere selling everything speedway – badges, scarves, rosettes and flags, it was all there. Not forgetting the stalls tempting you with the whiff of a burger or hot dog.

Whilst wanting to take all this in, the first priority was tickets, as we'd travelled without any in the hope we'd be able to get them on the day. Fortunately we could, although if they had sold out, there were certainly enough touts lurking around.

After getting our tickets, there was just enough time to sample a burger and get the obligatory programme and rosettes, proclaiming our allegiance to both Michael Lee and (ex-Stars) Simmo, before entering the stadium.

I can still vividly remember entering the stadium and making our way around that concrete corridor under the terracing to our entrance. We climbed those steps and Wembley slowly opened out in front of me. Having only seen it on TV previously, even as a 13-year-old, I was lost for words and just stood there looking around at a packed Wembley. The green of the soccer pitch, the white of the fence and starting gate standing out boldly against the rich, red shale. The many colours of the crowd, all displaying their team's scarves and hats. I distinctly remember we were in amongst a group of White City fans. Our view was excellent, on the first bend, with the starting gate directly in front of us.

The meeting was a good one, wide open, with several incidents. Ole Olsen, the new World Champion, said in an interview afterwards that it was the hardest final he had been in. The result could have been so different had Simmo's number one bike not blown up just before the meeting. And what can you say about Dave Jessup? Engine failures in both 1978 and 1981 cost him dearly – almost certainly a podium finish in '78 and maybe even the top spot.

For every race, we found somebody to cheer for and the following day we could hardly speak. Our voices had almost completely gone. It was then back on the coach, past the crowds and queues spilling out of Wembley Park underground and back to Norfolk. Our man hadn't won but I didn't care because it had been a brilliant day.

For a first meeting, the Golden Jubilee World Final takes some beating.

Rob Peasley: I'm a second generation fan. My dad started going to Oxford around 1956 (he would have been nine or 10-years-old). He started taking my mum in 1968, although she stopped going for around 10 years after the birth of my younger brother in 1975. I suspect my first speedway meeting was as a baby in 1973.

My first memories of speedway stem from around 1979. It was a wet year and Oxford ended up staging a lot of Sunday afternoon meetings, in addition to Thursday evenings, to catch up. I do have vague memories of seeing the likes of George Hunter, Les Rumsey, etc, in action for the Cheetahs. Incidentally, to begin with, I thought Les Rumsey was a woman, because Lesley was also a girl's name!

The first distinct meeting I recall is the Pip Lamb Benefit, held at Oxford in October 1979. We were standing on the back straight. It was split into two Pairs competitions – one involving British League riders, while most of the Oxford team rode in the National League event. The British League competition was won by Bruce Penhall and Bobby Schwartz – and Bruce became one of my early heroes.

But the meeting that completely and utterly hooked me was an Inter-League Fours qualifier at Oxford in June 1980, featuring Poole, Eastbourne and Wimbledon, in addition to the Cheetahs. Thanks to Dave Perks and Derek Harrison, Oxford finished third and beat BL Wimbledon. It was the first time I filled in a programme (I still have it at home) and I recall Gordon Kennett pulling a huge wheelie as he completed a maximum for Eastbourne.

After that, I went to every Oxford home meeting in either the school holidays or on a Sunday. I wasn't allowed to go on a school night, but used to get up early the following morning and study my dad's programme. From 1984, a year which saw Oxford not only switch to the British League but also to Friday nights, I was allowed to go every week.

Garry Hutson: Belle Vue v Hull on July 21, 1979. I was given a season ticket by someone who couldn't use it.

Brian Burford: In 1979 for a cup match between Swindon and Birmingham at Blunsdon.

Michael Lee and King's Lynn general manager Martin Rogers in the Wembley pits during the Golden Jubilee World Final.

My dad took me and I have a vague recollection of going once before, but can't remember it. My father was a motorsports fan and competed in time trials, rallies and other things after the War - only at amateur/club level for fun. He also went to speedway at Swindon before he got married.

I was a big Barry Sheene fan and I used to watch *World of Sport* on ITV. That's when I first saw speedway and after Dad told me all about it, I wanted to go. So I badgered him and the cup match was the first meeting I really took note of – Phil Crump became my favourite rider after that first night. Having been to other motorsports events, what I loved most was the fact that I could see the whole race and the aroma was hypnotic.

However, as a teenager, if I hadn't been to the 1981 World Final, I am not sure I would still have been going because that meeting sort of cemented my devotion. I discovered how magical a big meeting could be – the atmosphere, the venue, the excitement, the anticipation and the fact that a major trophy was on the line, all added up to

Eventual champion Ole Olsen leads from Michael Lee, Ila Teromaa and Jerzy Rembas in the 1978 World Final.

an addictive cocktail that I couldn't get enough of. After that, I attended as many major events as we could as well as regularly attending at Swindon, Reading, Oxford and then Sheffield and Belle Vue.

Debbie Howland: In late 1979 at Canterbury, which was within walking distance of my house. My best friend from school had been going with her mum since she was a baby and I finally gave in and went. I remember the first race because she had never told me about turning away when the riders came past and I got covered in shale. I said I couldn't see the point if you missed half the racing, so I wouldn't be going again but, of course, I did and 34 years later, I'm still going.

Christian Weber: My first experience of speedway in the UK was the 1985 World Final at Bradford. My dad took me along and we went on an organised trip, flying into London from Munich, and then by coach to Bradford.

That year, we had two German riders in the World Final, Egon Müller and Karl Maier. I remember I was rather disappointed with the whole meeting, which was my first-ever individual speedway World Final. First of all, the so-called 'Wembley of the North' was no comparison to the real Wembley, where all the previous World Finals in the UK had been held. I had expected Odsal Stadium to be much bigger and more plush.

I was further disappointed that this final was staged as a daytime event, in the afternoon, which took away much of the atmosphere. There is no doubt in my mind that there is truth in the saying that 'night time is the right time' for speedway. It looks so much more spectacular under artificial lights.

One particular moment I recall from that day at Bradford was when, whilst wandering around the stadium, I bumped into Kenny Carter. He had not reached the World Final that year and was working as a co-commentator for ITV. Other than that, the meeting did not give me much to remember.

Three years later, I had my first taste of league speedway in

England. I was in London, attending a National League match at Plough Lane between Wimbledon and Eastbourne, and a couple of days later at Waterden Road I saw the first leg of the KO Cup Final between the two London clubs, Hackney and Wimbledon.

I enjoyed those two meetings, but remember that even then I was rather shocked by the poor attendances and the run-down state of the stadia.

Living in Germany, the first meetings I ever attended were long-track events. My hometown club Plattling wanted to build a speedway track at the time but for some reason it never happened, and we still have our 835m long-track to this day.

With speedway arriving in our area relatively late, it wasn't until the summer of 1977 that I saw my first speedway race. It was a World Pairs semi-final and there was such a huge crowd at Pocking. There were riders I had never seen or even heard of before, and they were just as good or even better than our stars. This meeting was an eye-opener for me in that speedway was even more exciting than the long-track racing I was used to.

On this Sunday afternoon at Pocking in June 1977, the German pair of Egon Müller and Hans Wassermann won the meeting ahead of Australia's Phil Crump and Billy Sanders, with Finland's Kai Niemi and Ila Teromaa third. I was rather disappointed that, as usual for me, the Germans were the best (as they were so often when I saw them on the long-tracks), but I didn't realise at the time how big an achievement this was for Germany in a speedway World Pairs event. Müller and Wasserman went on to win the bronze medals that year in the final at Belle Vue.

One other thing I remember about my first real speedway meeting was how pleased I was when I read in the programme that Scotland would be competing. It was exciting because I had never seen any Scottish riders before. I think it would have been Jimmy McMillan and either George Hunter or Bert Harkins in this meeting, but I became very disappointed when the announcer at the track said the Scots would not be riding as they had allegedly missed the Channel ferry. They didn't make it in time for the meeting and they would be replaced by a Germany B pairing of local track reserves.

As it turned out, this was the very last time that Scotland was to be included as a nation in its own right in the World Pairs championship. After missing the boat – literally! – on this occasion, they have so far never regained their place.

Richard Simmons: It would be season 1981, April 9, Ipswich v Eastbourne. My mates wanted me to go along and see what it was all about. I was 13 at the time. But I did attend meetings when I was only a few weeks old as both my parents were regulars at Ipswich and took me along. Apparently I used to sleep all the way through.

Phil Chard: As a teenager, I went to Weymouth in 1982. I can't remember my first actual meeting, but have vivid memories of my first major disappointment, which coincided with my dad Cyril's first 'live' meetings.

It was Wildcats' gut-wrenching two-legged 96-95 National League KO Cup Final defeat against Exeter in 1983.

Weymouth, with big guns Steve Schofield, Martin Yeates, Simon Cross and Stan Bear, were huge favourites, but the team failed to perform lower down the order.

A young Alun Rossiter was the difference, notching 10 in the second leg at the old Wessex Stadium to lead Falcons, including Rob Ashton, Rob Maxfield, Kevin Price, Keith Millard, Steve Bishop and Michael Coles, to a far more comfortable success than 96-95 suggests.

Weymouth, who also included Gordon Humphreys, David Biles and Chris Martin, were my

The first race of the 1985 World Final at the revamped Odsal Stadium in Bradford. From the inside, Kelvin Tatum, Viktor Kuznetsov, Egon Müller and Armando Castagna.

team. They had been ever since my school friend Jay Eastwood, the audacious former Weymouth, Poole and Somerset track photographer, got me a Wizards programme from their 1976 season, the one with the eye-catching bright purple front cover. Sports-mad, I'd never come across a team in any sport who wore bright purple. Happy days!

Bridport-born and raised, I had no way of travelling to speedway until I bought my first car in 1982, so had to make do with reading the programmes Jay got me, while, in the late 70s, also listening to Bristol's home meetings on local radio.

But the long wait to see live action was definitely worth it, as speedway has been my number one live sport ever since.

Chris Young: The 1983 Northern Riders' Championship at Belle Vue is the first meeting I remember. I was four at the time and can recall just seeing these blurs whizz past me, thinking nothing of it, but then that glorious smell hit me and that was it, I was hooked – even at the age of four.

Chris Camp: I was enticed along to The Groveway stadium in late June 1983 by a gent my then partner and I had met when we all worked one of the bars for the series of David Bowie concerts at the Milton Keynes Bowl. It was his enthusiasm and passion for speedway, and the Knights in particular, that convinced us to attend and on a damp Tuesday evening, we watched our first-ever meeting, a junior event.

What struck me most was the atmosphere and the welcoming nature of the crowd. Little did we know we were about to be welcomed into the legendary 'Milton Keynes Knights Barmy Army'.

That was the start of what was to become an on-going love-hate relationship with speedway. I love the people and the sport but hate the way it's run and not much has happened over the years to change my view.

That first season was certainly a trying time where the Knights were concerned, as were most seasons, but especially on that terrible night in September when Craig Featherby lost his life at Peterborough. We hadn't known him long but the loss was terrible and felt by all the riders and supporters alike. However, even in the darkest times, the riders were on hand to share the pain and sorrow and I well remember a conversation with Charlie McKinna below the stands that seemed to encapsulate everyone's thoughts and feelings at that time.

Vitek Formanek: Since I come from Pardubice in the Czech Republic, where all the major stars competed in World Pairs, World Team Cup and Golden Helmet meetings during the communism era, I dreamed about coming to England to watch 'real' speedway. After the Velvet Revolution, my obvious choice was going to England. At Easter 1990, I arrived in London to be picked up by my friend, Graham Reeve, who took me straight to Swindon for a meeting which was – surprise, surprise – rained-off!

My first real action came at Coventry, where I signed a petition to allow the banned Mike Lee back into racing. I loved everything there, even the tea without sugar.

A really memorable night came the following day at Reading, where I met Jan Andersson, who I had known from Pardubice. He was very friendly and gave me 15 pounds "to enjoy my stay", which was such a wonderful gesture. I never forgot that. Trevor Redmond gave me a tenner, too, and my then wife spent the money on an electric kettle, so she was in seventh heaven!

Glenn Collins: Sittingbourne Crusaders v Buxton Hitmen on October 22, 1995 at the old Iwade track. I was taken at the age of five by my mum and dad. He had been a massive speedway fan since he first went in 1950 at Harringay and mum tolerated it, but has since come to love it. Every Sittingbourne meeting Dad would go to, I'd always ask if I could join him and remember being really excited about being allowed to go.

The first thing I remember is standing by the pits and the smell of the bikes as they were warming up. Of the match itself, I remember watching on the first corner, getting covered in shale every race and loving it. David Mason got a full maximum and the next day in the garden, I was out on my little bike pretending to be a speedway rider.

Jenna Johnston: The first ever meeting I remember attending was the Premier League KO Cup Final in 1999 at Arena-Essex, who were riding against Edinburgh. However, I have been told that I was taken to Sittingbourne when I was a lot younger.

As a 12-year-old, I had never seen anything like speedway before, as it is a sport which, I'm afraid to say, is not very popular with the younger generation. I remember being so excited watching the riders whizzing round the track and the atmosphere was electric, as both teams wanted to win, which did result in a bit of a fight between the two teams in the pits.

Edinburgh won and we were able to see them presented with the cup. I was also able to meet a few of the Arena riders that night to get autographs and I've still got the programme with their signatures on. After that night, I was hooked, just like my family and especially my dad, whose first meeting was at West Ham many years ago.

Matthew Lawrence: It was the Isle of Wight at home to Newcastle in 2006 and the Islanders won 57-35. I was there on holiday and had never watched the sport before or really heard about it, so I decided to go along and see if I liked it and instantly caught the bug.

Steve Schofield couldn't prevent Weymouth losing the KO Cup final against south-west rivals Exeter in 1983.

2 TEAMS AND TRACKS

Where did/do you watch speedway most regularly? What was/is your favourite away track to visit?

Maurice Plowright: I worked at Eastbourne from 1933 up to 1939 as a waterer, then raker, then in the pits as a 'pusher-offer' to Tiger Hart. I almost never watched at any other track.

Ken Carpenter: I was Sheffield's track photographer from 1983 to the beginning of 2006, when I retired to Crete. The first bend didn't give the close contact between riders which photographers want but it gave plenty of passing and loads of fast racing action on its big, wide sweeping circuit. It was at Sheffield that I met and photographed a man my dad used to tell me about when I was a kid – Frank Varey, El Diablo Rojo (the Red Devil), who had made such a big impact when racing in Argentina before the war.

Mick Bird: In 1946, it was Wembley on Thursdays. However, pay day for my dad was Friday and when Harringay (who rode on Fridays) opened in 1947, we began supporting them.

Cedric Read: My favourite away track is probably Belle Vue's Hyde Road, dating from my first visit in 1949 to support Birmingham in their opening fixture as a first division team. Such was the demand that four special trains were run from New Street to Manchester, then special buses to Hyde Road. Birmingham lost 49-35 and we arrived home at about 4.00am.

Keith Walker: Sheffield's Owlerton is the finest stadium of the 30-odd I have visited over the years but my favourite away track was the 'proper' Belle Vue at Hyde Road. With its iconic wooden grandstand and sweeping track, it was the perfect venue to watch Chris Morton and Peter Collins carving up the opposition.

Tony Webb: I remember Norwich as my favourite away track, though. It had round-the-boards racing and it was a track you could race on. We first went there for a World Championship round to support Les McGillivray and the Rockets fans were unhappy that the announcer could not pronounce his surname correctly.

Philip Dalling: Although I always enjoyed going to Exeter, for sentimental reasons, I probably have to plump for Cradley Heath as my favourite track, with Leicester's Blackbird Road as a close runner-up. Why? Atmosphere, excellent racing, just the feeling that these were real speedway venues in towns where the sport was part of local life.

David Walker: Obviously, it was going to be Coventry which was my home base. Despite a lot of stick over the years, it did have some superb racing on many occasions. One thing that sticks in my mind is the almost military precision of the presentation, all the staff, in uniform, marching out onto the centre green to the strains of Rimsky Korsakov's Flight of the Bumblebee followed by the National Anthem. The whole meeting was ruled with a rod of iron by Charles Ochiltree. It might now seem a bit old fashioned, but the innate sharpness of the presentation, with the whole stadium smart and tidy, centre green grass cut, announcements you could hear and understand, plus Alan Walker (no relation) belting out a Bees war cry, gave speedway an excellent image, which a lot of modern promotions could learn from.

Richard Parsons: I loved going to White City every Wednesday cheering on the Rebels. We were only there for three seasons but we did achieve a lot, winning the league in 1977 (in the days when most points meant you were champions). It was so great when we won the league at Wolverhampton and how many coaches did we take that day? It's the only meeting I remember where the red and blue riders were booed and the away riders were getting all the cheers.

My favourite away track was Coventry. I simply loved that place. I know people moaned that it was a gater's paradise but for the big meetings like the British Final, nobody did it better. You just felt you were watching a proper speedway meeting because Charles Ochiltree knew how to put on a show.

Charles Ochiltree, who knew how to put on a show at Coventry, with Mitch Shirra.

Paul Hiscock: I did enjoy Romford's all-too-brief existence at Brooklands where Ross Gilbertson was a class act. It was an experience to behold as riders raced past you within touching distance if you were mad enough to stand that close to the track. I'm not sure, even to this day, how they managed to get the place past the Noise Abatement Society in the first place.

Tony Lethbridge: From the start, there was only one track and one team - Exeter Falcons. My dad, Ted, always said that the first place he ever took me in my pram was to the County Ground for a lap of the track. Later on, when Ted became track curator, I did many more laps at the wheel of the water cart and the tractor.

Ted saw the first meeting there in March 1929 and I was involved on the last night in 2005, so between us we must have seen almost everything that happened there.

Now, after a six-year break, I get my racing fix at Plymouth, where the racing is the best I've ever seen.

Jeff Davies: I watch speedway most regularly at Coventry (I became their track photographer in 1984 and I'm still there every week). My favourite track was the old Belle Vue. There has never been another track quite like it but I do enjoy the racing at Peterborough. It's a great race track, very fast and great for pictures.

Mike Keir: Wimbledon was my spiritual home but I didn't start doing aways until 1975. I had no special favourites but something eventful always happened on trips to Ipswich.

Rod Haynes: My favourite away track for racing was Belle Vue, especially up in the stand when the second-half finals were between Ivan Mauger, Soren Sjosten, Tommy Roper and A.N. Other.

Dennis Lindo: I went to Cleveland Park every Thursday from 1961-1964 and was devastated when the track closed at the end of 64. Eric Boothroyd attempted to run Middlesbrough on an open licence in 1965 but it didn't last long. When Ron Wilson re-opened the track upon the introduction of the Second Division, I was again there every Thursday until 1977 when I moved to the Manchester area and began supporting Belle Vue.

John Pharaoh: When New Cross closed down for good in mid-1963, Wimbledon became my regular team. But I enjoyed being able to travel around the London area tracks where you could watch speedway practically every night of the week (plus Sunday afternoons at Rye House!).

Bob Radford: As Reading team manager, my favourite away tracks to visit were Oxford, Hackney and Wimbledon – because the Racers almost always won there! As a spectator, the old San Bernardino track in California produced the best speedway I ever saw. Here in the UK, I loved the old Clay Country Park at St. Austell.

Pete Rout: As a Witches fan, King's Lynn was always a favourite track to visit because of the local rivalry, the great racing and – dare I say it – I really enjoyed watching Terry Betts and Ian Turner in action against us. I also remember the big crowds and being showered with shale when standing close to the fence.

Gary Moore: As a Glasgow fan, you got used to watching the 'Stripes' at different tracks, so Blantyre's one and two, Shawfield and now Ashfield have been my regular fix of speedway. Powderhall will always be my favourite away track. Being so near, it was obviously the first away track I visited and I was blown away by it, due to the fact that I was used to the spartan surroundings of both Blantyre tracks. Bearing in mind I was still a kid, there was something magical about Powderhall, whether it was a sunny, hot summer night with its perfectly manicured centre green and bright red shale or my personal favourite, a cold and dark, atmospheric October night with the coloured fairy lights twinkling in the blackness. Powderhall will always be special to me and, being addicted to old programmes as a kid, Norrie's excellent stall under the main stand made it all the better.

Steve Casey: Sheffield is my favourite track. I could never make up my mind which was the quicker, Sheffield or the old Hyde Road. The facilities at Owlerton are fabulous and the track is super quick with spectacular racing. I've always said I would love to see a GP there.

Geoff Theobald: The plush, glass-fronted grandstand on the finishing line straight at Wimbledon and flower pots on the centre green; the class of Ronnie Moore and Trevor Hedge, not to mention Jim Tebby (!).

But then we discovered 'Ttraxcitement' in E15. 'Make it a Date, Friday at Eight' at Waterden Road, and we did with some regularity from the early 70s onwards. A great track, brilliant, largely home-grown young racers . . . and Leaping Len!

Howard Murphy: I loved going to Halifax, for the great crowds and seeing the third and fourth bends full of Belle Vue fans. Later on, it was a brilliant track for getting action photographs from the outside of the fence. The shape and banking of the track were unique.

Robert Wiles: Canterbury's Kingsmead Stadium was fairly basic with little in the way of facilities but that didn't matter to me. The track was larger than average at 390 yards which made for quite fast racing and I have some very happy memories from there.

John Farr: My favourite away track was Hackney, despite me never catching one of Len Silver's 'lucky' coins! I always believed that Hackney was a fair track on which a good rider could pass others, inside or out.

Pete Butler: The Belle Vue fairground was always great on BLRC night (which was always during the football season) as supporters would use the go-kart track to exercise their club loyalties, I remember one incident when a Newport fan's yellow and black cap flew off during a race and, although it landed off the racing line, everyone made a detour to run over it. At the end of the race, it was in shreds.

Greg Unwin: The best modern day away experience for me is Rye House. A drink or two in the Rye House pub next door to the stadium followed by fish and chips inside the stadium is a very enjoyable prelude to the speedway package provided by Len Silver and his staff. Len always acknowledges the presence of the Plymouth fans behind the first bend. It all adds up to the enjoyment of the race-night experience. Alas, this is followed by a five-hour drive home to Plymouth!

Tony Barnard: My local track was Halifax but my favourite was Sheffield. Why? Because you could go to the pits where you could see clearly what was going on. At Sheffield, the pits were/are next to the main stand with a clear view of the riders.

John Vine: Cradley Heath was my favourite opposing track as it was close to my home in Bromsgrove. The racing there was second to none but it was one of the few tracks where opposition riders had to be smuggled out of the stadium for supposed unfair riding.

Ray Griffiths: Wimbledon. I went initially for chips and doughnuts but Tommy Jansson changed that! I eventually became a Wimbledon junior rider. My favourite track was Hackney – Barry Thomas and Dave Morton around the boards at Waterden Road were amazing.

Chris Gosling: I mainly went to King's Lynn. As Martin Rogers once said: "Speedway was probably the most exciting thing to happen there since King John lost his crown jewels in The Wash in 1216." I was hooked almost from the start and went there as often as I could until emigrating to Canada in 2003.

Arnie Gibbons: Powderhall is my favourite. I saw some fantastic matches there (notably an Edinburgh v Long Eaton cup tie in 1994). However, my first visit to Powderhall was the most memorable. Leaving Leicester station at 8.00am, four or five of us travelled via Birmingham New Street to Edinburgh Waverley. Unfortunately, as the journey progressed, it became increasingly obvious that we were in for a wet day. On arriving in Scotland's capital, we stopped at a 'greasy spoon'. Bob got a tin lid in his portion of baked beans – slightly disturbing! Having established that the meeting was, indeed, off, we decided to trudge through the rain to Powderhall. On the way, we bumped into a car of Leicester fans, and briefly retired to a pub.

At the track, we were rewarded with the sight of a back straight under water and an invitation to the Monarchs Supporters' Club post-match disco (which had been brought forward in the absence of a meeting). I remember being told by Brett Saunders that we were mad to travel all the way to Scotland for a challenge match. When a speedway rider says you are mad, it's time to doubt your sanity!

The overnight return trip was a noisy one as we shared the train with hordes of Scottish rugby fans heading towards Cardiff Arms Park for a Five Nations match. After spending the early hours of the morning on New Street station, we finally arrived back in Leicester at 8.00am on Saturday. So at a cost of £14 (£28 for Tony, who was too old for a young person's railcard) we had 'enjoyed' the pleasures of a Monarchs disco, an eventful journey and the camaraderie created by our shared experience.

Mike Turner: We visited Halifax every meeting and made our way regularly to Hull on

Wednesdays (great fish 'n' chips from The Kingfisher on the A63), Sheffield on Thursdays and Belle Vue when we had an opportunity. The old Belle Vue had atmosphere and mostly good racing and you could visit the fun-fair to amuse the kids.

Paul Rickett: I'm biased but Owlerton's my track and some of the racing we've had down the years has been awesome. That's not just the Sheffield boys like Doug Wyer, Reg Wilson, Arnie Haley and Shawn and Kelly Moran but some of the sport's legends like Ivan Mauger, the fabulous Peter Collins and Hans Nielsen. It's a fabulous racetrack and some of the racing is unequalled, especially when the big names get the chance to race there.

As for away tracks, I always enjoyed Halifax, probably because we usually won around The Shay. I remember the first time I went there and stood with a mate on the first turn, in the days when you could reach out and pat the riders on the back as they came around . . . back wheels flying past just inches away, none of this namby-pamby six metres distance rubbish.

We decided to bob down under the wooden fence as the four riders thundered into the first turn. Unluckily, when I bobbed down, there was a great gap in the wood and the black shale splattered through and left a big black stripe across my face. I looked like a negative of Adam Ant. Happy days.

Rob Glover: I watch nearly every home meeting as a season ticket holder at Peterborough. Berwick is my favourite away track, a great track that has many racing lines – just how speedway should be. What makes the difference are the locals, what a great community they are.

Rob Peasley: It used to be Oxford. I saw a total of 655 meetings there. I used to love meetings at Cowley. Our perfect oval was a very fair track – maybe a little too fair. Unless the Cheetahs had a really good team, we tended to struggle because of the lack of home track advantage.

Oxford's record was quite odd - lots of league titles, but otherwise more likely to be in the bottom half of the table than the top. It was quite fun when Waggy (Nigel Wagstaff), promoter at Oxford between 2003 and 2005, piled on the shale and made the track super-duper grippy to give Oxford a rare home track advantage.

Nick Nicklin: With Dudley Wood less than two miles away from our family home in Quarry Bank, it was clear that I'd become a Cradley fan. The stadium was not pretty and its lack of facilities a long-standing joke amongst fans from other clubs. The open air toilets and the mobile classroom style bars, brought in on a 'temporary' basis in the early 60s, all added to the character of the place, and who remembers the barn type building situated on the second bend/back straight that burnt down in the late 70s in mysterious fashion?

The concrete terracing along both straights was adequate and gave a great view of the track, creating a terrific atmosphere when full on big match nights, but the lack of cover, especially down the back straight, meant rainproof gear was a must.

The track itself, in my opinion, made for some great racing, with its length and shape providing the right mix of technicality and speed. It was fair to both Heathens and visiting riders alike.

The Shay at Halifax, with its steep banking and close proximity to the fans, made for spectacular and fast racing. The banking, finished neatly with an unforgiving steel safety fence, favoured the brave and I remember one hot May Bank Holiday morning in 1978, when the Heathens visited Halifax, home star Mitch Graham, blazed to a terrific 10 points including three hard earned race wins. Time and again, he disappeared into the dust on the back straight, roared up the banking on the third bend and blasted around Cradley's star men to come down the home straight yards ahead. He failed to make the gate once that day and earned all of his points from the back and I still consider this to be one of the most switched on and bravest performances I've ever seen.

Again, the stadium facilities at the time weren't great, but the view of the track was brilliant from anywhere in the stadium while the Pennines in the background provided a spectacular backdrop that could always be used as an early warning system as they disappeared into the cloud when the weather was closing in.

Andrew Skeels: Quibell Park in the 70s, then Ashby Ville from 1979 after Scunthorpe had relocated. I moved to London in 1982 and joined *Speedway Star* in the summer of 1983, after which Wimbledon, Hackney and Rye House would have been my regular haunts. Nowadays, with no local track to where I live in Surrey, I probably see as many meetings at Scunthorpe's Eddie Wright Raceway in a season as I do anywhere else.

My favourite track to visit is/was Edinburgh, in both the Powderhall and Armadale eras. Edinburgh is one of my favourite cities in the world and an 'Edinburgh weekend' is an opportunity to combine three of my favourite things: speedway, football and pubs!

Jenna Johnston: I used to go to Arena-Essex or, as they are now known, Lakeside because it is my most local track. During the time I went there, I got more involved in the club, from selling raffle tickets to running Andy Galvin's 'Two Bob Club' and also working in the pits with Rose as tea lady for the riders, mechanics and track staff which I really enjoyed as I got to see all the action first hand. My favourite away track is Mildenhall. I love the surroundings, sitting on the grass hills, watching the racing while children can play in the playground. The track is small and the racing always close and you are able to see into the pits.

Martin Neal: We became regulars at Rayleigh as soon as I was old enough to go. I remember the crowds were so big that we used to park on the other side of the busy A127, dart across the dual carriageway and then weave our way through the light industrial units to the entrance.

I used to stand on the banking and peer down at the away side of the pits between races. I heard Eastbourne's Eric Dugard use the F word after a bad race one night – I was only eight or nine and I was horrified!

The competition for places at reserve was really tough and we became big fans of Red Ott – great name and a real appetite to race. As a result, we had a real downer on Peter Cairns who became our man's big rival for a place in the team. I still feel bad about that now.

We hardly missed a meeting in 1973, which proved to be the last at the Weir. Still, they went out on a high, or so I thought. After the final meeting, they were presented on the centre green with something called the 'Wooden Spoon'. I was delighted. It hadn't been a great season for results but they'd still won something!

We went as regularly as we could to Rye House when the Rockets moved there for 1974, although in those days, before the M25, it wasn't an especially easy or quick journey. My mum and dad were shocking navigators too and viewed using a map as an admission of failure, so it was rare for two journeys to Hoddesdon to be the same.

We dabbled with Crayford when it opened as it was closer and there were some familiar faces in the team and in the manager's office but the viewing wasn't great and neither was the racing.

I used to enjoy going to Mildenhall before they reshaped it. It was small but almost round so it was fast. There was no dog track then so you were right up close to the action and the atmosphere was electric.

3 FAVOURITES

Name your three most favourite (not necessarily the best) riders, and why you have chosen them.

Eric Marchment: My greatest regret is that I never saw the great Vic Duggan and having followed speedway for nigh on 80 years, three favourites is a very small number. First has got to be Jack Young, World Champion in 1951 and 1952, although he didn't have as long a career at the top as a lot of the other champions. To me, he was the greatest rider of all time and could have been champion in any era. Then how do you choose from Ronnie Moore, Peter Craven, Barry Briggs, Tommy Price, Tommy Jansson, Jason Crump and Anders Michanek? OK, I'll take Ronnie, Peter and Barry.

Maurice Plowright: George Newton (New Cross). From 1936 onwards he was world class, a spectacular leg-trailer. Rube Wilson (Crystal Palace), one of the earliest foot-forward riders, who I believe was even before Ginger Lees. Bob Lovell (Harringay), a foot-trailer of great promise who always willingly answered all my many questions.

Dennis Hoppe: My first hero was Aub Lawson and I made known my admiration for his semi leg-trailing style by writing to him. He replied, almost by return, with a handwritten letter, which I treasured for many years. He was a true gentleman of the track. As I worked in London, I also attended meetings at New Cross and in time came to look forward to seeing

Aub Lawson, a true gent on and off the track.

my second hero, George Newton, another old-style leg-trailer. He certainly knew how to thrill the crowds. Although Vic Duggan of Harringay fame ruled the tracks during this time, his foot-forward approach lacked the excitement of the old-timers' wide sweeps. In this category, I must include another leg-trailer who always pleased the crowd, Odsal's Ollie Hart.

Ken Carpenter: Kelly and Shawn Moran. I've seen both of them change their line three times (outside, inside, and outside again) on the same bend. They had complete mastery of the bike as if it was a part of them. I never saw either of them do anything dirty or dangerous and they were both always generous in victory or defeat. Peter Collins, because there was never anything more exciting than seeing his last bend dives through the inside to snatch victory at Hyde Road. Mike Patrick's photo of him locked up using only one hand, while removing a rip-off with his left hand, has got to be the best shot ever of the great PC.

John Hyam: Keith Harvey, Ernie Price and Jack Parker. Harvey, a 50-year-old South African making a 1946 comeback at New Cross, because he gave me sixpence when I helped him by carrying the bag with his leathers to the dressing room door. Price, who rode for Bradford in the immediate post-war seasons, because he wore spectacles and brown leather boots. Jack Parker was simply the greatest ever rider.

Wally Loak: Peter Craven, the Wizard of Balance; Nigel Boocock never knew when he was beaten; and Dewayne Keeter, the India rubber man!

Ron Byford: My first hero was Ron Johnson. Ron How and Peter Craven came pretty close but if I had to pick three, it would be Ronnie Moore, Barry Briggs and Peter Collins.

Peter Jackson: Danny Dunton, who went into 1949 as a novice and then qualified for the World Final in 1950. Sadly, he never recovered from that awful smash at New Cross. Vic Duggan, of course, my dad thought a lot of him. Ove Fundin was always a great, hard rider.

Ken Wrench: I am going to exclude all the Belle Vue riders – there have been so many great ones and I have been far too close to many of them over the years. Of the non-Aces, I would select Ronnie Moore, a really relaxed rider; Malcolm Simmons, a classic stylist who

Danny Dunton (left) in the 1950 World Final with Split Waterman and Vic Duggan.

could cut through the field whilst looking as though he wasn't trying; and Hans Nielsen, the out-and-out professional.

Keith Barraclough: In the 1965-85 era at Halifax, my two favourite riders were Eric Boocock and Kenny Carter, closely followed by Eric Boothroyd and Ian Cartwright. Boocock was so consistent, a good gater but also very good from the back. Carter was a brilliant, exciting rider who would probably have been World Champion had he not had so many injuries and bad luck.

The third of my favourites is from the 1949-51 era. It could have been Vic Emms or Arthur Forrest but, as a young boy, my real favourite was always Jack Dawson. He was never a heat leader, only a second string/reserve, but to this day, whenever I reminisce with the 1949-51 programmes, I always look for Jack Dawson's score before any other.

Lucy Burton and friends with West Ham's popular Cliff Watson.

Lucy Burton: My favourite riders were Cliff Watson, Aub Lawson and Howdy Byford. They were all very friendly and they also had a lot of time for the supporters. On a couple of occasions, I was lucky enough to be invited to have tea with Cliff Watson when he was lodging with the Fearman family.

Cedric Read: Graham Warren – a real daredevil and the most exciting rider I ever saw; Ole Olsen – the epitome of the classic, professional rider immaculately turned out, a master of team-riding and a natural leader; Frank Smith, of Coventry and Stoke, a part-time rider who also held down a full-time job. Frank, and riders like him, provided the backbone of British league speedway.

Keith Walker: Oliver Hart – for his glorious round-the-boards technique, coupled with his own obvious enjoyment; Shawn Moran – a little wizard, especially when partnering Kelly at Sheffield; Ricky Ashworth – hanging off the bike, more than on it, but the undisputed master of Owlerton.

Ken Taylor: My first favourite was, and this is the late 40s, Bill Kitchen, the Wembley captain. I was in Newcastle and supported the Diamonds but each year at the end of the season, there would be a gala night at Brough. The place used to be bursting at the seams, with maybe 12,000 or so crammed into that small stadium. There would be four or five top first division stars, such as Jack Parker, Split Waterman, Eric Langton, Vic Duggan and Kitchen invited for the second-half and the Newcastle riders would be pitted against these top men. Although one might say they were just exhibition races, it enabled us in the north to see the star riders from London. My second rider is from the mid-to-late 50s and into the 60s, Ronnie Moore, who was also the firm favourite of my late wife Sheila. She had a few, Ivan was in there, but RM was her No.1, so I'll also go for him in her memory. A good rider from the 50s and 60s was another of my favourites, Ken McKinlay. Ken rode for Leicester and later for West Ham, a very successful team in the mid-60s, and it was whilst he was at Custom House that I got to

The spectacular Graham Warren with Birmingham boss Les Marshall.

know him. A particularly happy memory was the rained-off 1965 British Final scheduled to take place at West Ham on Tuesday, August 24. Along with some work colleagues, I took time off and travelled down from Leicester, only for incessant rain to cause the meeting to be postponed. Ken was by himself that night and it was suggested I travel back to Leicester with him to keep him company. It was great for me to accompany West Ham's No.1 in his Vauxhall Victor Estate with all his bikes and equipment!

John Chaplin: Unquestionably, they are Vic Duggan, Jack Parker and Graham Warren. Duggan was the smoothest, neatest, most clinically efficient and stylish winning machine I have ever seen on a speedway bike in all my 67 years watching the sport. Parker – because of his overwhelmingly outstanding personality – if ever there was a star, it was Parker. Warren – for his dashing skill and spectacular approach to his racing. He could win on any track in any conditions.

Tony Emmott: My star rider was Arthur Forrest, known as the Black Prince in his shiny, black leathers, who could do no wrong in my eyes. He was virtually unbeatable at Odsal and I recall his clashes with the likes of Jack Young, Ronnie Moore, Peter Craven and Ove Fundin. I was fortunate to be at Wembley when Arthur came third in the World Championship in 1956. His namesake, Arthur Wright, would be my second choice. He rode for England and made one or two World Finals but was always overshadowed by AF. My third would be Peter Craven and what more can be said about this great rider?

Odsal's Arthur Forrest resplendent in his shiny black leathers at Wembley.

Glynn Shailes: Jack Young, Barry Briggs and George Craig. Young was just amazing, since he wasn't particularly good at the start and to watch him just pick off the opposition was sheer 'poetry in motion'. Briggo was much the same, since he wasn't particularly fast from the tapes and just made it to the front by sheer hard work. George Craig had one and a bit seasons at Swindon and built up a wonderful repartee with the crowd. Bob Kilby was, of course, the greatest in my opinion but he became a good friend and whilst both my wife and I loved to see him in action, he was thought of as a good friend rather than a rider.

Oliver Chapman: Ken McKinlay – for many years, he was Leicester Speedway. His equipment and black leathers were meticulous. In the early 60s, I was asked to deliver a letter to Ken in his workshop and was astounded by the tidiness and cleanliness of the premises. I would have willingly eaten a full English breakfast served on the floor! Graham Plant – I followed him from a very early age, when he used to skid a mini motorbike around the petrol pump island at his dad's garage (Health & Safety was not around at that time). When on form, he could overtake riders with ease, like a hot knife through butter.

Ian Barney – not a good gater, but provided much excitement with his round-the-boards manoeuvres at Peterborough.

Michael Mayo: Ove Fundin – probably the greatest rider of all-time, in 1960, the holder of more track records than any other rider, and the hardest rider to pass in any race, Ove being the most fantastic gater. Ronnie Moore – a silky smooth rider who could gate well and also win a fair proportion of races from the back. His undoubted ability should have gained him more

Graham Plant was capable of beating anyone on his day.

than two victories in World Finals, where he never had the best of good fortune. Barry Briggs – a swashbuckling rider who possessed a fantastic will-to-win which he exhibited in all of his races, whether they be league matches, Test matches, open meetings, World Championships or second-half trophies.

Tony Webb: My all-time favourite will always be Vic Harding, the rider I was closest to. I was possibly one of the last people he spoke to on that fateful night, June 8, 1979, when he tragically lost his life at Hackney. He was what I would call a rider's rider. After Vic's death, speedway lost its gloss for me. I used to worry about the parts we (Shaleway Products) were making at the time and the responsibility for ensuring our products would not cause an accident. Silly, I know, but that's how it affected me. So many people will never forget that tragic night.

My second rider is Mike Lanham. I got to know him well as his in-laws were neighbours and would pick up spares for him. He was such a gutsy rider and he did well to recover from his horrific accident at Leicester. And my third rider is Garry Middleton. I never realised the true story about Garry until I discovered his family members and his grave in Brisbane. Garry had the potential to be a champion. If only it had been recognised there was a medical condition that in today's world would have been treated, he would have achieved his aims.

John Cross: Peter Craven must be in my list of favourites, he was always so popular. I will also mention Len Williams of Leicester Hunters who seemed to have a very unusual style which I know, along with his brother Stan, originated at Sheffield. From the modern era, I will name Mark Loram, who I always admired because he many times had to battle from behind to win his races and always gave other riders enough room.

Vic Harding lost his life in a crash at Hackney in 1979.

Ray Cresp enjoying himself at Long Eaton in 1965.

Philip Dalling: As a young fan, I always enjoyed watching Maurice 'Slant' Payling. He was unpredictable but, on occasions, spectacular, and also one of the many riders of the 60s who was always happy to chat to supporters. Ray Cresp was a great favourite of mine in the mid-60s when, on many occasions, he stood between a weakened Long Eaton side and complete oblivion. Ray always looked like my idea of a speedway rider. I suppose I am showing a real bias, sticking with Long Eaton/Leicester, but I cannot leave out Ray Wilson from my list. From the very start, he looked the part and I believe his presence at Long Eaton during hard times for the Archers made a huge contribution to keeping the fans coming through the turnstiles.

Tim Templeton: Ronnie Moore – his natural talent on a speedway machine was unsurpassed, poetry in motion. Also, he's such a nice bloke, never harps on about his achievements, took his world titles as "just another meeting" and as long as he has a beer and a fag, he's happy. Barry Briggs – just the opposite to Ronnie in some ways. He was hard, he'd hustle and bustle his way to the front if he wasn't already there, but just look at his consistency over a long period of time when there was only a fag paper between him Fundin, Knutson, Craven, Moore and Mauger. He couldn't have been around at a more competitive time. Darcy Ward – the guy leaves me speechless. I watch him most weeks and I've never seen anything like it. He seems never to have issues with set-ups, tracks or anything. He's looking for his partner within yards of leaving the tapes. He will be the complete package, the best in the world, if he chooses to be.

Bert Harkins: Going back to my schooldays in Glasgow, Junior Bainbridge, the fiery Aussie who rode for Glasgow; Ken McKinlay, who, when he rode for the Tigers, was almost always last out of the gate and first past the chequered flag and had immaculately polished black leathers and a chrome-plated JAP (that impressed this schoolboy); and Ronnie Moore, who I had never seen ride at that time but from photographs he was always neat and stylish with his right elbow up and left elbow down. Many years later, I met and raced against Ronnie and we became friends, but I have never told him I used to collect photographs of him!

Ronnie Moore, one of the greatest natural talents.

David Walker: Having seen an enormous number of great, good, average and poor riders in 61 years, some stick in your mind more than others. Ronnie Moore – the greatest natural talent I have ever seen on a speedway bike, an opinion backed up by Ivan Mauger and Barry Briggs, so maybe I'm in good company. Despite seemingly being far less dedicated than many others, I was always amazed by Ronnie's incredible track craft, with his ability to find lines and grip that others couldn't.

Per-Olaf (Peo) Soderman – one full season for Coventry, averaging over 13 points per meeting, plus sixth place in his first World Final. A superb talent that never seemed to reach fruition, which still has me grinding my teeth as one of the great 'might-have-beens'. His second and third seasons were much less impressive, mainly due to his frequent absences.

Arthur Forrest – as a youngster, all sorts of things impress you. In my case, a gleaming, polished and chromed bike, with a man, not in any old black leathers, but a set as shiny as that bike. Wow! No wonder they called him the Black Prince, and an excellent rider too.

David Brassington: Sverre Harrfeldt – when he was riding for West Ham, he was No.2 in the world for one season and his brother Henry was a member of a church I attended at the time; Stan Stevens of New Cross – such a friendly guy who would always come out to chat to people during the meetings; Greg Kentwell of Halifax – I was working with a friend of his who managed to get me into the pits at Wembley during a league match between the Lions and the Dukes and I remember what a great thrill it was to chat to a rider during an actual meeting.

Mike King: I would have to list my three favourite riders as Ivan Mauger, Mark Loram and Tai Woffinden. Mauger was the ultimate professional and Loram, with his gritty determination, was one of the hardest triers in the game. Woffinden quickly embraced these attributes and all the other qualities needed to reach the very top.

Richard Tyrrell: Ove Fundin was always worth watching at Oxford. He had the reputation of being so good, you couldn't miss his visit to see if any Oxford riders could beat him. Actually, Ronnie Genz did do just that one night, but I always admired his 'killer' instinct. Peter Collins was also worth watching. Oxford were in the second division at the time but I always went to see Reading, Coventry or Swindon v Belle Vue to watch PC. I was on holiday in Guernsey when he won his world title and the shopkeeper thought I was demented when I jumped around the shop having read the result in the Daily Mirror. And, of course, the one we called 'The Great Man' at Oxford, Hans Nielsen. It was an absolute joy to be around when he was in his prime and we followed Oxford all around the country at that time.

Aussie Jack Geran was a big favourite at Exeter.

James Easter: Briggo, who personifies adventure, charisma and bravery; John Cook, perhaps the most all-round perfection on a bike; and John Louis, who was Mr. Ipswich. He always handled his racing and his on/off track personality to perfection. I owe him a great deal and, sadly, he knows it!

Andy Wilkinson: How can I possibly limit it to three? Ten, 15 or 20 would be just as difficult. I have a Wimbledon bias but how could I not include Trevor Hedge, Edward Jancarz, Jim Tebby, Rudy Muts, Buzz Burrows et al. OK, Ronnie Moore, Tommy Jansson and Reg Luckhurst. All three were loyal Wimbledon riders and they were exciting riders who you knew, if they didn't make the gate, could still come through to win.

Tony Lethbridge: I've been lucky enough to have seen and met many great riders, so I respect anyone who can properly race a 500cc speedway bike. Working on the inside, you should not have favourites but of course you do. You just try not to let it show and some people are more likeable than others. The three I have chosen are Jack Geran, Vaclav Verner and Richard Green. Stylish Jack was one of my earliest heroes, along with the great Neil Street. In what other sport can your childhood heroes become your friends? When Jack was made president of the WSRA, he asked me to make the traditional introductory speech at his inauguration. That was a great honour, the more so that there were five World Champions present. Vaclav and Richard are two of the most exciting riders I've ever seen, and I'm proud to call them friends. I saw Richard hit a bump at Milton Keynes in 1992, become airborne and spin around a full 360 degrees before landing back on two wheels and finishing the race. I was on the centre green and near enough to see him raise his eyebrows at me as he passed, even though he was still wearing goggles!

Richard Bott: Peter Collins, Ivan Mauger and Kelly Moran. PC because I have known him since he first started and became his business manager, but mainly because he was so good to watch. He did so much for British speedway before and after he won the World Championship in 1976.

Ivan because he was the complete professional. He left nothing to chance and was an out-and-out winner who always wanted more. He was also a great team captain and inspiration wherever he went.

Of all the riders I saw at Hull, when I was press officer there for 10 years at the old Boulevard track, Kelly was the most exciting. Bruce Penhall was brilliant and a great World Champion but Kelly was just a 'born' racer, like PC. Such a tragedy he died so young.

Paul Ackroyd: My favourite riders as a supporter, not as a referee, would have to be Chris Pusey, who was unbelievable at both Belle Vue and Halifax and was probably one of the best-ever at team-riding; Henny Kroeze, who was the first rider to get a 21-point maximum in a league match; Bob Kilby, who was always brilliant around the northern circuits; and, of course, Eric Boocock who was No.1 for Halifax.

As a referee, I didn't have favourite riders but many gave me great pleasure to watch, in particular Kenny Carter, and Shawn and Kelly Moran.

Roy Blanchflower: My all-time favourite has always been Jack Young, who made speedway look so easy. No.2 is Bob Leverenz of Norwich, who was such a good rider, home and away. I knew Bob very well, I also cleaned his leathers. as I did for many of the Norwich team. No.3 is a very exciting rider, double World Champion Peter Craven, who, whenever he came to Norwich, would always take time to speak to you.

Stephen Jinkerson: Jeremy Doncaster, an all round top guy, willing to talk to the fans no matter how busy he was and a hard, but very

Henny Kroeze made history with his 21-point maximum.

fair rider; Kelly Moran, what a character! He could beat anyone on his day; and Emil Sayfutdinov, who has it all – guts, determination and a really likeable fella as well.

Bryan Newbold: Without doubt, my favourite rider is Ray Wilson. He was my first real sporting hero and the inspiration for me desperately saving all my earnings to buy a speedway bike of my own. Second on my list is Ivan Mauger. Never the most popular, or indeed exciting, of riders, but Ivan was the ultimate professional. Many of his opponents were beaten before the tapes had even been released. Third is Malcolm Brown. Never a superstar, Malc was one of those frustrating second strings who could beat the best in one race (Ole Olsen, for instance) and trail in last in the next. But he was a great character on and off the track. I still remember his famous stripteases in front of the Blackbird Road grandstand. Characters like Malcolm are sadly missing today.

Paul Jeffries: I have to go way back and say my No.1 was Clive Featherby. Never a world-beater, but truly unbeatable on the inside line around Owlerton in his heyday. Of the world stars, Ronnie Moore, the master of Plough Lane. Even if I never saw him in his pomp as

Ever the joker, Malcolm Brown.

World Champion, what a privilege it was to see even his later seasons here. And of the World Champs I've seen, it just has to be Ove Fundin – simply the best.

Doug Nicolson: Graham Coombes – one of Trevor Redmond's 1964 Tigers. A great, little all-action rider who never gave up. Won the Scottish Cup for Glasgow at Old Meadowbank on a night when it seemed to be going wrong big time. Somehow, he withstood George Hunter's challenges for four laps and had Hunter's tyre marks on his arm at the end of the race.

Mick Powell – a vital member of Glasgow's glorious 'double double' years (cup and league winners) in successive years. Few cornered quite as fast as Mick. I will never forgive promoters Sands and Snedden for sacking him at Ashfield.

Phil Crump – watched him progress from a promising second division rider to World Finalist. A great racer. Pity he never came to Glasgow. He was considering it apparently but Neil Street persuaded him against it due to all the travelling it involved.

Colin Pratt after winning the London Riders' Championship.

Karl Fiala: Colin Pratt, who was my local motorcycle hero and he was very good (if you know what I mean, kinda like, sort-a-thing!); Tommy Jansson, so smooth and stylish with so much potential; and Ivan Mauger, because he was the best and most professional.

Mike Keir: Bert Harkins, the charismatic Scot, was one I could instantly identify with. I used to dress for meetings in clothes that matched the colours of his leathers. Well, it was the 70s! Kai Niemi rode for us (Wimbledon) for a few seasons in the early 80s and formed a dynamic partnership with Malcolm Simmons. He'd left by 1985 but I cheered him on at the World Final that year and he scored 11 points. Todd Wiltshire – I remember his debut at Wimbledon, when he got better with every ride. I watched him at tracks he'd never seen before and he'd run *a la*st in his first ride but you could see him weighing up the track from the back. Then he'd go out and win all his other rides, no matter who else was on the start-line. At the 1990 World Final, everyone in the stadium thought he was there just to make up the numbers, except me, and I wasn't the least bit surprised to see him win his first two rides and end up on the rostrum.

Rod Haynes: Roy Trigg, for his stylishness; Alan Knapkin, for his pure skill; and Arnold Haley (later to be a team-mate of mine at Sheffield) for both his style and skill on a bike, not forgetting his sheer all-round class, which was perhaps wasted along the way.

Dennis Lindo: When I first went to watch the Middlesbrough Bears, Eric Boothroyd had been brought into replace the injured Wal Morton and he quickly became my first sporting hero. I first saw Chris Morton ride at Cleveland Park when he represented Ellesmere Port. I don't think he scored many points due to poor machinery but I remember thinking he displayed a lot of determination. And Ivan Mauger, for his sheer professionalism and single-mindedness. I often walk or cycle past the house where he lived in Woodford, Cheshire and every time I think to myself: why didn't he ride for Middlesbrough instead of Newcastle?

Ian Martin: Jim Airey was stylish and very pugnacious and I appreciated that he would always

The top three in the 1990 World Final – Per Jonsson, Shawn Moran (left) and Todd Wiltshire, who did much more than 'just make up the numbers'.

fight for every point. Graeme Smith was my favourite all-time rider and made speedway look so easy. He had an 'armchair' style and the way he stuck to the white line was phenomenal. Russ Dent was with us (Sunderland) throughout our four seasons of racing in the 70s. He scored the most points over the years and was very loyal to Sunderland. I admired that loyalty.

I must mention a fourth rider whose escapades will never be forgotten – 'Crazy' Jack Millen, 'The Villain'. What a character, hard as nails and with a determination to win that I have rarely seen in anyone. Jack was probably the most memorable Sunderland rider in both of our incarnations (60s and 70s).

I thought I would take a liberty here and name my three favourite away riders too. First would have to be Bruce Forrester, you would have thought Sunderland was his home track, he rode it that well. He was a truly nice person too. One day, Elizabeth and I turned up very early at Cleveland Park for a meeting that night. Bruce pulled into the car park, spotted us, chatted to us and then he actually took us in and showed us round the stadium, including the pits. I thought this was a tremendous gesture. In the years just before Bruce sadly passed away, he attended our Sunderland Speedway reunion - a wonderful man and a true gentleman.

Jack Millen was a larger than life character at Sunderland.

Second would be Taffy Owen who, when he won a race at Sunderland, used to do a lap of honour with a big grin on his face, which infuriated the home supporters. Finally, Frank Auffret and Tony Childs. Their duels with Jack Millen were epic.

Stephen Hawthorne: Ivor Brown, the top rider in a poor Cradley Heathens team and loyal to the club; Bernie Persson, as Brown, plus he finished second in the World Final in 1972 and had a tremendous celebration at Dudley Wood on his return; and Erik Gundersen. Seeing him come to the club and progress to such great achievements was special. He always had time for the fans and made himself one of us.

Harry Ward: Everyone's favourite, Kelly Moran. Not only did I pound the motorways to

watch the most stylish rider I have ever seen, but also he was a really nice bloke. I remember watching him at Oxford. In the pits, Hans Nielsen was a bit aloof, arms folded, watching the racing far from the fans, but next to me was Kelly, chatting away to fans, having a laugh and signing autographs. Next, Norman Hunter because he was so good at Hackney in 1963, then transferred to the Hammers and became a real star; and finally, Christer Lofqvist, simply because he was the closest thing to Peter Craven I had ever seen. A quiet, shy, nice man and a Hammer to boot.

Steve Johnston: Brian Leonard, Christer Lofqvist and Olle Nygren. Brian was my first favourite, riding at No.6 for the Hammers. I still have my child's body colour with a No.6 on the back! I think I liked Olle because he held the Hammers together so many times and his white boots also caught the eye. Christer

Ivor Brown held Cradley Heath together for many years.

because, apart from being a sensation upon his arrival at Custom House, I also helped my cousin run his fan club for a couple of seasons until he went to Poole in 1972.

Andrew Edwards: Peter Collins, Simon Wigg and Erik Gundersen. PC was probably the best natural rider on a bike I have ever seen, other than Michael Lee. And people forget it was his progression from junior grass-track up to World Champion which inspired a generation of British riders – not all world champs, but glorious British lads who filled our teams and our hearts for years and years at that time.

Wiggy was the best two-wheel sportsmen ever. Full stop. What a professional. I produced his official press releases for many years, speaking to him regularly on a late Sunday night as he drove back from some distant East European grass-track, long-track or speedway. So I got to know him and his family well. A wonderful, warm human being who never stopped talking about his passion for our sport.

Erik was a very special little man. Extremely intelligent, which came across in his riding and in his zest for life. A deep thinker, who taught me more than other riders, what it takes to be a successful rider. His diary was pretty full, but he always had time to talk and explain speedway matters.

Bob Radford: They are three of the greats but the choice is for many reasons. It would be easier if I could name 30, I admire and like so many.

Barry Briggs was my first hero as a Southampton rider. He moved to Swindon and came to visit me in hospital after a bad motorcycle accident in 1965. Later he advised me when I became a manager at age 22 and he remains a lifelong friend who always talks speedway up. Bruce Penhall was probably the most charismatic speedway rider of my lifetime. He was exciting, personable and looked like a pop star. Again, very good to be in his company and he was, all too briefly, great for the sport. The third choice is unbelievably hard between Ivan Mauger, Ole Olsen and my choice, but I will go for John Louis who is still my all-time favourite British rider. What he and John Berry achieved at Ipswich, along with many others, was incredible.

Derek Chalmers: First must be Brian Collins, a prolific scorer and a team player. He took me under his wing, first in the pits, fuelling and oiling his bike, then showing me how to ride a bike, an experience I will never forget.

Peter Carr was an Edinburgh Monarchs hero, a natural rider with talent to spare and never gave less than 100 per cent. Joe Screen, another natural, and I will never forget the wheelie he pulled at Peter Carr's testimonial at Armadale when he stood the bike vertically on the back wheel and did two laps at walking pace.

David Hoggart: Carl Stonehewer has been a friend since the Long Eaton days. He is the first rider I put money into and he repaid my faith a thousand times over and never once took me for

Les Collins became a No.1 in his own right at Leicester.

granted. He has always been appreciative, he had some brilliant results and we had some great laughs too. Graeme Smith was someone I idolised and I worked as his mechanic. We went everywhere together and Graeme was very influential in my formative years (particularly driving!). He was focused and worked very hard at the speedway craft. I learned a lot from him but, sadly, we fell out and have never made up – a regret to this day but we cannot turn the clock back. Ronnie Moore – 'Mirac' by name and Mirac by nature. I'd never seen him ride until his return to Wimbledon second time around and I can remember walking down Garratt Lane to the stadium and both sides of the road there were speedway fans hurrying along to get a glimpse of this enigma. The car park was heaving and the crowds around the riders' cars were incredible, all trying to get a glimpse of Ronnie. I went with a pal from work who hadn't been to speedway for four or five years but he wasn't going to miss this. The welcome was overwhelming and a rusty Ronnie, on a JAP machine, scored a handful of points. I couldn't work out what all the fuss was about until maybe a month, six weeks later when he came good with a bang – points everywhere, incredible skill and speed to pass from nowhere. He was one of the very few riders that I would travel to see. He was that good.

Martin Rogers: Les Collins because of what he achieved and what he did for us at Leicester;

Terry Betts, who was so influential at King's Lynn and helped fuel my enthusiasm for and involvement in speedway; and of the modern brigade, Jason Crump, who time will surely define as one of the best there's been.

Pete Rout: Ivan Mauger, for his star quality, professional approach and success in the sport; John Louis, especially in the early years when he was still learning speedway, but beating many of the established star riders on the way; and Tony Davey, spectacular to watch, he never gave up and is one of the nicest blokes you could wish to meet.

Tony Davey leading Peter Collins in a Golden Helmet match-race at Ipswich in 1978.

Steve Casey: Cyril Maidment, my first hero. Belle Vue were going through a terrible time after the death of Peter Craven. The launch of the British League in 1965 seemed to be perfect for 'Maido' who would regularly pass people with his legendary 'hook back' on the last corner. Ivan Mauger was my next idol for bringing the Aces back to the forefront of speedway again. His record for Belle Vue, home and away, was incredible. It was a talking point when he dropped a point and the battles with Ole Olsen were always worth watching, especially when the mind games at the tapes were in full flow. Mark Loram was fabulous to watch on his visits to Kirky Lane. He could pass anyone and I loved the fact that he wasn't a gater and was always working the bike and making moves that didn't look possible.

Geoff Theobald: My all-time favourite, as he was for so many Hackney fans, has to be Barry Thomas. A lovely bloke, for so long he was worth the price of admission alone at Waterden Road. You forgave him the odd poor race because he gave his all and would come from the back in fabulous fashion in his next. He may not have had the best equipment, nor been as professional as some, but he epitomised what the Hackney team was all about. Bo Petersen would be next, just edging out Zenon Plech, because he rode more seasons. Tall, yet so spectacular on a bike, he was not in the normal Hackney mould – he was a young foreigner who came good, a Hawk who topped the national averages. He had immaculate equipment and he could score big on the away tracks. My third would have to be Andy Galvin who, for a spell, was a Kestrels legend. Blond, fast, fearless, the captain, National League top dog. For a while, he was on a par with Wimbledon's Todd Wiltshire. The tragedy was that he didn't push on to the heights his Aussie rival did, but he surely had the ability.

David Beresford: I could choose a hundred but my three favourite riders are Eric Broadbelt, who let me help him in the pits (even though I was useless) and introduced me to the speedway world behind the scenes; Reg Wilson, a great rider and leader and a humorous, straight-talking

Yorkshireman; and Shawn Moran, who was a skilful and spectacular rider and popular with all fans.

Mark Wilkinson: This is really difficult and I have changed my mind many times. The likes of Joe Screen and Chris Harris readily came to mind, but I've not actually seen them race in real life much, so I'm concentrating on riders I've actually seen in action regularly. Colin Cook – spectacular, 100 per cent effort, a long career and, to me, he was 'Mr. Speedway' and always will be; Ray Wilson – I missed seeing him in his prime, but Heat 1 at Blackbird Road always had an extra edge of anticipation; and Ila Teromaa – a much needed ray of light during some indifferent years for Leicester. It was a pleasure (and a change) to see a rider progress so well.

Robert Wiles: Reg Luckhurst – when I became properly interested in speedway, he was, to put it politely, in the second-half of his career and was riding at reserve for Wimbledon. He was, however, still a top grass-tracker and could give the likes of Ivan Mauger, Ole Olsen and Anders Michanek a serious run for their money at events like the annual Speedtrack at Lydden Hill. What made it so special to me was that the top speedway men arrived with their full-on Jawa long-track machines and Reg had his JAP-powered, home-built, grass-track bike. He was a very stylish rider on both shale and grass and it came as no surprise when I researched his speedway career a little to find that he was a former World Finalist. Oh, and Reg could sing a bit as well! Barry Briggs – unfortunately, I didn't get to see him race very often and I'd never been to Swindon, but the pictures and match reports in *Speedway Star* and national press and TV coverage built him up to legend status in my eyes. Ross Gilbertson – I first saw Ross when he rode for Romford. The Bombers team of the time seemed stuffed with ex-Division One riders and seemed quite glamorous to us country boys at Canterbury. Ross always gave the Canterbury riders a hard time at Kingsmead and was considered to be something of 'a villain' as a result. He was fast and tough and tended not to take any prisoners on track. At the end of 1970, Canterbury lost two heat leaders from the team that had won the Division Two title. Gilbertson joined the team for 1971 and proved a revelation.

Ross Gilbertson (on bike) as Canterbury captain in 1972. With him (left to right) are: Les Rumsey, Ted Hubbard, Trevor Jones, Charlie Benham, Johnnie Hoskins (promoter), Graham Banks, Dave Piddock, Barney Kennett, Russ Osborne (team manager).

Malcolm Ballard (centre) with Eastbourne and Young England team-mates Dave and Gordon Kennett in 1971.

From the sinister, all-black leathers he wore when riding for Romford, he changed to colourful blue and yellow to match the Crusaders' colours. His uncompromising riding style didn't change, though, and now wearing Crusaders' crossed swords, he instantly changed from villain to hero in my young eyes.

Alan Jones: It's too easy to pick the riders who score the most points but, having said that, I'm taking the easy way out and going for Ray Wilson for his tenacity, bulldog spirit, box office appeal and pure excitement whenever he was in a race. During Ray's tenure as captain of Leicester it was a golden era when the team should have delivered at least one league title. However, travelling away from home to watch Ray was a joy and he made you feel proud to say to anyone that you were a Lions supporter. Secondly, Rolf Gramstad stood out for me. Unwanted after a spell at Swindon, the Norwegian came of age at Leicester and rocketed up from reserve to heat leader in his first season. A career-ending injury in 1981 was a sad day and, whenever I think of him, it is the sight of Rolf taking a high-line around the Tote Bend at Blackbird Road in full flight. As for the third nomination, it has to be John Boulger who arrived at Leicester as a second string and gradually climbed to become the No.1. He ousted Ray Wilson from top spot in 1973 by delivering consistently high scores, which enabled him to emulate 'World Cup Willie', in itself a marvellous achievement by anyone's standards.

Ken Burnett: Malcolm Ballard – so fast and hard, made rapid strides in the sport in a short space of time, a top guy and against the Kennetts, even in the second-halves, you knew it was going to be as good as the races in the earlier match because he didn't do second places; Tommy Jansson – great to watch, a real star of the future who was robbed of becoming World Champion; and Peter Collins – pure class on a motorbike.

Pete Butler: Richard May, Pierre Brannefors and Per Jonsson. May was my schoolboy hero who shone for Reading in the Division Two days but he was never a trapper throughout his whole career, so earned most of his points from the back. I was gutted when he left Reading to join Poole in 1976.

Brannefors had a short spell as a Racer but his robust take-no-prisoners riding was a highlight in a period of little success on the team front. I made a Brannefors programme board, which featured him in action with a rider and bike crumpled against the fence in the background. It had his name in bold, black letters above the slogan: 'He's hard. Rock hard.' Among my fellow Racers fans, it was known as the 'hard board'. It also had small black silhouettes of riders with red crosses through them and adjacent was the name of his latest victim. At the end of the season, it resembled a fighter ace's fuselage and among the names were his best friend Bjorn Andersson and team-mate Jan Andersson! As for Jonsson, it was a privilege to see someone come into the team as an 18-year-old (the SCB did not want to give him a work permit, as they deemed he was not good enough) and progress to that glorious night at Bradford in 1990. Everyone knows how good a rider he was – he could pass anyone at Smallmead – but his team-riding abilities, and especially his partnership with Dave Mullett, showed he had a team ethic to add to his individual greatness.

Greg Unwin: It is hard to pin down my favourites over 45 years to just three riders. My first favourite was an Aussie rider who joined the Devils in 1968, Chris Bass, and like most of the Devils team, he was a 'junior' at Exeter even though he was 28 at the time. Mike Cake was the big favourite at Plymouth but Bass proved to be every bit his equal. It was a shame that an injury limited his BL2 appearances for the Devils to only 10 matches, but his 10.15 CMA spoke for itself. In 1969, he joined BL1 outfit Cradley Heath, where he was a steady second string. He seemed to drop off the radar when he returned to Australia in 1971. My second rider is the one and only Ivan Mauger. His gating and first bend riding made him an instant favourite of mine when I first saw him riding for Belle Vue. When Ivan joined Exeter in 1973, the news was announced on the local Westward Television and I couldn't believe it. The World Champion was to be an Exeter rider. On hearing news of his signing for the Falcons, I danced a jig around our living room – my late mother thought I had gone crazy. My third choice, American Scott Autrey, came to my attention as a team-mate of Ivan's. When Ivan moved on to Hull, Scott was already a firm favourite and highly popular at the County Ground. He soon established himself as the Exeter No.1 as his average was well over 10 points by the time he reached the 1978 World Final at Wembley. A special train was chartered by the Exeter Supporters' Club and as it started its journey from Plymouth, three friends and I were able to choose the best seats having a whole carriage compartment to ourselves. Scott was to finish on the podium in third place. We speculated for many years afterwards as to whether he would have done better if not for a broken bike frame held together with a split pin. I thought he was never the same rider after he moved to Swindon in 1980.

Tony Barnard: Eric Boocock, Nigel Boocock (when the brothers met on the track, there was always fireworks) and Barry Briggs. After a Halifax v Swindon meeting once, they interviewed Briggo on the centre green and he commented of Eric Boocock that "we have a future World Champion in the making", which was praise indeed from a star rider of the time.

Richard Lambert: Chris Julian was my favourite, a real character or what? He came from Cornwall and once was allocated by Rider Control to Glasgow – pre-motorway! He was supposed to be riding for Cradley Heath at Wolves one day but went missing. Just before the off, he was found asleep in his A40 in the car park. One time, he gated at Belle Vue, but hit the same pot hole on each lap and ended up last.

John Vine: When Newcastle closed at the end of 1970, Mike Parker, the Wolves and

Chris Julian (left) with Cradley Heath colleagues Bob Andrews and Roy Trigg in 1968.

Newcastle promoter, brought the great Ole Olsen to Monmore Green. He was so good that it became unusual to see him beaten ever, so it was exceptional to say the least when Dave Jessup, who was in tremendous form, went out and beat him twice in one night. Olsen was a superb team rider and one night he was riding at Coventry when Bill Powell (his mechanic and the ex-Belle Vue rider) had been persuaded to come out of retirement. Powell had obviously been told to gate and Olsen would team-ride him round, which he duly did. My second favourite rider was Hans Nielsen, another of Wolverhampton's top riders. You almost knew he was going to win a race before it started, or so it seemed at the time. With an average of 9.30, he still couldn't beat the great Olsen's best of 10.93, which any Wolverhampton rider will find hard to get anywhere near. My third favourite rider has to be either Sam Ermolenko or Peter Karlsson. I liked Sam for his never-say-die attitude. You knew he would never give up if there was any chance at all of winning. PK was, and still is, a very smooth rider and his line around the Wolverhampton track is an example to all other riders.

Ian Glover: Brian 'Barney' Kennett, a hard man of the sport but a team rider who put bums on seats; Graham Banks, an unsung team man in the engine room of the Crusaders and every team needs one; and Mark Loram, local lad, 110 per cent racer, team man and top bloke in my book.

Richard Mason: My favourite rider in the 60s was Middlesbrough/Teesside's Tom Leadbitter, who my parents got to know well from the local scrambles in the Midlands area. I remember him as Teesside captain and star rider, sat in the corner of the pits with all the fans pressed up to the fence to see him. He would then spot us through the fence and come across for a chat. In his later years when he returned to riding moto-cross, I actually got to race against him. A really great bloke and a character sadly missed. In the 70s, my favourite was Peter Collins. At last, after what seemed many years of being a speedway fan, we had a British rider who we all knew was going to be World Champion. Just a pity he didn't dominate for longer in view of the ability he had. My 80s favourite was Kelly Moran. From the first time I saw him go around Sheffield, I just loved the way he rode.

Paul Kerry: Peter Craven – no more need be said. I was inconsolable for days after he died in September 1963 and had the action shot shown on the back cover of *Classic Speedway* (issue 23) pinned on the underside of my desk lid at school after cutting it from *Speedway Star*. Kenny Carter – an unbelievable racer, should have been a multiple World Champion. He could beat anyone, anywhere in the world. But something was lacking, and we all know his tragic finale. Eric Boothroyd – like me, a Halifax man. He's seen it all over the years. In the 50s, he rubbed shoulders with the world's best in the hurly burly of league racing and had an international career too. In the Provincial League, he was a colossus, THE man to beat but, incredibly, missed out on the PLRC to Len Silver. Then he came to The Shay . . . at 40-years-old, the

Tom Leadbitter with the product all speedway nostalgia addicts wishes could be bottled and bought to preserve happy memories of that distinctive aroma.

perfect captain for the newly-formed Dukes. A much respected local man, I once saw scrawled on a hoarding outside The Shay the slogan, 'Boothroyd for PM'. 'Nuff said!

Paul Watson: Terry Betts, my childhood hero, daring and spectacular; Martin Dugard, for his will to win; and Henka Gustafsson, who I truly believe missed the gate so he had to overtake the field on the last two laps of a race at King's Lynn.

Chris Gosling: Ian Turner was a fantastically entertaining rider who happened to move in just up the road from us in Gedney. When Ian first started riding, you just didn't know what was going to happen. He was very spectacular and, in the beginning, he often fell, but when he stayed on, he got better and better. We got to know him and my brother accompanied him to many meetings as his helper. At his best, he was simply breathtaking. I remember him in a televised match against Ipswich in June 1978, going from last to first in each of his opening three rides, narrowly missing out on a maximum in his fourth after being baulked by Michael Lee. My other two choices are Chris Morton and Peter Collins. Morton was a racer, as you can see from all those fantastic videos on YouTube of the World Team Cup meetings. I was fortunate enough to be there and see those big sweeps around the boards. He rode King's Lynn as well as anyone, although Collins probably rode it even better than Morton and had a lot of success there, both in individual and World Team Cup meetings, but especially in league meetings for Belle Vue.

Carol Stock: Peter Collins is my all-time favourite. He was so spectacular to watch, especially as he nearly always had to battle from the back. My good friend Kelly Moran is sadly missed. He was a natural on a bike and made riding speedway look so easy. He had his demons in life, but rarely did they interfere with his on-track ability. I was only nine-years-old when Martyn Piddock died in the Lokeren Disaster in June 1970, but I will never forget him. He was tall for a speedway rider and always wore an orange scarf around his neck. He

was an up-and-coming youngster with tons of ability. He had represented his country and was just making a name for himself when tragedy struck. I believe he would have been World Champion.

John Brownhill: My first favourite was Clive Featherby but my second is a man who grew up with his family in the same village as myself, Grenoside in Sheffield. He left school and worked as a milkman and also did farm work. His family were into motorbikes and to buy his first bike, a JAP, he had to sell his mini-van. Helped by a number of friends and his brothers, he went to various so called 'training schools' where little tuition was offered in most cases, but did eventually become good enough to sign for Sheffield. Initially, he was loaned to Ian Thomas' new track at Workington, then a season later to Hull, before being recalled to Sheffield where he spent 10 years, some as captain.

The formation of a Second Division saw the emergence of a large number of very good British riders – so many, in fact, that to earn a Union Jack body colour was recognition that you were somebody. The rider, as you have probably guessed by now, is Reg Wilson and he went on to ride as a British Lion on tours to Australia and New Zealand. Unfortunately, he suffered two broken legs during his career, which held him back, and he would, I think, have benefited from a season at a smaller home track too.

Spectacular and determined Nigel Boocock.

Reg achieved so much and I was fortunate to be a pits helper for him at many meetings up and down the country. My third favourite was another Yorkshireman and a tremendous racer, spectacular and brave, one Nigel Boocock.

Richard Clark: I've been very, very, lucky to have met so many of the greats through working for *Speedway Star*. And even luckier to have forged fantastic working relationships with a few. It's difficult to narrow it down to three. Mark Loram, Leigh Adams and Greg Hancock have all gone out of their way on so many occasions for me and I always enjoyed watching them race, but will equally always be in debt to Jason Crump, for example, and I loved his out-and-out determination on the track. Likewise Billy Hamill. Chris Morton, PC and Chris Louis are great 'thinkers', as is Crumpie and as was Wiggy – Simon Wigg – all great riders whose company I've always enjoyed. Ivan Mauger and Barry Briggs are equally fascinating company and brilliant on-track in their heyday. Erik Gundersen, what an inspiration and such a lovely man (and wife and daughter!). Being in a band with Boycie (Craig Boyce), Dicko (Martin Dixon) and Humper (Ian Humphreys) was great fun, too. Bertola (Bert Harkins) has been a memorable travelling companion. Chewing the fat with Simon Cross, Michael Lee, Alun Rossiter, Gary Havelock, Shane Parker, Joe Screen, Jan O. Pedersen, Jeremy Doncaster, Malcolm Simmons, John Davis, Colin Pratt, Kenny McKinna, Phil Crump was never less than educational and they've all supplied some great moments on-track. Spent some great northern trips in the company of the likes of Alan Mogridge, Barry Thomas, Andy Galvin, Paul Bosley, Trevor Banks, Roger Johns, Kevin Teager, Mark Baldwin, Steve Payne, David Blackburn, too. Don't mean this to be a cop-out answer, simply spoilt for choice.

Richard Parsons: On his day, Gordon Kennett could beat anybody. The master white-liner, he was so good around Wimbledon. I loved it when he got his normal 12-point maximum there and how the Dons fans loved him! I have always wondered, if White City had stayed open for another three years and Gordon hadn't become a diabetic, would he have reached more World Finals and gone one better than 1978? Erik Gundersen – one of the greatest riders of all-time? I loved it at Bradford in the 1985 World Final when he shut up everyone who said he was just a gater by swooping past Shawn Moran and Lance King in Heat 20. Then he kept his nerve to win the run-off for his second crown. I'm not ashamed to admit I cried the day it all came to an end with that crash in the World Team Cup Final. Peter Collins – what is there to say about Peter that hasn't been said already? We all know he couldn't gate to save his life but what excitement he brought when he didn't. I was so lucky Peter won the world title the first year I went to speedway and I can still remember Trevor McDonald reading it out on the ITN news.

Keith Wiggins: Bob Humphreys was a cut above other riders and was responsible for so many maximums for Milton Keynes. He would team-ride the Knights' No.2 home after creating a gap to let him through. Ian Clark once did a last lap, last-to-first at The Groveway by ramming the throttle open and vowed he would never do it again, but he did – quite often! Jason Crump was my son's favourite, as well as mine. He was just class and the master of Alwalton. He could overtake anywhere.

Rob Scrutton: My favourite riders include Mike Lanham, who was a real racer, not the best gater, but he certainly was a good passer. I remember Mike and Dennis Sigalos getting a 5-1 to win the match for Ipswich, 49-47, at King's Lynn in only the second away match I had driven to, Dennis getting Mike home for a win when he had a puncture on the last lap. Ben Howe signed for the club when he was 16 in the face of competition from other tracks. Ben had made several interval appearances when he was only 15, recording some quick times. He was another slow starter and clever passer who had some exciting meetings at Foxhall. Billy Sanders was another favourite of mine after winning the first heat of the opening home meeting of 1972 against Hackney after coming into the race when Sandor Levai broke the tapes. Billy managed to hold off Bengt Jansson for the win and followed that with another win in the reserves' race in Heat 2. All of this at 16-years-old with very little track time at Foxhall behind him. He certainly made an instant impression and it was so very sad how things ended for both Billy and subsequently his son Dean.

Peter Lush: Bert Harkins – the Wembley captain after Ove Fundin left. One of my heroes and a great leader for the Lions who stayed loyal to the club.

Sverre Harrfeldt – one of our stars in the second season at Wembley. He was a thrilling rider for the Lions. I wish I had seen him at his peak. Tony Davey - a very hard choice for third out of various Ipswich riders. With John Louis and Billy Sanders, he was at the heart of the original

Mike Lanham pulled off match-winning heroics for Ipswich.

Merv Janke became a big favourite with Glasgow fans.

Ipswich BL1 team. He didn't have as high a profile as Louis and Sanders, but overcame a horrific injury in 1972 and served the team consistently well for many years.

Gary Moore: This is really difficult as I have so many favourites, but I am going for Merv Janke, Shawn Moran and Steve Lawson. Merv was, and still is, my all-time favourite rider. During the first meeting at Blantyre, a rider bounced off the fence and shot across the centre green, causing all and sundry to scarper. I obviously didn't know who he was at the time but the wee guy with the long blond hair and yellow scarf billowing in the wind turned out to be 'Merv the Swerve' and I loved watching him race. When I was a boy playing on my BMX, I 'was' Shawn Moran, who in my eyes was the most stylish rider I ever saw. I even had the number plate on the front of my bike, which were all the rage at the time, the STP stickers, I used to take the front brake calipers and lever off and have the remaining lever hanging low *a la* Shawn, and that was me off to the red ash football parks for a skid. One of my most treasured memories was the night he honoured Jim Beaton with his presence at Jim's well-deserved Testimonial. Seeing 'Shooey' blasting around Craighead Park was an absolute sight to behold. My third rider is Stephen Faulder Lawson – enough said!

John Baxter: Boston legends Arthur Price and Jack Bywater are two. Right from the first meeting we went to, we loved them both. Stylish, but friendly to fans and we really got to know them. Plus, Terry Betts of King's Lynn, a fantastic rider and brilliant with the fans.

Mike Turner: The 70s and 80s had so many good riders, it's hard to recall them all and everyone had their own favourites for so many different reasons. If you twist my arm, three stand out for me. Bo Petersen, riding for Hackney, always seemed to enjoy himself at Halifax, both riding for his team or as a guest. He always looked comfortable on a bike and at home on the sweeping banked bends of The Shay. Ivan Mauger because he had everything: skill, intelligence, common sense and the ability to psyche out other riders. Last, but not least, is Mick McKeon, sometimes a heat leader for Halifax but a great team rider, always great entertainment value and a nice bloke to boot.

Paul Rickett: Shawn Moran – a real full-blown, chocolate-covered speedway legend. When Shawn arrived at Owlerton as a raw teenager from Hull in late 1980, he struggled and we all thought Ray Glover had signed a duck-egg. But once he clicked into gear, he was simply fantastic to watch. I still look at the first turn now and can picture Shawn hurtling around the boards. He made the mistake of coming back to Sheffield nearly a decade later and it was so difficult to watch him struggle with his mental gremlins. I interviewed him for *Speedway Star* when he finally gave up in 1993, saying he just didn't want to get hurt anymore, and it was the toughest, most heartbreaking speedway conversation I've ever had. Arnold Haley – one of the real stars of what was an excellent Sheffield team in the early-to-mid-70s. Arnie was a thrill-a-second rider and a real character to boot. Doug Wyer – as the betassled Flyer (or

'Chuggy Dougie' as he was known when he missed the gate) will always tell people: "Nobody went for a tiddle when I went to the tapes" (or words to that effect). That sums him up really.

Andy Povey: Anders Michanek – my first ever Reading hero; Jan Andersson – Mr. Reading Speedway, a brilliant and loyal clubman and not a bad rider either; and Phil Morris – another loyal clubman for Reading and has always been helpful to me in my media work.

Paula Peirce: Kenny Carter – a true Brit, I loved his style; Lars Gunnestad – a brilliant team man for Poole, I had the great pleasure of helping during his testimonial year; and Gary Guglielmi – my first rider crush (I was only seven!)

Debbie Howland: Mark Loram, Kevin Howland and, nowadays, Chris Holder. Mark because he was Canterbury's mascot, so I've known him since he was a small boy and watched him become World Champion; Kevin, because I married him; and Chris because, like Mark, he's a great racer, never gives up and always seems to have time for the fans.

Eddie Garvey: Down the years, there have been a good few that I have had more than a healthy respect for: Billy Hamill, Shooey, Erik Gundersen, Screeny, Stoney, the Smiths (Andy and Paul) and Michael Lee, to name but a few. But if you were to ask me to pin my colours to the proverbial mast, then I would have to say Peter Collins, Chris Morton and Tommy Jansson. PC has been my hero from the first time I ever saw him race in the 1974 World Pairs Final; so spectacular and different to everyone else in the way he was turned out, those multi-coloured TT leathers that seemed to appear at the rate of two sets per season and the fantastic designs that accompanied them. Mort is not much older than me, he was 19 in 1976 when he qualified for his first World Final in those blue, white and red leathers that had his name down both arms. Not much more than a kid himself at the time, he all but matched Peter round the sweeping bends of Hyde Road and beyond. Tommy Jansson will live long in my memory, although I only had the chance to see him ride in the flesh on a handful of occasions. Swedes were banned from British racing in 1974, so my memories of Tommy come from the visits of Wimbledon and individual meetings such as the Peter Craven Memorial Trophy and the Players No.6 Classic at Hyde Road. His style was spectacular for a tall rider and, like PC, he had the flowing neck scarf billowing out over his shoulder. Then he was gone. I will never forget the *Speedway Star* headline I read as I walked to school in Abbey Hey that morning: 'Tragedy Of Tommy'.

John Murphy: Three favourite riders is tough, as I respect all riders who are skilled and brave enough to race speedway. But my first choice is Dave Baugh of Bradford, my first speedway hero. Tough, consistent, black leathers, fearless, dependable and a demon from the back. Second up would be Bruce Penhall, for reasons that would match up with most other fans. He took the sport beyond the track but the downside was that it was not for long enough. He was the nearest speedway has had to a 'George Best'

Gary Havelock on the night he became World Champion at Wroclaw in 1992.

figure. Finally, Gary Havelock. I was lucky enough to get to know him and work for him a little before and after his World Final win. He was loved by the Bradford fans and only by looking back does one appreciate how good he was. I still see the odd negative comment regarding Wroclaw '92 but I suggest they should re-acquaint themselves with his consistency throughout the whole year.

Roger Johns winding up for another blast round the boards.

Gary Miles: Barney Kennett was Mr. Canterbury. As any Crusaders fan would tell you, he was the man to watch. Guaranteed entertainment, especially his tussles with Kelvin Mullarkey. Kelvin Tatum was Mr. Professional, a polished performer who helped make speedway the professional sport it is today. An excellent ambassador for the sport. Gary Havelock was Mr. Controversial. He did it his own way.

Martin Smith: Billy Sanders – you never forget your first hero and he was mine. Billy was an incredible rider and a colossus for Ipswich over many years. Dennis Sigalos superbly navigated a challenging period leading the Witches into a new era. Majestic sweeps around opponents on the fourth bend at Foxhall linger happily in the memory. Alan Mogridge – I think he personified the 'working man' rider who loved speedway and rode for the sheer thrill of it, to the immense pleasure of supporters. Brave, exciting and unpredictable, often all at the same time, he was a joy and great fun to watch.

Alex Mackenzie: I was mesmerised by Tommy Jansson's talent. He seemed to be from a different planet and was so skilful and safe. His early death was tragic; Roger Johns was a legend at Plough Lane. He wasn't great at gating but he would wind it up and come flying round the outside. I swear that Tomasz Gollob could not have done it better. Peter Collins – when people ask me who my favourite sportsman is, I tell them I can't separate PC and Seve Ballesteros, they were both so talented and exciting. PC was so skilful, he could do anything on a bike and so determined he would never give up.

Craig Saul: They are all heroes in my book and so many have also been great to me in terms of agreeing to pit-side interviews at a moment's notice and dealing with the occasionally inane or repetitive questions that are thrown their way. That said, and without wanting to omit anyone, there are three riders that do stand out, and for differing reasons. The first is Andy Buck. I first saw Andy when I attended a National League match between a powerhouse Ellesmere Port and struggling Scunthorpe at Thornton Road in 1985. I remember him scoring a hatful of points, many from the back, to take the Stags to within spitting distance of a huge upset. Scunny closed their Ashby Ville doors just a few weeks later, and Andy headed south to Eastbourne, where he played a pivotal role in what quickly became a golden era for the Eagles. I also have to include Hans Clausen, dubbed the 'Golden Bullet' at Alwalton because of his blond locks. Hans is such a lovely, warm individual. Proof of what a nice guy he is came when we were both attending a Grand Prix round at Coventry in the early days of the series. I saw him from a distance of around 20 yards, waved to attract his attention and say hello, and he made a point of coming over to shake hands and chat. What's so big about that, you ask? Well, I was seated in the main stand and Hans had to work his way from the aisle across a whole row of supporters to get to me. They were 20 very long yards. Anyone else would have just waved back and carried on with his business. Another super guy is my third choice, Chris Neath. Chris has been a huge 'go to' guy during my time at Rye House, always available for an interview and a journalist's dream because he always knew how to make his points succinctly, create an angle and drop in some key sound-bites along the way.

It was a great personal honour to be able to 'helm' his Testimonial meeting at Rye House in 2008, and such an unfortunate situation to see him forced to the sidelines right at the start of the 2012 season.

Chris Rowsell: John Davis – when I first started going to Reading, John was the glamour boy of the team and readily identifiable, with a distinctive bike, leathers and transport. This was emphasised even more when Dave Lanning wrote his press releases. After Dave Jessup left the club, John became No.1 and whilst he had an annoying habit of drifting wide between the third and fourth bends at Smallmead, he was always my favourite. I know that some (John Berry for one) considered that he wasn't super-talented, he put in good service for the Racers and made the most of his talent. Peter Collins – I first became aware of Peter at the 1976 World Final, which I saw on TV. I knew he was an exciting rider and that England hadn't had a World Champion for some time. It was great to see him win that year and when I finally got to see him in the flesh, it was really eye-opening. Here was a top class rider who didn't make the gate, but won lots of

Chris Neath was a journalist's dream at Rye House.

races. What more can you want? Tim Hunt was never going to be a World Champion but, on his night, he could beat the best. Sadly, he could also lose to the worst, but either way you could guarantee you would get 100 per cent effort from Tim. He suffered some terrible injuries, which eventually reduced his effectiveness and brought on his premature retirement. He could lose his temper, which always provided entertainment for the crowd, and some of his attempts to beat the two-minute warning had to be seen to be believed, including many a 'grass-track' manoeuvre across the centre green to reach the starting gate in time.

Andrew Gallon: Kenny Carter – a pukka Halifax hero who could mix it on the world stage; Piotr Pyszny – not the best rider the Dukes ever had, but a real trier. I remember one race in which he had a puncture on the final lap. He somehow managed to finish in a scoring position and came to a halt in front of me near the pit gate. His rear tyre was mangled and smoking and the bike looked a wreck. I never went in for autographs but I did pluck up the courage to follow him to his van after one home meeting and get him to sign my programme. Shane Parker kept Middlesbrough afloat single-handedly on many occasions during his stint with the Bears and, from a journalist's point of view, was always good for a quote.

Steve Wilkes: John Jackson – the master of Thornton Road, he was almost unbeatable in the 70s even when visiting with Crewe. Not noted for his passing but a class act to watch.

Unfortunately, he lacked the self-belief to make it big in the British League. Tom Owen – the king of the National League in the late 70s, he was never the same rider after he broke his leg in 1979 and, like Jacko, he preferred to ply his trade in the NL for easier pickings. Jason Crump – a worthy three-time World Champion, he would have won more except that he had Tony Rickardsson to contend with for a number of years. He is one of the few riders who could ride the Belle Vue track, which is not noted as being a favourite amongst many riders. A class act and once he had curbed his fiery temper in his early days, showed what he could do on the world stage.

Tim Allan: Mark Loram – whilst riding for Poole, Mark obviously became World Champion

and it was fantastic to have the pleasure of watching him every week and see him spend so much time with supporters of all ages. His homecoming with the trophy was out of this world and to be playing the music and announcing while Clive Fisher was on the centre green, really stands out for me. Simon Wigg was well before his time, he always had immaculate equipment and was such a professional sportsman. Again, watching him at Weymouth in the early days, on the grass-track and visiting Poole as a Cradley Heathen, he always stood out as a class act from day one. Stan Bear was always a joker. In the early days at Weymouth and then at Poole, he gave the fans many laughs and controversial incidents along the way. A good team man and a huge character, something that is missing in today's speedway.

John Jackson mastered Gunners' Thornton Road track.

Rob Peasley: Hans Nielsen – an obvious choice but I have to pick him first. He was remarkable, you could almost put three points by his name before every race when he was at his peak. He made it look easy. He gated first in 90 per cent of his races and left the opposition standing on the first lap the other 10 per cent of the time. A combination of raw talent, professionalism and dedication. We'd go away to Cradley, who had a heat leader trio of Erik Gundersen, Jan O. Pedersen and Simon Cross, and Hans would demolish the lot of them. On top of all that, he was a very nice guy. After he won his second world title in Amsterdam in 1987 (my first-ever trip abroad to see speedway), he was the guest of honour at the Blenheim Fun Park which, living in Woodstock, was within walking distance for us. Despite him being a double World Champion, no-one knew who Hans was, apart from us. We were decked out in our Oxford gear and his eyes lit up when he saw us because he had someone he could talk speedway to. We were chatting to him for ages. I couldn't believe it – Hans Nielsen, who I considered to be God almighty, was chatting away to my mum, dad and me! Marvyn Cox – Mr. Entertainment. Never knew when he was beaten. 'Cocker' at his best (circa 1986-87) was a sheer delight to watch. At Oxford, you always knew when the move was going to come, because he'd go wider around the first and second bend to build his speed up. The crowd knew it and would begin to roar, as Cocker stormed around his opponent on the third and fourth turns. Jens Rasmussen – I hesitate before picking all three riders from the same era of Oxford Speedway, because I have many other favourites as well, such as Tony Langdon,

David Smart, David Steen, Armando Castagna, Todd Wiltshire, Jan Staechmann, Lawrence Hare, Chris Mills, Craig Branney, etc. And a special mention to Mick Fletcher, because he took me around on his bike at Oxford in 1981 as a treat for my eighth birthday (which also turned out to be a treat for him, because it was also his birthday that week and it was the first time a child had asked to go on his bike rather than the likes of Dave Perks and Derek Harrison!). But, in the end, it has to be Jens 'Razzer' Rasmussen. Or 'Rambo' as Peter York christened him, due to his 'hard man' tactics. He was one of the old school who gave it out, but took plenty in return. I lost count of the number of times Tommy Knudsen fenced him one night (although Hans gained revenge on behalf of Jens in the Golden Helmet match-race by running Tommy up to the fence and leaving him hanging there!).

Nick Nicklin: Despite appearing in a team of star riders in his time at Dudley Wood, the quiet, unassuming Dane Kristian Praestbro would appear in my top three riders. His career seemed to be going nowhere at Belle Vue when Dan McCormick made him his surprise first signing in 1978, but he quickly upped his game at Cradley and became a reliable second string, always capable of jumping out of the start to win a crucial race when necessary. Off-track, he was the consummate professional and was instrumental in securing the services of Erik Gundersen for Cradley, setting the future World Champion on his way by acting as both mentor and landlord in 1979. Steve Bastable was just breaking into the Cradley team when I began watching at Dudley Wood but he improved dramatically over the next couple of seasons to become Cradley's No.1 in 1978. He was a really spectacular performer with arguably the best set of leathers seen anywhere at the time. The black

Old school hard man Jens Rasmussen.

and white chequered outfit was quite eye-catching and unusual and so, too, was one of his sponsors at the time, the TGWU trade union. Unfortunately, he suffered a badly broken ankle in May 1979 after a terrible three-man pile-up at Leicester involving John Titman and Erik Gundersen. To my mind, he was never the same again after that accident but I was pleased to witness Steve's big success in the British Final of 1981 and of course his return to the Cradley team in 1986, albeit in more of a supporting role. Alan Grahame was another rider who tasted success in the British Final when famously coming second to brother Andy in 1982, but it was as a team man with the Heathens that Alan gets my third vote. I always felt Alan was largely underrated in the Cradley team but the team's success in the late 70s and right through the 80s owed much to the big points that he scored from the third heat leader position behind the Penhalls, Gundersens and Pedersens. Alan was a very skilful rider, hard but fair, who could pass inside and out and never knew when he was beaten.

Martin Neal: I'll go for Ivan Mauger, the big star when I was a kid and the all-time best in my opinion. I remember asking him for his autograph after he'd fallen off at the Lydden International Speedtrack in the early 70s and, fair play to him, he signed my book. Andy Smith was the most tenacious rider I've ever seen. Never knew when he was beaten and a joy to watch. Andrew Silver was the King of the National League in the mid-to-late 80s. Fast, stylish and a great bloke. I can't believe he didn't go on to become a major star on the world stage.

Dean Felton: Sam Ermolenko is my all-time favourite rider. He was a legend at Wolves and in the couple of matches I got to ride with him, he always tried to help me and give me tips. I booked him for the Buxton air-fence fund meeting in 2013 and he was more than willing to help out which, sadly, can't be said about some other so-called legends. Jan

Alan Grahame played a terrific supporting role to the stars at Dudley Wood.

Staechmann is my second favourite rider. His bikes were always immaculate and he was such a professional but he is a really friendly guy. When we rode together for Stoke, if I could make a start, he would team-ride with me and always offered help and advice.

Mark 'Buzz' Burrows is my third choice. Buzz was, until the day he retired, a rider who scared the life out of me on track. I hated out-gating him – you would hear him coming behind and you wouldn't dare to look back because he would be there on your back wheel, usually with his front wheel in the air! I don't think I ever rode so fast as when I had Buzz behind me. He is a really good friend, though, and a great bloke too.

Brian Longman: My first speedway hero was Zenon Plech. I've always admired flair riders who would throw caution to the wind and try to pass another rider and Zenon was one who would definitely do this every time he took to the track. My all-time time favourite is Barry Thomas, a rider who would often miss the start and then spend the next four laps trying his hardest to get to the finish line first. A loyal rider who gave everything to Hackney Speedway. Down to earth in persona, Thommo is my all-time favourite rider, no question. A while later came Andy Galvin, who led Hackney to their most successful seasons. A fantastic captain and No.1 who was exciting to watch and had the skill to pass other riders and get his team-mate through for a 5-1, sometimes by means that would wind up the opposing supporters. He was the kind of rider who you would much rather have in your team than riding for the opposition. I remember he was getting stick off the Stoke fans when we lost to them in 1988. He proceeded to beat their top rider in the Silver Helmet match-race and then got off his bike in front of the main stand and took an exaggerated bow in front of them. Classic!

Andrew Skeels: Mark 'Buzz' Burrows - has there ever been a more wholehearted and entertaining rider? 'Big' Arthur Browning – one of my heroes as a schoolboy on the Quibell Park terraces, a real character and a truly talented motorcyclist; Nigel Crabtree – captain of the Scunthorpe team in 1983, the first year we ever had a decent side, and the epitome of a true team man.

Brian Burford: No contest here, my favourite was Kelly Moran. The most talented speedway rider I have ever seen and one of the nicest fellas too. To be able to count him as a friend later in life, well, it doesn't get any better than that. He was no angel, but I travelled everywhere watching him race. I've seen him do things so effortlessly that it made Hans Nielsen and their ilk look like amateurs. I enjoyed Shawn as well and though he wasn't as spectacular as Kelly, he is a brilliant guy all the same. My other favourite is Billy Hamill, who I tipped to win the world title the second time I saw him race. At his best, he was a very exciting, full-on, aggressive, attack, attack, attack, racer. Again, someone who I got to know personally and watching him win the world title in 1996 was great. With Team Exide, the fairing, the motor home and the Kenny Roberts tie-up, he tried to bring the sport into the new century and he was way ahead of his time because even now they're still not up to that level with regard to sponsors, marketing and promotion. However, he was partly responsible for my change in attitude toward the sport because I was present when he had that accident at Swindon in 2005, when he sustained multiple injuries. I witnessed its aftermath: the hospital,

Mark 'Buzz' Burrows was always a wholehearted trier.

the recovery, the psychological impact and I never felt the same about the sport again. I still enjoy it when it's good, but it changed my perspective of those guys out there. Heroes is an over-used word, but I respect them all and critics of the sport just don't appreciate what these guys are putting on the line when they go out there. It's difficult picking a third. I have a lot admiration for Peter Collins, Scott Autrey was a great rider and one of the most interesting people I have ever met or know, but I really enjoyed watching Phil Crump, Leigh Adams, Jan O. Pedersen and Tony Rickardsson. I'd have to go with Sam Ermolenko, though, because of the way he came back from that multiple leg injury in 1989. Not only did he come back, but he completely changed his style – he had to because he couldn't ride the same as he did before. He was more precise and not as loose – that's quite something to change your style and come back better than ever and win the World title. From 1991-95 he was amazing.

Christian Weber: As a boy, I remember that my first favourite rider was Anders Michanek. I am not really sure why, perhaps it was because of the Swedish race-jacket he wore (the three crowns), which fascinated me at the time. Michanek was a new name appearing at our local long-track meetings in about 1974 or '75 when he was introduced as the World Champion and I loved that there was suddenly a new name upsetting the (in my mind) established stars like Poschenrieder, Godden, Olsen, Wiesbock, etc. Later on, from reading speedway magazines, I learned more about the sport and found out that racing was taking place in some really obscure places. I got fascinated with the South African speedway scene, which I have followed closely ever since. At the time, the best South African riders were actually two Rhodesia-born lads, Peter Prinsloo and Mike Ferreira. Rhodesia (now Zimbabwe) was, of course, an even more obscure place for speedway but they had some pretty decent riders, in particular Prinsloo and Ferreira who were going very well for a number of years, even in the British League. I followed their results very closely. Pity that neither of them ever got into a World Final.

Stylish Alan Sage starred in Crayford's mid-70s revival.

Derek Barclay: Peter Collins was the greatest rider I've ever seen and ever likely to see. I first saw PC on my first visit to Plough Lane – it was the 1974 Wills Internationale and having only seen Division Two racing up to then, the whole occasion took my breath away. PC won that night and became my favourite instantly. My biggest ever disappointment was in 1977 when I got on the Tee-Mill Tours bus in the Wimbledon Stadium car park to head for Gothenberg where Peter was nailed on to retain his world title, only to read of the injury he'd suffered. And he still managed second place. Alan Sage – so many Crayford favourites, but Sagey was the top man for me. Silky smooth but a great racer and just immaculate in every way, his record of not missing a match for seasons on end is one which should get him more recognition when they write speedway history books like this. Mark 'Buzz' Burrows – I suppose I'm known as Buzz's biggest fan and that's about right. When he joined Wimbledon in 2003, I knew of him and a great race at Arena-Essex when he visited with Stoke a year or so before was in my memory but, other than that, I thought he was probably just a journeyman. How wrong I was. Buzz is the second most exciting racer (behind PC) I've ever seen and he became a modern day legend of London speedway. He became a good friend too and I would follow him anywhere to see him ride, even after the Dons folded. It was such a shame that early in his career, he lacked the sponsorship/financial backing because, as better men than I have commented, he had the raw potential to have got to the very top.

Jez Coupland: Dave Mortiboys came on loan from Coventry to Boston and always gave 100 per cent. Sometimes he would go out and beat the opposition's heat leaders and then other times be lucky to last four laps. You just didn't know what you would get. Dave Piddock was another rider Boston picked up when nobody else wanted him. His style was so smooth and silky when he got his confidence back after a serious injury. Gary Guglielmi came on loan from Coventry as a very raw rookie in his first year over here and, oh boy, was he wild. But before long, he showed his class and was soon racking up the points for the Cudas.

Robert Griffin: My favourite rider always was, and still is, the great man himself, Ivan Mauger, a true professional and a perfectionist in everything he did, right down to the inner tubes on his bike and to all the nuts and bolts.

New Zealand pulled off arguably the biggest shock in World Team Cup history with victory in the 1979 final. Here is the team from White City that day (left to right): Roger Abel, Bruce Cribb, Trevor Redmond (team manager), Larry Ross, Mitch Shirra, Ivan Mauger.

The only things worth winning in speedway are the World Final, the World Long-track Final and the World Team Cup – everything else is nothing more than a substitute for not winning the big ones. Ivan is my hero. I look up to him even now because he is the best rider who always knew what he was doing. He has given me pleasure throughout all my years of following speedway. You might think that watching Mauger win the World Final on many occasions is worth its weight in gold, but not so. For me, the best meeting ever was watching New Zealand win the World Team Cup at White City on September 16, 1979, when they beat Denmark. Every single heat was so tense that I was shouting in the stands, watching almost in disbelief as I wondered if this little nation could pull it off - and they did. Afterwards, I walked to the pit entrance and saw Mitch Shirra, who invited me through the pit gate where I did actually meet all the riders, including his Kiwi team-mates Mauger, Roger Abel, Larry Ross and Bruce Cribb. I even held the trophy with Mitch, which really made my day. That World Team Cup Final meant more to me than anything else in speedway and I was so proud to be known as a little Kiwi boy for that afternoon.

Richard Simmons: The Moran brothers and, from Ipswich, Preben Eriksen. Shawn and Kelly were just masters on a bike and were superb to watch wherever they were riding. I took to Preben when I first started going to watch Ipswich. The first thing that struck me was the name, because I had trouble saying and spelling it, but he was great to watch. I was gutted when he left for Wolverhampton in 1984.

Chris Camp: Kevin Smart never knew when he was beaten and was one of the most exciting and genuine riders I've ever met. Home or away, you could always count on Kevin giving his all and he was one of the few real exponents of the art of team-riding. To see him and Keith White or Nigel De'Ath team-ride at The Groveway was something quite exceptional. Simon

Keith White knew the best way round Milton Keynes.

Wigg was possibly the finest ambassador British speedway has ever had and he was born to ride a speedway bike. He always had time to talk to the fans and on the many occasions I met or saw him, he never had anything other than a smile on his face. On a bike, he was great to watch and anytime he pulled on an England race-jacket you could see his chest pump out with pride. Keith White was a fine captain, rider and one of the best exponents of team-riding when the fancy took him. I recall a Four Team Tournament at Peterborough when, with Rob Henry climbing all over his back, he provided a textbook example of riding the white line. Keith knew the best way around The Groveway, where he was almost unbeatable on his day, and all this supposedly in the twilight of his career.

Vitek Formanek: I had many friends among the riders, so to single out just three is impossible. I loved Kelly Moran, he was nice to talk to and lovely to watch; Simon Wigg was very stylish and friendly and he was, apart from Tim Hunt, the only speedway rider who wrote me a handwritten letter; while my first hero was John Davis, who was very helpful in introducing me into the world of speedway. He was always there for me and we are still friends, even after 33 years.

Matthew Lawrence: Chris Holder dropped only one point in the first meeting I watched and was the most entertaining rider. At such a young age, you could see he would go far in the sport. Jason Bunyan scored a five-ride maximum in the first match I saw and he has always came across as a great character off the track, regardless of his scores on it. Nick Simmons was, quite simply, Isle of Wight through and through and someone you knew would always give 100 per cent in every single race.

Jenna Johnston: Carl Stonehewer, Andy Galvin and Lawrence Hare. Stoney always put his fans first because he knew that, without them, he wouldn't have been the rider he was. Galvin was such a character and used to make me laugh when I worked in the pits. And I think Lawrence is an inspiration to other people who have sustained serious injuries in terms of how you can still lead a normal life.

4 CLASSICS

Of all the meetings you have attended, do you have one memorable classic that stands out from all the rest? And can you single out one particularly great race that will live longest in your memory?

Ken Carpenter: The last World Final at Wembley, in 1981. What a great atmosphere. It took me back to my childhood. I still can't forget the referee's decision to exclude Kenny Carter after Penhall brought him down at the World Final in Los Angeles. It was such a blatant example of sucking up to the home fans, the American TV audiences, Hollywood and sponsors. One of my greatest disappointments was Shawn Moran choosing the wrong gate for his run-off with Per Jonsson for the 1990 World Championship at Bradford, much to the disappointment of just about everyone in that stadium.

I shall never forget the bad accidents I have witnessed. It is very hard to remain professional and keep shooting when people you know and like are injured and maimed in front of you. But, like a war photographer, you just have to do your job, record what is happening and let the editors decide what or when photos can be published.

There was the 1984 World Under-21 Championship at King's Lynn, where Leif Wahlmann, a nice young Swedish boy, was killed in front of me, his mum and girlfriend. The fans went mad at me because I kept snapping but a week later, much to my astonishment, I got a request for photos from his mum.

Erik Gundersen's crash in Heat 1 of the 1989 World Team Cup Final really affected me badly. I had to go back to my darkroom and spend the night processing photos, not knowing if he would survive. My phone never stopped ringing with requests for pictures. This was in the days before digital and I had an agency 'wire man' drum-scanning my prints wet out of the dishes. When I saw the Scandinavian papers later, the photos looked very poor, blurred and grainy. I felt like a vulture preying on somebody else's misfortune. I didn't want to profit from this terrible accident, so I gave all my earnings to charity.

At this time, I was pestered by a well-known national 'red top' with financial inducements to get photos of Erik in his hospital bed. I kept telling them that I wouldn't take another picture of Erik until the day he got out of bed and walked again. And that is what happened. I was there the day he walked to receive a cheque for Pinderfields' Stepping Stones appeal from Ron Baker, representing the championship's sponsors Sunbrite Smokeless Fuels.

As for memorable moments, how about Kenny Carter celebrating a victory after only three laps during a BLRC at Belle Vue. He claimed someone had waved the chequered flag at him! The fans loved it and offered to give him a calculator.

Craig Pendlebury head-butting a critical fan. But, being a gentleman, he took his helmet off first!

Reg Wilson, the greatest team-rider ever, nursing Mark Fiora home for a 5-1 after Mark got a puncture at Owlerton on the last lap. Although the race slowed right down, no-one could get past Reg.

No sign of the tragedy that ensued as *Speedway Mail* photographer Ken Carpenter captures these happy Exeter fans on the first bend terracing as King's Lynn show their support for the Falcons' two contenders before the 1984 World Under-21 Championship. Swede Leif Wahlmann and Dane Frank Andersen. Leif (nearest camera) looks relaxed as he leads the pre-meeting parade wearing the No.1 body colour.

Standing on the track on the first bend at Belle Vue at the request of the infield presenter Dick Barrie, photographing some fans on the terrace, when the referee let the tapes up. I've never moved so fast in all my life. I threw myself over the fence with a load of cameras wrapped round my neck and fell in an untidy heap just as the bikes roared past and the shale hit the fence. Dick thought it was very funny. The ref clearly hadn't checked the track before releasing the tapes and that experience seemed to confirm what most fans think – some refs do need glasses!

There were many great races but I shall always remember Kenny Carter beating Bruce Penhall for the Golden Helmet at The Shay. What brutal, close and exciting racing that was.

Eric Marchment: The 1960 Internationale at Harringay; Bruce Penhall's 1981 Wembley win; seeing Peter Craven fall in the 1963 World Final and not knowing it would be his last; a young Ronnie Moore challenging Jack Young for the match-race title at Wimbledon in front of a capacity crowd; and Ronnie and Barry Briggs' titanic battle for the Golden Helmet. A

Things begin to go wrong on the first turn as Andy Smith loses control of his bike, careers towards the outside and 'collect' Leif's back wheel. Andy and another rider rush to the fallen Leif's aid, but he died from his head injuries.

race to remember for all-time has got to be the 1957 Briggs v Fundin run-off for the World Championship, won by Briggo, and his famous comment when interviewed afterwards: "It was either me or the Swede," which I think was to the point.

Maurice Plowright: A meeting in about 1935 when a team of US riders, led by Putt Mossman, made a one-off appearance. It was the first time I ever met an American. A match-race in about 1936, when Rube Wilson rode all four laps shoulder-to-shoulder with Lou Burger (Belgium) and they dead-heated in 76 seconds, just one second outside the track record.

Ron Byford: Wimbledon youngsters Denis Gray, Barry Briggs and Ronnie Moore scoring most of the points in the 1951 National Trophy win at Wembley; Ronnie winning his first World Championship in 1954; or the Daily Mirror International Tournament Final at Wembley in 1973 – England 39 Sweden 39, and a run-off between Peter Collins and Anders Michanek which Collins won after 'Mich' was excluded for foul riding. Match-races between Ron How

Heat 1, first bend of the 1989 World Team Cup Final at Bradford and Erik Gundersen's life is about to change forever. Ken Carpenter's pictures shows how very tight it was between all four riders (left to right) – Erik, Simon Cross, Jimmy Nilsen and Lance King – going into the corner. The second image illustrates how Erik made it across from gate four but as his back wheels locks slightly, Lance and Jimmy had nowhere to go to avoid a dramatic collision.

and Ove Fundin were always a joy to watch but the race I pick is from the 1978 World Final at Wembley when Ole Olsen and Gordon Kennett passed Ivan Mauger on the third bend, one inside and one outside, just before Ivan slid off into the fence. I was on the edge of my seat for the whole four laps.

Peter Jackson: Cradley Heath v West Ham, October 23, 1965. West Ham had to win away to clinch the first ever British League title. I went with a mate on one of the many coaches travelling to Dudley. There was a great atmosphere, which was shattered for us in Heat 1 when Ken McKinlay stalled at the gate and Cradley got a 5-1. After six heats, the score was 18-18 but then the Hammers pulled away to win easily by 47-31.

Ken Wrench: The 1973 KO Cup Final run-off between Peter Collins for the Aces and Anders Michanek of Reading. The lead changed hands on every bend with PC winning. Hyde Road was the perfect track for that sort of racing. There was one event that I will always

A massive tangle of men and machines as Erik (far left) is sent crashing to the ground, whilst Lance goes airborne and Jimmy goes over the 'high side' . . . as back marker Simon is a split-second away from joining the carnage.

Medical staff rush to the aid of the stricken riders. Erik (left) lay motionless and would be placed on the critical list at the local hospital, where he underwent a long period of rehab and happily learned to walk again. Lance escaped with a badly strained neck, but all four riders were ruled out of the rest of the meeting. The crash – and Erik's life-threatening injuries – cast a huge shadow over this showpiece occasion, which is remembered for all the wrong reasons rather than the last time England (or Team GB) won the world team trophy.

remember – not for the racing, but for what came later. Chris Morton won the 1980 Inter-Continental Final at White City. On the way home, large numbers of fans from different tracks stopped off at Watford Gap services. Mort and his wife Jackie walked in and, regardless of what team colours they were wearing, everyone stood up and cheered him. That seems to encapsulate what speedway supporters are all about.

Lucy Burton: I used to belong to the West Ham Supporters' Club ladies darts team and one year we won the cup. We were presented with it on the track by Jack Young. That was a great night. In September 1950, Aub Lawson raced Jack Parker for the Sunday Pictorial Match-Race Golden Helmet. It was the best of three races and after it stood at 1-1, Aub won the third race and the Golden Helmet. There must have been 90,000 in the stadium that night and the atmosphere was incredible.

Cedric Read: My classic meeting took place on August 30, 1948, the Daily Mail National Trophy knockout competition, Birmingham v West Ham. Hammers were top of the first division while Brummies were mid-table in Division Two and definitely the 'country cousins'. As expected, West Ham had easily won the first leg at home 67-41 and arrived at Perry Barr with understandable confidence. A record crowd of 28,400 greeted both teams but no-one could have guessed what was to follow. Heat 1, with Graham Warren and captain Stan Dell taking maximum points, set the scene, as Warren also equalled Dell's track record. It was followed by 5-1 after 5-1 and by Heat 7, the deficit from the first leg had been cleared. The whole Birmingham team were inspired and went on to win every heat, 13 by 5-1 and the other five by 4-2. Five of the team returned double figures to end the match 85-23 – Birmingham's highest score ever.

Keith Walker: The 1990 World Final at Bradford. The large crowd overcame Odsal's biggest drawback, which was a lack of atmosphere with the normal sparse attendance. The racing was superb that night and Per Jonsson's success crowned a brilliant meeting, despite my hero Shawn Moran being beaten in the run-off.

Andy Povey: A few Reading away wins over the years, but the 1990 World Final at Bradford has to be head and shoulders above all of them. Per Jonsson beat Shawn Moran in a run-off for the title and Todd Wiltshire was on the rostrum in third place. That meant Reading had

The England team and manager Len Silver parade before the 1973 Daily Mirror International Tournament final against Sweden at Wembley. Riders (front, left to right): Eric Boocock, Martin Ashby, Peter Collins, John Louis. Back: Malcolm Simmons, Ray Wilson, Terry Betts. Only Booey looks nervous.

the numbers one and three in the world – something I always dreamt would happen.

The run-off in the 1990 World Final between Per and Shawn Moran was not a great race by any means, but lives in the memory just because it was so nerve-racking before and during the race. Seeing Per cross the finishing line released a lot of emotion.

Steve Wilkes: The 1990 World Final at Bradford. I remember going to watch Oldham Athletic FC in the afternoon and then making the short journey over the Pennines. Kelvin Tatum was the best hope for an English victor but once Hans Nielsen gave him a shove in his third outing, it was all over. Unusually for a World Final, there was plenty of passing and to top it off a run-off to decide the World Champion.

Ken Taylor: It was June 17, 1967 at Coventry, a Great Britain v Sweden Test match which

Shawn Moran leads Per Jonsson during the 1990 World Final at Odsal.

Vic Duggan shows off the 1948 Speedway Riders' Championship trophy at Harringay.

finished with a win for the Swedish side by 62-46. It's not so much that GB were poor that night, they were not, but Sweden produced some world class stuff.

John Chaplin: Well, it should be the night, in 1948, when Birmingham, then second division, knocked first division league leaders West Ham out of the National Trophy by scalping the Hammers at Perry Barr 85-23. And it should have been the 1948 Speedway Riders' Championship Final at Wembley. It was my first time in the incredible Empire Stadium atmosphere, which was truly intoxicating. Maybe that's why I only remember the noise but little about the actual racing and how Vic Duggan won the title. It was neither of those. I was staying in London and the night after Wembley was taken to Harringay, Duggan's home track. Before the match against Wimbledon, Vic was paraded before his home fans with the trophy he had won the night before. Spotlights beamed down on this smiling figure in incredibly shiny black leathers, infusing the occasion with the utmost glamour and sparkle. And then there was the fabulous thrill of experiencing for the first time world class league speedway and being in the presence of such top stars as Duggan and Wimbledon captain Norman Parker – names I'd only read about in magazines. The great Duggan lived up to his reputation that night by winning all his eight races. Of course, they had second-half events then.

As for a particularly great race, the British Match-Race Golden Helmet challenge to title-holder Jack Parker by Graham Warren in 1949. It created so much interest that 43,000 crammed into Perry Barr for the first leg. Graham had a slight lead on Jack in the first race but then, on turn three, Graham picked up drive and turned over, ending up in the fence. Exactly the same thing happened in the second race. This time Graham injured a foot which kept him out of the Australian team for the following week's Test. Parker finished alone and, as I recall, equalled the track record – on a flat tyre. Jack later told me: "Well, he was inexperienced."

Tony Emmott: It must be the 1956 World Final at Wembley when Arthur Forrest took third place. I wish I had retained the programme. In 1957 (I have a scrapbook from that year) there was a Test match at Odsal, where England beat Australasia 55-53, which was a cracker before a large crowd. Alan Hunt (England) took Bob Duckworth (Australasia) on the last bend of the last heat to give England victory. It was a mystery to me why Arthur Wright was in the England team, but Arthur Forrest wasn't.

Robert Rogers: The first-ever clash of Great Britain v Russia at Wembley in July 1964. The fans chanting, 'We want the Russians' at the end of the match, calling for them to do a parade lap so they could show their appreciation.

Bryan Newbold: I would have to pick the 1981 World Final at Wembley. I travelled down with my dad and my then wife's aunt and uncle. As we didn't have a Leicester rider to cheer on, we decided we would support Bruce Penhall and each of us purchased BP rosettes, scarves, etc, to show our backing. All of us, that is, except the uncle, who decided he would cheer on Kenny Carter. So, decked out in our adoptive colours, we made our way round to the third/fourth bends, where we found we were right in the middle of what seemed like thousands of Cradley Heath fans. Three of us blended in perfectly in our Bruce Penhall colours, whilst one very lonely figure had to spend the entire meeting amid a sea of green and white, wearing his Kenny Carter colours!

Steve Casey: A bit predictable, I'm afraid. The 1981 Wembley World Final was brilliant. Scorching night, a full house and brilliant racing. I don't think anyone realised how badly

Bruce on top of the world at Wembley, above the two Danes he conquered in such thrilling style, Ole Olsen (right) and Tommy Knudsen. Below, Tommy Knudsen (2) and Bruce Penhall (11) going for it in Heat 14 at Wembley – one of the great races that made it such a memorable occasion.

prepared the Wembley track had been for World Finals until this one. 'Uncle' Len Silver had prepared a great track which allowed the racers to strut their stuff. The atmosphere was electric and Bruce Penhall was a deserving and worthy World Champion. I'm sure his clashes with Tommy Knudsen and Ole Olsen are on most people's list of favourite races. It was also Erik Gundersen's first World Final and he was so unlucky. He was super quick until an engine failure ruined his chances. I drew Chris Morton in the sweepstake we had on the minibus on the way down. Mort was in great form leading up to the final, so I was quietly confident, but he had a nightmare as he struggled to make a decent start all night. I know for a fact he has never watched the video of that final because he was so disappointed with his performance.

My greatest race is predictable again, I'm afraid. The run-off for the 1973 KO Cup Final at Hyde Road after Belle Vue and Reading had tied on aggregate. Peter Collins and Anders Michanek passing each other on every corner of every lap. I should add, though, that I have been privileged to watch racing at a few Polish venues and some of the races I have seen at Bydgoszcz, when Tomasz Gollob has been at his outrageous best, had to be seen to be believed. Gollob's list of 'best races' must be enormous.

Bob Radford: The 1981 World Final at Wembley, partly because I was the centre green presenter but also because, for once, the most exciting rider won – Bruce Penhall. The old stadium was already decaying then, but its loss was a hammer blow to speedway.

My race is, predictably, the classic run-off between Peter Collins and Anders Michanek for the 1973 KO Cup. Reading's Tilehurst Stadium was already being demolished, PC had his clutch and throttle on the same hand due to injury, Anders' magneto had packed up and he was on Bernie Leigh's bike. They say the lead changed hands 16 times, but it seemed like more. It was such an epic that it took me almost an hour to absorb the fact that Reading had lost the chance of a league and cup double.

Peter Lush: The 1981 World Final. I only decided to go at the last minute and had a place high up on the terracing on the third and fourth bends. Wembley was packed and it was a fantastic spectacle and atmosphere. I'm glad I was there for what may be the last-ever meeting at Wembley. But if they can stage speedway at the Millennium Stadium, we live in hope of a Grand Prix in north-west London.

Mike Turner: One meeting which will always stand out for me and the family is the 1981 World Final at Wembley. My first final, the last at Wembley, first win for Penhall, first appearance for Kenny Carter and a truly memorable weekend in London. It had it all. I can remember clearly being the last in our enclosure and a friendly policeman asking us to leave. Fantastic!

Mention Carter and you will invite controversy, but he provided one race to be savoured at The Shay in the form of the Golden Helmet challenge against Bruce Penhall. Wheel-to-wheel stuff with both riders concentrating on the racing and, being at The Shay, it meant you were closer to the action as well. I can recall the last bend bumping and bashing between the two of them.

Paul Jeffries: No-one who was there can ever forget the majesty that was the old Wembley – the twin towers, the awesome scale of the stadium – and I'd have to cite Ove Fundin's fifth title win there in 1967, in that run-off with Bengt Jansson. One of THE great meetings.

As for one great race, I'll go for Wembley again and the tension of another unforgettable night there, in 1973, the match-race decider between Peter Collins and Anders Michanek. Still argued about to this day. But hey, that race didn't finish, so let's go for another one: Tony Rickardsson's legendary 'Wall of Death' ride outside Jarek Hampel, at Cardiff in 2005. How did he do that?

Doug Nicolson: West Ham v Oxford in 1969 – a great meeting and superb racing between two teams who were in the lower half of the table. Guys like Reeves, Jarman and Samuelsson rode out of their skins that night for the visitors.

My great race? Nils Ringstrom hanging on to second place ahead of Bernie Persson to ensure Glasgow beat Edinburgh 40-38 in the last league meeting between the two at Old Meadowbank. Tigers had a 10-point lead which Edinburgh whittled down with two tactical sub rides, leading to a last heat decider. It would have been a travesty if Glasgow hadn't won

Six times World Champion Tony Rickardsson pulled off an unbelievable move at Cardiff in 2005.

that night. Ian Hoskins described it as "the cruellest cut of all" and while it didn't definitively stop Edinburgh winning the league, it certainly went a long way towards it.

Mike Keir: April 13, 1984. A Friday. The previous night, we (Wimbledon) had lost at home to Oxford, and this was the return fixture. Well, what chance did we have at their place if we couldn't beat them at home? The Dons were inspired that night, particularly John Titman as I recall, and we turned them over.

I'm not sure about one single race, but I used to love watching Ed Stangeland at Plough Lane. He rode a different line to anyone else and used to come around the outside of people on the first and second bends on lap three or four.

Rod Haynes: I've seen many classics over the years, but will choose any of the late 60s matches at Belle Vue against Sheffield. There was also my own involvement in my initial league season for Scunthorpe v Peterborough in August 1972, when we defeated the Panthers by a solitary point against all the odds.

I saw an outstanding race for the 1994 British title when Mark Loram and Chris Louis knocked the stuffing out of each other before Mark triumphed, all on the day Ayrton Senna was killed.

Dennis Lindo: The meeting that stands out most for me was at Hyde Road between the Aces and Coventry. I can't remember what year it was but Ole Olsen was riding for the Bees. Every race was a nail-biter, really hotly contested with riders passing and re-passing on almost every corner. There is also a meeting I remember for the wrong reason – I wasn't there. I'd got into a bit of trouble with my dad and didn't want to face him, so I ran away and missed the speedway that night – it was the Provincial League Select v Norwich at Cleveland Park in 1963. Peter Craven guested for Norwich in the absence of Ove Fundin. This was my one and only chance to see the Wizard of Balance and I blew it. I had to rely on Uncle Tom's description of the meeting. He told me that Craven was brilliant and just took everyone on the outside. Nobody could get near him all night. Sadly, this was only a week or so before he

Peter Craven

Jack Parker

Freddie Williams

Ove Fundin

Ronnie Moore

Barry Briggs

Bjorn Knutson

Olle Nygren

Christer Lofqvist

Bengt Jansson

Anders Michanek

Tommy Jansson

Bernt Persson

Soren Sjosten

Ivan Mauger

Nigel Boocock

Ray Wilson

Eric Boocock

Terry Betts

Jim McMillan

Bert Harkins

Arnold Haley

Chris Pusey

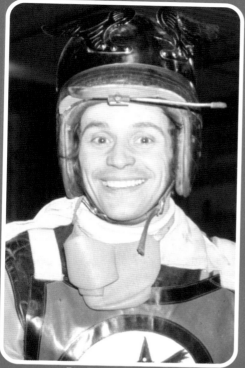

John Louis

Dave Jessup

Martin Ashby

Bob Kilby

Ole Olsen

Pete Smith

Barry Thomas

Dave Morton

Chris Morton

Peter Collins

Gordon Kennett

John Davis

Doug Wyer

Reg Wilson

Malcolm Simmons

John Boulger

Phil Crump

Billy Sanders

Mitch Shirra

Michael Lee

Scott Autrey

Bobby Schwartz

Ron Preston

Dennis Sigalos

Bruce Penhall

Shawn & Kelly Moran

Sam Ermolenko

Kenny Carter

Andy Smith

Joe Owen

Neil Evitts

Simon Wigg

Kelvin Tatum

Jeremy Doncaster

Andrew Silver

Martin Dugard

Gary Havelock

Tommy Knudsen

Jan O Pedersen

Jan Andersson

Jimmy Nilsen

Hans Nielsen

Erik Gundersen

Per Jonsson

Leigh Adams

Jason Crump

Tony Rickardsson

Greg Hancock

Joe Screen

Chris Harris

Scott Nicholls

Lee Richardson

Mark Loram

Tai Woffinden

The ever spectacular Peter Craven was such a massive loss to the sport in 1963.

lost his life in a track crash at Edinburgh. How I regret not getting to that meeting and seeing that amazing little man race.

The race that lives longest in my memory is the one between Peter Collins and Anders Michanek to decide the 1973 Speedway Star KO Cup, but there is also one other race I still think about. It took place at Cleveland Park during a Teesside v Scunthorpe meeting. Tigers' Frank Auffret, who was sometimes a little wild and scary, fell off but the race continued and Frank picked himself up, rode like a man possessed and actually won the race. I've never witnessed that before or since.

Steve Johnston: My all-time favourite meeting was the 1972 World Final at Wembley – my one and only visit to a final and it was the night Christer Lofqvist finished fourth. It seemed at one point that he might even win the title, but one poor ride ended that dream. As a 12-year-old, I was so proud of 'my rider' and shouted myself hoarse. The atmosphere, the packed underground train, the whole night was magic.

Ian Martin: My most memorable meeting was the 1972 World Final at Wembley. My favourite rider then was Barry Briggs and I was terribly upset when he had his accident. I honestly think Barry would have won that year had it not been for his pile up with Bernt Persson and the two Russians.

Harry Ward: In 1980 at Cleveland Park, when Rye House needed a win from either that meeting or the following day at Glasgow to be crowned NL champions. Karl Fiala was fantastic from start to finish and his last race win meant the Rockets were champions.

Bill Halliwell: Belle Vue v Leicester, 1971 . . . you know, the one with the punch-up! Not for the fight, though, more because it was the first time I saw the Aces lose at home.

John Pharaoh: My first Wembley World Final, in 1963. It was mind-blowing to see so many people effectively camping out in the car park after the meeting. There was an amazing atmosphere, although I don't remember any of the racing, apart from Peter Craven having a bad night and even falling in one of his heats.

Andrew Edwards: The 1976 World Final when Peter Collins won at Chorzow in front of 120,000 spectators. That's right, 120,000, a figure which has never been beaten. The atmosphere was electric looking down on that huge track in that super-heated bowl that made such World Finals never to be forgotten. It was only my third World Final reporting for *MCN* and we had an English World Champion. That year, we also had Barry Sheene as World Road Race Champion and George O'Dell was World Sidecar Champion. Golden days.

The best race I ever saw was the last heat decider at Sheffield in the 1973 Daily Mirror International Tournament match between England and Sweden (the same teams met again later in the final at Wembley). Lining up were Peter Collins and Eric Boocock for the Lions and Anders Michanek and Tommy Jansson for the Swedes. On the last lap, Collins blasted round the outside of Michanek while Boocock did the same to Jansson to win the race 4-2 and the match 40-38. It was all picked up by the ITV cameras too and that understated commentator Dave Lanning said: "Fantastic, what a climax, Dan Dare or Doctor Who couldn't have planned it better."

David Hoggart: The first ever British League Division Two Riders' Championship at Hackney in 1968. My parents had moved us from the North-East to the South-East just eight weeks earlier, so to go to this fabulous London venue and see Graham Plant, one of the local heroes at Middlesbrough (Teesside), win was just unreal. My brother and I shouted ourselves hoarse waving our big T programme boards and red and white bobble hats that Mum had knitted. That was what speedway was about – atmosphere.

Anders Michanek and Ole Olsen took the top two positions in the 1973 Pride of the East, but it was third placed Zenon Plech (right) who stole the show.

There are so many great races to choose from and I feel privileged to have witnessed some brilliant racing over the years. Graeme Smith beating Taffy Owen at Derwent Park; Carl Stonehewer's winning ride in the PLRC at Sheffield, likewise Ricky Ashworth; and in Graeme's time at Sunderland, every race that the late Jack Millen rode in.

Martin Rogers: Leicester 42 Coventry 36 in the British League on August 26, 1980 – our first season at Blackbird Road and the first time the Lions had beaten the Bees in six years. It was a 'dancing in the streets' type of night. Zenon Plech giving the other three riders, including the then pre-eminent Ole Olsen, a 30-yard start and then rounding up the lot of them en route to one of his four wins in a spectacular 1973 Pride of the East at Saddlebow Road. At that time the most exciting rider in the world, Zenon punctured in his other ride and missed the top spot but he made the meeting and the locals up there still talk about it.

Geoff Theobald: Hackney v Exeter, 1977 and the Heat 13 final race, final bend by Thommo (Barry Thomas) that saw him roar round the team-riding Scott Autrey and the great Ivan Mauger to scupper the 5-1 the visitors needed to get a point, and probably win the league. More importantly, it won the match for the Hawks.

There is also Wimbledon v Hackney at Plough Lane on June 26, 1980. They used to say that 'Happiness is 40-38' but this was a 41-37 away win for the Hawks, with a final race last-to-first for Bo Petersen that saw Len Silver standing proudly on the victory parade tractor. It was personally memorable as my late wife was expecting our first child that day. The way she was jumping up and down as well during that last race, it was something of a surprise that my daughter didn't arrive for another three days!

Mark Wilkinson: England v USA at Wimbledon in May 1980, a 54-54 draw. Team speedway at its best and two sides packed with top riders. OK, some were past their peak but it was a terrific match.

The England team before their epic 1980 Test against the USA at Wimbledon. Standing, left to right: Eric Boocock (co-manager), Peter Collins, Malcolm Simmons, John Davis, Michael Lee, Kenny Carter, Ian Thomas (co-manager). Front: Chris Morton, John Louis, Les Collins. The Lions went on to complete a then unique grand slam of individual, team and pairs world titles that year.

For my race, I go back to the British Final at Coventry in 1975 and the run-off for fourth place between Ray Wilson and Martin Ashby, with a World Final place being the winner's reward. My programme note says: "A bit close" – testimony to my talent for the ironic understatement because the two of them swapped the lead back and forth until Wilson's swoop off the final bend. I recall being a wreck afterwards.

Kevin Fall: The 1975 British Final at Brandon, Ray Wilson v Martin Ashby in the fourth place race-off. Ray gated but Martin never gave up and inched closer and closer, eventually passing Ray on the inside on lap four. Somehow, Ray found enough to edge it by half-a-wheel on the line and qualify for the World Final after being excluded in his first ride. There was a huge crowd and that race brought the house down.

John Farr: There's only one meeting which really stands out in my mind – the England v USA, first Test match at Wimbledon in 1980. It ended in a draw, 54-54, but it was the racing. In virtually every heat, there was passing, re-passing and passing again. The lead changed hands so many times, too. I wonder if someone, somewhere has that meeting on tape? I'd pay good money for it.

Robert Wiles: I never got to attend any recognised classic meetings, but I do remember the first Young England v Young Czechoslovakia Test series. Here was a team from behind the mysterious Iron Curtain – they were all clad in black leathers and had standard issue factory blue Jawa machines. However, they could all ride a bit and I remember hearing Canterbury No.1 Barry Crowson talking behind the pits after the meeting and saying that he was "hanging on for grim death" in his first ride when he tried to go round the outside of a team-riding Czech pair.

I've seen some very good, even great, races but the one that sticks in my mind was in the 1973 British Junior Championship held at Kingsmead. The hot pre-meeting favourite was Peter Collins and he duly won his first three rides. However, Canterbury star Barney Kennett had done the same, so the inevitable crunch race came. Nobody really gave Barney a chance against Collins but he rode the race of his life. The packed crowd roared him round every yard of the four laps until he took the chequered flag in the fastest time of the night. The sad thing for Crusaders supporters was that in his last ride, Barney could only manage third, so the title went to Collins by a point.

Alan Jones: I am going to plump for the 1969 Brandonapolis at Coventry. In those days, the field was better than a World Final – an often quoted statement but entirely true. I have referred to being proud to say you were from Leicester and that rang true again on a night when Ray Wilson went through the card. In one race, Barry Briggs' front wheel seemed to be invisibly locked onto Wilson's rear tyre. One error of judgement and the Swindon man would have been through but the Lions' captain rode a perfect four laps to beat him. When it came to the final race, Wilson and Coventry's Nigel Boocock had won four races apiece and Booey was out in the lead, only for Ray to pass the Bees idol on the third and fourth bends. Briggs, who finished third overall, went on to say that, in his opinion, no-one in the world would have beaten Ray Wilson that night.

Pete Butler: As the badge said, 'happiness is 40-38'. King's Lynn v Reading, 1980. Reading and Hackney are battling for the league title and the Racers have fought back from eight points down to only two behind with two heats left. Jan Andersson then passed Dave Jessup on the last bend to join Bobby Schwartz to secure a Heat 12 5-1 which put Racers two up. At this moment, most of the Reading fans' minds were drifting back three years when Mike Lee passed John Davis on the last bend in Heat 13 to win the KO Cup for Lynn, and the two were to meet again. I believe most had settled for a similar outcome (I had!) and the Racers securing a good away point, but this time JD turned the tables. I'll never forget the sight of Bobby Schwartz bouncing at the pits gate as JD secured two vital away points for the Racers. Happiness, indeed.

Greg Unwin: My classic meeting also includes my single great race and always stands out in my memory. It was an international meeting at Exeter between England and the USSR on Monday, August 23, 1971 and featured some household names in the England team, led by Nigel Boocock. Soviet Russia made two changes to their programmed team, plus five positional alterations, which made the filling out of your programme a spelling nightmare. With the Russians 42-36 ahead, England started an amazing comeback. After a 5-1 in Heat 16 from the Kilby and Ashby combination, the scores were tied at 48-48.

Heat 17 was to produce one of the most incredible races I had ever seen at Exeter. Boocock and reserve Barry Thomas were up against Russian pairing Vladimir Gordeev and Anatoly Kuzmin. Boocock suffered engine failure as Thomas and Gordeev battled for the lead. As the riders approached the third bend, Gordeev crashed into Exeter's famous steel safety fence and was catapulted over the top onto the terracing. There was a huge gasp and cries from the crowd before Gordeev gradually and gingerly got to his feet. As the dispersed spectators crept back to their original positions, track staff and medics ran from all directions to assist the stricken rider. They were tough, those Russians! Thomas won the heat from Kuzmin to give England the lead for the first time in the match at 51-50. Prior to this amazing race, Thomas had managed only one point. Ray Wilson was able to beat the Russians Vladimir Paznikov and Grigory Chlynovsky for a 3-3 tied heat as England finished 54-53 winners. What a turnaround and a great comeback by England.

David Beresford: Sheffield v Belle Vue (45-45) in a challenge match that saw Owlerton reopen on April 7, 1991 after several years of closure. A super meeting, hundreds locked out – thank you, new promoters Cliff Carr, Neil Machin, Louis Carr and Monaghan Creer.

Phil Rice: The 1962 World Final won by Peter Craven was the greatest classic for me. Those

Reopening day at Sheffield in 1991 and promoter Cliff Carr welcomes back Tigers' legends Reg Wilson and Doug Wyer before the match against Belle Vue.

jam-packed Provincial League Riders' Championships from 1961 onwards were great meetings and the first few British League Riders' Championships were wonderful events in front of big crowds. Barry Briggs' successive titles and a win for Len Silver in one of the earlier PLRC finals stick out. I was also fortunate enough to be at Katowice when Peter Collins won his only world title in 1976. I bought about 40 programmes for about 2p each and sold them for 50p apiece.

But despite all this, the classic race for me was at Liverpool in a second-half in 1960 between Dave Dodd and Willie Templeton. They passed and re-passed each other for five laps and then had to do it all again. The re-run was just as good but I can't now recall who won!

Steve Wilks: I was fortunate enough to go to the 1978 World Final at Wembley. A wonderful occasion, so many people there just out to enjoy themselves and won by the great Ole Olsen.

Not a great race, as such, but I was at Hackney v Reading when Dave Jessup was excluded

Action from the 1993 title decider at Wolverhampton, where home pair Peter Karlsson (inside) and Mikael Karlsson try to keep Belle Vue's Jason Lyons and Carl Stonehewer at bay. The victorious Aces after regaining the BL title.

for unfair riding. Reading walked out of the meeting and Hackney won the re-run 5-0 and also won the last two races by the same score.

Richard Lambert: The day Cradley Heath reserve Ken Wakefield led then World Champion Bjorn Knutson for three-and-a-half laps . . . but then fell off.

John Vine: My most memorable meeting, for all the wrong reasons, was the final match of 1993 when Wolves met Belle Vue to decide the league championship. Wolves had been riding high for most of the year until a series of accidents to Graham Jones, Charles Ermolenko, Ronnie Correy and Phil Ashcroft caused an alarming drop in points. Gordon Kennett and Mikael Karlsson were brought in but the writing was on the wall in October when Sam Ermolenko broke his leg. Even so, everyone thought all was not lost and the meeting went to the last race with Belle Vue doing enough to win the title. We all went home feeling very deflated.

Ian Glover: Canterbury v Mildenhall on October 14, 1978, which finished 48-30. It was a 'must win' meeting for the Crusaders and by sufficient race points to overhaul the mighty Diamonds of Newcastle to claim the National League title. There was an electric atmosphere and it was a very emotional night in view of the rollercoaster season at Kingsmead.

The race that lives longest in my memory to this day is a very sad one – Graham Banks' last ride for the Crusaders in a league match against Newcastle on May 3, 1978. It was a titanic race, with the great Tom Owen losing on the line by less than half-a-wheel. Graham lost his life the next day on a local grass-track, his other great love.

Dave Ede: London derbies were always needle matches and I remember West Ham v Wimbledon at Custom House in 1967, I think. Dave Lanning stirred up the Dons fans by introducing Olle Nygren as "the dirtiest rider in the British League", which certainly had the desired effect. We all just thought that Olle was hard, like Sverre Harrfeldt, Norman Hunter and others. Hackney v Wimbledon matches were always memorable, if only for the aroma. The Waterden Road track was between the gasworks, a perfume factory and the Seameal fish processing plant – and that's without the Castrol R in the pits! Len Silver always put on a good show, as only he could, and a close score was guaranteed with two evenly matched teams.

A race that stands out for me was when Ronnie Moore and Jim Tebby team-rode to a 5-1 over World Champion Ivan Mauger at Wimbledon – boy, was Ivan miffed!

Paul Tadman: Ivan Mauger was involved in the race of the century for me. Mauger and Scott Autrey were in Heat 13 for Exeter but Hackney's Barry Thomas passed them both on the last lap on the fourth bend to give Falcons' closest rivals White City the league title.

As for great meetings, I can't answer that. The Czechs at Romford, various Superama stagings at Hackney, the 1980 Test match at Wimbledon between England and the USA, the 1981 World Final at Wembley – there are just too many to choose from.

Paul Kerry: A classic meeting for me was at Belle Vue in 1964, Great Britain v Soviet Russia in a Test match. It was my first sight of so many world-class riders together in one meeting. There was a massive crowd, Barry Briggs was unbeatable and Ron How and Ron Mountford scored highly for GB. A shame it was so one-sided, but for my first international match, it was unforgettable.

For a great race, I go back to Halifax v Coventry in May 1965, Heat 12. The score was Dukes 32 Bees 34 and we had Eric Boocock and Eric Boothroyd out against the unbeaten Nigel Boocock and Howie Booton. The two Erics gated first and team-rode for four laps to keep Nigel in third and score a 5-1 which made it 37-35. The place was in uproar and I was utterly beside myself. A 3-3 in the last heat and we'd snuck it 40-38. Absolutely incredible and I'll never forget it. I can't remember which Eric won, but who cares!

Carol Stock: The 1975 World Final at Wembley. The rough track was dry and dusty, so some unhappy fan(s) got onto the dog track, grabbed a hose pipe from somewhere and watered the speedway track on the outside. Peter Collins was in the next race, Heat 9, on gate four. Although he made a reasonable start, he hit a slick (watered) patch on the first turn and could not recover the ground he lost on Ivan Mauger, Phil Crump and Anders Michanek. It lost him vital points for the championship. I was gutted for PC, as I was sure he would win that night.

Richard Clark: England 54 USA 54, 1980 at Plough Lane was exceptional, and with little

The race that wrecked Peter Collins' world title hopes in 1975. PC is on the outside and about to lose vital ground on (left to right) Phil Crump, Ivan Mauger and Anders Michanek.

known footage of it available nowadays, I'm having to rely on the addled brain cells to assure me it was as good as I think it was.

As for a great race, I'm not sure of the year, but it was a National League Riders' Championship at Brandon. They had cobbled together a mini-track in the car park and you were allowed to have a whizz round on mini-bikes. Neville Tatum and Peter Johns insisted I had to exchange elbows with them so, reluctantly, I agreed. There was actually little chance of the elbow bit when we set off because they disappeared while I wobbled away at a pace akin to a near-comatose snail. Even at this pace, however, my bike found the outer fence an irresistible magnet, so I spent who knows how many laps bouncing off said fence while those two terriers, 'Nev the Rev' and 'Johnsy', kept buzzing past me on the inside. However, when the yellow flag came out to signify one more bruising lap up against the fence for me, it signalled a frantic last dash for those two, which ended with them in a heap. I powered past them at half-a-mile an hour and took the chequered flag before bouncing off the fence in a final flourish!

Chris Beard: Mildenhall v Scunthorpe, NL play-off final, second leg, in 2011. A truly amazing comeback by the Fen Tigers, only to fail at the final hurdle with some top class racing thrown in.

Adrian Stockwell: The 1973 Wills Internationale at Wimbledon. It was a warm, sunny Spring Bank Holiday Monday and the Internationale, widely regarded as second only to the World Final in prestige, was again being staged at Plough Lane with a line-up fit to grace any World Final. A massive crowd estimated at 20,000 soaked up a simply thrilling evening's racing, highlighted by home favourite Tommy Jansson's Heat 1 and third place run-off wins over Ivan Mauger and culminating in the greatest race I've ever seen, the crunch Heat 19 Ole Olsen v Anders Michanek encounter which Olsen had to win to force a run-off for the title. Those 60 seconds of speedway magic is indelibly seared into my memory. The excitement and experience of that meeting has still never been surpassed in my many years of following speedway.

Ole Olsen, Anders Michanek and Tommy Jansson – top three in a classic 1973 Internationale at Wimbledon.

Julia Wilson: I have two meetings that stand out. One was the 1978 World Final at Wembley for two reasons – it was my first World Final and Ole Olsen won it. I also remember a very wet Midland Cup Final at Wolverhampton one October. It was a double-header and the Bees were riding second. The rain started in the first match and by the last heat of the night, everyone was drenched. As the race finished, Ole rode up to the trophy, picked it up and rode straight back to the pits.

Stephen Williams: My memorable classic meeting is the 1976 BLRC at Belle Vue. We got in at the last minute and it was a huge crowd. I was 13 that October and it was a birthday present. Barry Briggs showered us with shale early on as we stood right up against the fence between the first and second bends and Ole Olsen won. What a perfect present!

Keith Wiggins: Rye House v Milton Keynes on July 1, 1979. Rye House were favourites for the league and always seemed to score 50 or 60 at home but the Knights pushed them close in what was a morning meeting. Rye jumped into a massive lead but some good tactical substitutions and great riding by Bob Humphreys, Derek Harrison and Andy Grahame saw the Knights fight their way back. The Rockets didn't clinch the match until Heat 12 and a last heat 5-1 to Milton Keynes saw it finish 40-38. Then we all went off to White City for the Commonwealth Final.

Rob Scrutton: The classic meeting I can remember was Ipswich's away KO Cup match at King's Lynn in 1981, raced over 16 heats. The Stars included the world numbers one and two in their team, Michael Lee and Dave Jessup, who scored a 5-1 in Heat 14 to give them the lead by 45-39. Dennis Sigalos came in for a tactical substitute ride to partner Kevin Jolly to a 5-1 of our own, which was followed by another 5-1 for Siggy and Mike Lanham (with a puncture) to win the meeting 49-47.

My greatest single race was the run-off for third place between Ivan Mauger and John Louis in the 1975 World Final at Wembley. Ivan was on the inside gate, John on the outside but Ivan tried a few mind games by returning to the pit gate after almost lining up at the start. John was left at the gate awaiting Ivan's return but was able to maintain his concentration and was first away from the trap. Despite Ivan's passing attempts, John was able to claim third place to the delight of the fans, becoming the first English rider to claim a World Final rostrum place since Peter Craven in 1962.

Gary Moore: I was going to go for Ivan Mauger's Farewell to Scotland at Powderhall, but instead I'm going to plump for the first leg of the 1994 all-Scottish KO Cup Final between

John Louis and Ivan Mauger before their run-off at the 1975 World Final.

Edinburgh and Glasgow. It was one of those October nights at Powderhall, cold and dark with a huge crowd packed in creating an electric atmosphere – an 'old school' speedway night. The meeting itself was perhaps not a true classic, but it was hugely entertaining nonetheless. The first heat was a classic, though, as Les Collins produced a ride straight from the gods, coming from the back to blast around both Tigers on the final bend to bring the house down, as only he could. Two more races that have always stuck in my mind are Colin Caffrey beating Dave Perks, who was one of the league's top men, at Blantyre One in 1981, and Micky Powell keeping both Greg Hancock and Billy Hamill at bay around Shawfield in 1995. They were snapping at his heels for all four laps, but Mick held on as the crowd got louder lap-by-lap. The place erupted when he crossed the line ahead of them.

Arnie Gibbons: I'm tempted to say the 2009 World Cup round at Peterborough but, in the interests of nostalgia, I'll go back a little further to Reading's second league championship-winning season. In 1980, Reading had slipped up at home to Cradley Heath in the first leg of a KO Cup tie, so the second leg at Dudley Wood on August 21 seemed like a formality. It turned out to be a classic encounter. A John Davis/Ashley Pullen 5-1 over Erik Gundersen in Heat 13 put Racers two up on the night. After Bobby Schwartz won Heat 17 to complete a seven-ride 21-point full maximum, the only one in Reading's club history, the aggregate scores were 105-105 with one heat to go. Jiri Stancl led the deciding heat for three-and-three-quarter laps before Bruce Penhall stormed round the outside for a draw on the night and a two-point win overall for the Heathens.

Paul Rickett: September 17, 1974. Leicester 23 Sheffield 55. It was my first visit to Blackbird Road on what was a soggy September night. Of course, having a friend who's an opposition fan, it's that much nicer when your team stuffs theirs. On a rain-drenched track, covered in sawdust, Sheffield were awesome from the moment Bob Valentine shot out of the trap to beat Dave Jessup in the first race. Valentine and Doug Wyer scored maximums and Reg Wilson had a paid full house as we recorded a club record away win.

For me, you will never beat the run-off to the 1985 Overseas Final at Odsal. Dukes star Kenny Carter and 'our hero' Shawn Moran went to the tapes in a shoot-out for the title and the tension was amazing; considering the Yorkshire rivalry, there was more to it than just the

Overseas crown being at stake. Carter gated but Shawn crawled over his back wheel on the first lap and then swept underneath going into the third turn. Carter hugged his exhaust pipe for the rest of the race, tried the inside and outside lines, but Shawn held on by a bike's length and the place erupted. Brilliant.

Rob Glover: Peterborough v Reading in the second leg of the Elite League Grand Final – a fantastic atmosphere, large crowd and brilliant racing. The race that sticks in my memory has to be Heat 15, when Peterborough's Hans Andersen and Ryan Sullivan took a 5-1 over Greg Hancock to win the tie on aggregate.

Eddie Garvey: The 1976 Inter-Continental Final at Wembley was without a doubt the best I've ever seen. The heat, the colour, the smell, the thrills, the shocks – with the possible exception of the 1981 World Final, nothing has ever really come close to what I experienced that night in London. The exit of two former World Champions, Ole Olsen and Anders Michanek, PC on top of the rostrum and Mort sailing through to Katowice in a fashion that belied his age and experience, it was a true classic.

John Davidson: Not the most original response, but the Wembley World Finals of 1978 and 1981 most obviously come to mind. Both featured electric atmosphere and great racing on a track that was conducive to it. Penhall was magnificent in '81. In overcoming Tommy Knudsen, he defeated a young, very quick rider. In overcoming Olsen, though, he took on a master riding a virtually flawless race, on a track at which Ole performed better than just about anyone of his generation. I'm also fond of the World Pairs Final at Belle Vue in 1977. It was a beautiful summer night and Peter Collins and Malcolm Simmons put on a tremendous display of team-riding. Ivan Mauger sent the English duo to their only defeat of the night with one of the finest rides I ever saw from him. There were TV cameras there that night – somewhere out there, there must be footage floating around.

I can name two classic races, starting with Heat 4 of the 1978 World Final – Mauger v Olsen v Kennett. I was seated along the back straight, coming out of the second turn. I had a perfect view of the start and suffered heart palpitations as Mauger continually bumped the tapes. I felt sure he was going to break them, or miss the start completely. As it turned out, he flew out of the gate. The angle of the TV footage doesn't do justice to the leap Ivan made from the start. I'll never forget it, that charge to the first bend. It was a truly great race. Don't forget, Olsen came from a long way back. Ivan was clearly on a struggling engine, but rode a flawless line to keep two quicker rivals at bay. And then it ended. I slumped into my seat, disconsolate and said: "He's out of it. Ivan's lost his title."

The other race is one of the many battles I witnessed between Ivan and Peter Collins. This one was at Belle Vue, Heat 13 of a league match in 1975. On the back straight, final lap, Collins seemed to have finally overhauled Mauger after three laps of busting a gut trying to do so. But Ivan refused to let him go by, and it is one of the few occasions I recall seeing him straining in physical effort. The two of them peeled out of the final bend and flashed over the finish line together, almost inseparable. I felt sure the home-town boy would get the call – but he didn't.

Mark Sawbridge: My classic meeting was the 1978 World Final at Wembley; my classic race was Heat 4. I was 12-years-old and had never been to anything like that before. I went with a friend and his father on the supporters' train from the West Midlands. Wolves,

Birmingham, Cradley Heath and Coventry fans all crowded on board. I remember so much of the day, particularly when we got out at Wembley Central and the Coventry fans in front of us unfurled a giant banner which read 'Bionic Ole beats Lee Maugers'. (If you don't understand that reference to *The Six Million Dollar Man*, ask your parents.)

Heat 4 brought Ole Olsen, Ivan Mauger and Gordon Kennett together. Mauger gated, but seemed to be on a bike with 100cc less power than the others. He rode two-and-a-half laps trying desperately to hold onto the lead. Going down the back straight of the third lap, the three were all level as they charged into the third bend. Something had to give, and it was Mauger. Olsen went on to win the race and the meeting. Watching this race on YouTube still gives me goose bumps.

Richard Gilson: My favourite classic/memorable meeting took place on June 15, 1985 and is very simple: The mighty Cradley Heathens 38 Sheffield 40. I recall the headlines in *Speedway Star* about 'the result that rocked the speedway world'. I still look at the programme with a smile, just to remember and check that it actually happened.

Ian Shelton: I'll choose a run-of-the-mill British League fixture at Dudley Wood in April 1976, when Swindon were the visitors. It was a match that swayed to and fro, with Cradley well led by Bruce Cribb but having to cover for the missing John Boulger with rider replacement. Heathens were two points down going into Heat 13 and found themselves outgated in the decider by Martin Ashby and Bobby McNeil. Defeat looked inevitable. Then I learned all about the legend that was Bernt Persson. He stormed around Ashby and then piled under McNeil, who slid into the pits fence. The stadium held its breath as the red lights came on and we all awaited the ref's decision. McNeil was excluded and Persson and Bruce Cribb now faced Ashby in the rerun with a 5-1 still required for the win. Cribby made the start, with Ashby second, but once again Persson found a gap to pass Ashby and give the Heathens victory. I never saw the best of this Black Country legend but I will never forget that match.

John Murphy: For me it's not always just great racing but I suppose some aggravation and

Ivan Mauger and Ole Olsen in their thrilling clash at the 1978 World Final.

nonsense chucked in too. The 1981 World Final probably tops most fans' hit parade. Take away the two stand-out Penhall races, though and, in all honesty, there have been better meetings. But throw in 92,000, night-time, Wembley as it was and what turned out to be speedway's swansong beneath the twin towers . . . A quick mention for Bradford 48 Birmingham 30 in the Speedway Express BL2 KO Cup, 1973. We'd lost 47-31 at Perry Barr in the first leg but I believe Tony Featherstone clinched it for us at Odsal. Brilliant, although Boston cuffed us in the semis.

Martin Smith: The Four Team Tournament at Peterborough in 1991 for an Ipswich victory as unexpected as it was thrilling. On a glorious afternoon, the Witches rediscovered their self-belief and winning habit after a barren spell from the mid-80s. Central to this magical afternoon was an astonishing last-to-first ride by David

Ipswich after winning the 1991 Fours final at Peterborough. Standing: David Norris, John Louis (team manager), Ben Howe. Front: Tony Rickardsson, Chris Louis, Shane Parker.

Norris early in the final, sweeping past everybody in a daring, full-throttle burst over the first two laps. An inspirational ride that was hugely influential to the outcome.

Alex Mackenzie: Cardiff, 2007. The track was cutting up and bikes were being thrown around but Chris Harris got into the final and cut back to overtake Greg Hancock on the last bend of the last lap to win. Together with just about every person in the stadium, I jumped for joy. I saw Bruce Penhall win at Wembley in 1981 and won't forget that either, but this was better.

Craig Saul: There are several that stand out, for differing reasons. As a spectator, my favourite is probably the 1985 NL KO Cup Final, second leg between Ellesmere Port and Eastbourne. The Gunners were by then on the brink of claiming the league title, albeit at great personal cost, and everyone at Thornton Road that night expected them to overcome what I recall was a 12-point first leg deficit to collect the Cup. Gordon Kennett, Andy Buck and a blossoming 16-year-old named Martin Dugard had other ideas, and their superb riding helped to send the trophy to Sussex.

As an announcer, the Elite League title deciders at Peterborough in 1999 and 2006 were very special. If I had to choose between the two on a personal level, I would have to plump for the former. It was, after all, the first success, and one achieved with a 'super seven' who were great and easy to work with all season: Jason Crump, Ryan Sullivan, Sam Tesar, Mario Jirout, David Howe, Jan Andersen and Nigel Sadler. The Panthers had to overcome Belle Vue, which they did at a canter, but also hope that Poole would slip up at King's Lynn. Sky ran the two matches simultaneously, and we had a live visual feed in the pits – but no audio – to the events unfolding at the Norfolk Arena. I quickly cobbled together an improvised racecard so that I could feed my announcing colleague Edwin Overland the heat-by-heat line-ups ahead of each race, so that he could then provide an audio racing commentary for the crowd of what was going on at Saddlebow. No big screens in those days. The sheer emotion at our end of the A47 when the Stars clinched a last heat victory over the Pirates was simply unbelievable, and yet only the start of a week that also took in last race wins in the Craven Shield and KO

Cup Finals, plus an end-of-season dinner/dance presentation.

My favourite race has to be the second Golden Greats race that was included in Chris Neath's Testimonial at Rye House in 2008. Only recently retired from active competition, Sam Ermolenko had strolled to victory in the first heat ahead of Rob Woffinden and an even rustier Michael Lee. 'Mike the Bike' understandably opted out of the return encounter, leaving a straight-forward match race between 'Sudden Sam' and 'Woffy'. The 1993 World Champion was already track-side, preparing for another easy romp, when Woffy snuck up to me in the pits, a glint in his eye, and confided that there would be "a change of plan". Just as he said this, a rider decked in his colours exited the pits to join Ermolenko at the tapes. Sam clearly still thought his opponent was Woffy, and maintained that impression when he duly gated in front of his adversary. What he didn't expect was to be passed, almost as though he was standing still, down the back straight. Always the competitor, the Californian gave chase but totally over-cooked the third bend and ended up on his backside on the track as 'Woffy' completed the race on his own, and then pulled up next to me at the starting gate. With microphone in hand, I spluttered my apparent incredulity at how Rob had achieved his remarkable success, as the rider slowly removed his helmet. Imagine the look on Sam's face – and the reaction of the crowd – when the winner was revealed as none other than . . . Testimonial man Chris Neath!

Chris Rowsell: The one classic meeting that immediately springs to mind is the 1981 KO Cup meeting at Reading against Coventry. It had been a difficult season for the Racers, who had won the league in 1980, and took place with much unrest in the camp. John Davis had been wanting away for a while and, in fact, this turned out to be his final meeting for the time being. The Racers had lost the first leg at Coventry by 49-45, which was a good result, and going into the last heat of the second leg they held a 46-44 lead on the night, but were still two points down on aggregate. It was Davis and Jan Andersson against Ole Olsen and Mitch Shirra. The crowd was at fever pitch as the Racers duo sped away and repelled the attacks of both Bees for four pulsating laps, crossing the line first and second to get the necessary result. The crowd went crazy and it was probably the best night I've ever experienced at speedway.

Garry Hutson: The 1981 World Final at Wembley lives long in my memory for the racing and the whole atmosphere.

The one great race that stands out was from Belle Vue v King's Lynn, a league match in 1980. Dave Jessup gated and, as usual, held the bike down on the white line with Chris Morton giving chase. At one point, they were so close it looked like they were riding the same bike but Morton eventually went round Jessup for the win.

Steve Ridgway: But if I had to choose one classic, it would have to be the 1972 BLRC – a sell-out crowd (and I mean sell-out), squashed right against the fence at the start of the third turn. Tipping it down with rain, which glistened in the lights and nowadays would have had the meeting called off at lunch time. There was just enough room to duck behind the fence to avoid getting sprayed with liquid shale! I still have the programme, complete with a scraped off layer of Hyde Road third bend shale on it. But there were other memorable moments, like Barry Briggs' aerial acrobatics after tangling with John Langfield in the 1972 Australia v New Zealand match at Hyde Road; the Aces' 57-21 demolition of Exeter in the 1978 KO Cup, which most of us had written off after a 51-27 reverse away in the first leg seemed to make the return a formality; and in 1977, when, only a few weeks after they'd been uncharacteristically hammered 59-19 in the Cup, Ipswich returned to Hyde Road and duly won 52-26 – Aces' heaviest-ever home defeat at that point. I remember one of my mates turning round to us and muttering, completely deadpan: "They were lucky." A couple of weeks later, Exeter turned up and won 53-25.

Ask anyone who was there at the KO Cup Final in 1973 – you really did have to be there – and 'that race' stands out as if it was yesterday. But there were others, like PC winning a race against Newport in 1972 with only one handlebar, or guiding Robert Maxfield to an unlikely 5-1 over Ole Olsen against Coventry in 1979.

Tim Allan: I wouldn't say it was a classic but the Farewell Individual at Weymouth on Friday, October 22, 2010 will live long in my mind. All riders were former or current Wildcats, with fans' favourite Gary Cottham winning the meeting and bringing an end to a sad evening for the Wildcats.

Rob Peasley: The second leg of the 1985 KO Cup Final between Oxford and Ipswich, where the Cheetahs triumphed in a last-heat decider. The place was heaving – there had to be at least 5,000 people there and the meeting was on a knife-edge throughout. We may have won the league already that year, but Ipswich rode our place better than we did. The three previous Oxford v Ipswich matches at Cowley in 1985 had finished 36-42, 39-39 and 39-39. So, facing a deficit of four points from the first leg at Foxhall, the Cheetahs were up against it. Heat 5 took a few attempts to run and, by the end of it, Jens Rasmussen was injured and the culprit Jeremy Doncaster had become a panto villain in the eyes of Cheetahs' fans. With Andy Grahame and Klaus Lausch already on the injury list, we only had teenagers Ali Stevens and Troy Butler in addition to Hans, Wiggy and Marvyn Cox. But the youngsters came up trumps. as Stevens took Dennis Sigalos from behind in Heat 8 to join Hans for an oh-so-vital 5-1.

Nielsen completed a brilliant 15-point maximum by winning Heat 12, but Cocker ran a last and it was going to go down to Heat 13. With Rasmussen injured, Bernard Crapper (who knew the rules inside out) tried to pull a fast one by sending out Stevens. But the ref was having none of it – Ali had already taken his permitted maximum of five rides, so Butler had to go out instead.

John Cook and Doncaster squeezed out Wigg on the first bend and our hearts were in our mouths – were Ipswich going to snatch the cup by a point with a 5-1? Then came the fourth bend. Doncaster seemed a bit close to Cook and the American took his own team-mate out to the fence. In a flash, Wiggy and Troy were through, and the crowd erupted. We only needed a second place, but Troy, who had struggled all season in his rookie year, rode a blinder and Donkey couldn't even regain third. The Golden Helmet match-race had to be abandoned due to the jubilant Oxford fans spilling onto the track as soon as Heat 13 was over.

Stephen Roberts: The best single race I ever witnessed was in 1977 at Hackney between Gordon Kennett and Peter Collins. They rode shoulder-to-shoulder for the entire four laps and the referee couldn't split them, so he awarded a dead heat.

Nick Nicklin: Coventry v Cradley Heath, British League match on May 17, 1980. Coventry, at the time, had been unbeaten at home in the league for a number of years while Cradley were an improving side who had run the Bees close at Brandon in the two preceding seasons. A large crowd, as well as the ATV Sports cameras, were present to see the drama unfold as the Heathens pulled off a famous victory. Cradley had a trump card at reserve with Finnish ex-World Finalist Ila Teromaa taking three race wins, whilst cleverly being used by Heathens' team manager Bob Wasley to take the place of inexperienced Danish youngster Hans Albert Klinge at key times. The racing was enthralling and close throughout, with a rare dead heat in one race, but the incident that stands out the most for me was the exclusion of Ole Olsen in the crucial Heat 10. Olsen and

Oxford, with Troy Butler, the injured Andy Grahame and Simon Wigg at the forefront, on their victory parade after a dramatic 1985 KO Cup Final.

Alf Busk had secured a much-needed 5-1 for the Bees but Ole was excluded for losing his chainguard after an appeal by Heathens manager Wasley, citing a little used rule in the rulebook. Olsen, for so long a pantomime villain for Cradley fans, voiced his exasperation to both the referee and ATV frontman Gary Newbon whilst watching the race back on a TV monitor but it was all to no avail; the chainguard had come adrift and it was clearly from Olsen's machine. Coventry went into the final heat needing a 5-1 to win but Bruce Penhall and Phil Collins took the heat advantage to give Cradley the league points and end their neighbours' long unbeaten home record.

Having watched the sport for so long, it is difficult to recall just one race that stands out more than any other and I can think of at least three that are worthy of a mention. The first, from 1978, took place at Dudley Wood between Cradley's Bruce Cribb and White City's Kai Niemi and Gordon Kennett. This was when Niemi rode shoulder-to-shoulder with Cribb for four laps, with Kennett never more than a few metres behind until his engine failed on the last lap. Cribb and Niemi crossed the line together, their battle declared a dead heat by the referee. The second was a race from the Courage ATV Best Pairs, held at Dudley Wood in 1979. Cradley's two Americans, Bruce Penhall and Bobby Schwartz, were paired together and when they jumped out into the lead in Heat 3, riding side by side, against Wimbledon's Roger Johns and Colin Richardson, they looked set to cement their position at the top of the leader board. But Johns, after chasing for a couple of laps, surprised the Americans by bursting between them down the back straight. A close battle followed, with Johns taking the flag in a tight finish from Schwartz. The third was also from 1979, a great season for speedway at Dudley Wood, and again featured Penhall, by now the Heathens' undisputed No.1. The event was the Grand Prix Qualifying Round and saw Bruce take on the unfancied Vic Harding from Hackney in Heat 14. Penhall made the gate but was chased by Harding, who passed Penhall on the second lap. The two traded passes on lap three before Penhall finally established a winning lead. Harding had a great meeting, scoring 12 points, finishing third on the night, marking him down as a young rider to watch. How sad I was to learn of his death just a few weeks later.

Martin Neal: Two races that stand out for me are one in the 1986 Grand Slam Final at Arena-Essex and Bomber Harris' British Grand Prix win at Cardiff in 2007. The Grand Slam was on the day Argentina beat England in the World Cup finals with Diego Maradona's infamous 'Hand of God' goal. It was a hot day and I'd taken the work experience girl in the hope of impressing her (she wanted tickets for the tennis at Wimbledon but this was the best I could do). It was a long, drawn out and not especially exciting meeting (work experience girl not impressed). But in the final, contested by eight riders, Gary Havelock came from the second row of the grid and picked off everyone ahead of him in spectacular style to take the win.

Mark Simms: The league title decider between Wolverhampton and Belle Vue at Monmore Green in 1993. I had been out of work, so had no money and it was touch and go if my old car would get me there. At the eleventh hour, I decided I had to go. The way the meeting unfolded, with all the drama and that final decisive race, made for a truly awesome night.

My greatest race was Heat 8 in the 1982 Reading v Belle Vue BL match starring the Carr brothers. It was a real turning point in the meeting where I started to think we could win on the night and then ultimately go on to win the league. The Aces were on the wrong end of a 5-1 and with the conditions being poor due to rain, passing was never going to be easy. Louis passed one rider on the outside, then cut back and passed the other on the inside. This must have given Peter heart, as he forced his way into second for a family 5-1 in our favour. I can't recall who represented the Racers in the heat. It was our last league match of the season, we won 40-38 and it completed an 11-match unbeaten run that saw us top the table at season's end.

Graham Goodwin: Probably the Wolverhampton v Belle Vue 1993 league title decider. For a league title to go down to the last race of the season in the pre-play-off days was incredible. Belle Vue won the meeting by a single point and took the league title on race points difference.

One race that stands out in my memory was a run-off for second place in the BLRC at Hyde Road between Chris Morton and Shawn Moran in 1981. They passed and re-passed on every corner. And, of course, that final race in the 1993 league title decider was so tense.

Ila Teromaa, Cradley's match-winner at Coventry.

Brian Longman: Hackney away to Wimbledon in the 1988 KO Cup Final. There was a lot of rivalry between the two clubs at the time and for the Kestrels to win it at Plough Lane was extra special.

A race that lives in my memory is Barry Thomas against Exeter in 1977, when he passed Ivan Mauger and Scott Autrey on the last bend. The most amazing piece of speedway riding ever; it didn't matter one iota to us who had won or lost the league, it was pure guts and skill and we just went crazy afterwards.

Chris Fenn: The race I remember is the one all Hackney fans still talk about. It was in a very important meeting if you supported Exeter or White City, who were battling it out for the championship. Exeter had Scott Autrey and Ivan Mauger in the last race, needing a 5-1 to win, and they had it until the last lap when Barry Thomas swept through an almost impossible gap on the outside between Mauger and the safety fence. I was sitting on the rail that ran along the dog track on the fourth bend and had an excellent view. It was an incredible piece of overtaking and I've never seen anything like it since.

Andrew Skeels: Scunthorpe v Newcastle in 1975 at Quibell Park. Scunny trailed virtually all match, but inspired by Tony Childs, we came from six points down to take a totally unexpected 37-35 lead going into a Heat 13 last heat decider, which Keith Evans was winning over the Owen brothers to give us the victory . . . until his bike packed up (from memory, he shed a chain, but I could be wrong). The Owens were gifted a 5-1 and Newcastle won 40-38. I was 11 at the time, and devastated. And it only took us about another 200 years before we finally beat Newcastle for the first time. Or so it seemed anyway.

Newcastle's Tom and Joe Owen were gifted a 5-1 at Scunthorpe.

There's probably too many great races to single just the one out, although I do recall a particular race which was memorable for the wrong reason as one of the worst pile-ups I've ever seen. It was a dreadful crash at Milton Keynes' Groveway in 1983 involving Exeter's Rob Ashton and Knights' Steve Payne (who still is a good friend of *Speedway Star* editor Richard Clark and I). Payney broke his thigh.

David Golley: Oddly, a meeting that ended in disappointment – Mildenhall v Scunthorpe in the NL Grand Final in 2011. We had been thrashed at Scunthorpe, but in more twists and turns than a crime thriller, back at West Row the Fen Tigers took it to a last heat decider before the Saints just scrapped home. When people like Michael Lee, Chris Louis and Kevin Jolly say they've never known a meeting like it, you know you have witnessed something special.

For my great race, Mike Sampson and Danny Kennedy in a run-off for the Seyco Cola Trophy at Weymouth in, I think, 1975 or '76. They passed and re-passed each other on every corner, but I am ashamed to say I can't remember who won.

Derek Barclay: The 1977 Inter-Continental Final at the White City. I'm not sure the sport has ever reached that height since – a packed stadium in the heart of London, in the sunshine, Peter Collins simply awesome, the best in the world then and I'd argue the greatest individual performance ever.

My best race is a slightly odd choice. Also at White City, the year before, in the second-half final of the opening meeting, a challenge v Wimbledon: Gordon Kennett v Tommy Jansson. Gordon had beaten Tommy in a fantastic Heat 13 to win the match 40-38 for the Rebels and the second-half final saw them take on each other again. It was another brilliant race but this time Tommy prevailed. It was the last time I saw Tommy race, because he was dead within a few weeks and the tragedy of losing him makes the memory poignant too.

Richard Simmons: The 1984 British Final at Coventry and the 'Kenny Carter show'. Most people hated him and wanted him to fail but that night, riding with a broken leg, he showed everybody how it was done.

My memorable race is also from that meeting – Carter's last, when he lined up against the Collins brothers. He had to battle hard for the win but he made it. I also remember the Golden Helmet match-race held after the 1985 League Cup clash between Ipswich and Belle Vue for different reasons. It was the last time I saw the great Billy Sanders in action.

Phil Chard: Coventry 46 Poole 44, BSPA Elite League KO Cup Final, second leg, 2003. It was the cup final Bees had in the bag, but threw away in almost unbelievable fashion during an extraordinary last eight heats of the second leg. As the Poole reporter for *Bournemouth's Daily Echo*, I wrote for those Pirates fans lucky enough to have witnessed the astonishing turnaround from the Brandon terraces, it must have been one of those genuine 'I was there' moments. Pirates, protecting a slender four-point lead from the first leg, almost drowned in the first seven heats on a slushy, rain-saturated, track at Coventry. If it hadn't been so late in the season, October 25, and a cup final, there was no way the meeting would have started. The track resembled a Cambodian paddy field. But, despite Poole's protestations, go ahead it

Peter Collins inside Ole Olsen and Phil Crump on the way to victory in the 1977 Inter-Continental Final at White City.

WHITE CITY STADIUM
WOOD LANE, SHEPHERD'S BUSH, W.12

TURNSTILE
B

Individual Speedway
Championship of the World
Intercontinental Final
Sponsored by the Sunday Mirror
Sunday, 21st August 1977
First Race 4.30 p.m. - Gates Open 2.30 p.m
RESERVED £2.00

ENTRANCE
24

ROW   **L**   SEAT   №   36
To be retained, for conditions see back.

BLOCK
T

did and, inspired by Tony Rickardsson, Leigh Adams and Bjarne Pedersen, they somehow pulled off the mother of all comebacks from 14 points down on aggregate with eight races to go to win by two overall. I hadn't witnessed anything like it before. Nor, I suspected, had most of the 400 odd diehard Pirates fans, huddled beneath their brollies shivering on the first and second bend terraces. It was a spectacular fight-back, made even more special because it came completely out of the blue. It was one of those occasions when you had to have seen it with your own eyes to believe it. And even now most of the 4,500 people who were packed into Brandon then – fans, riders, promoters, team managers, track staff, ref, journalists, etc – are probably still struggling to believe it happened, more than 10 years later.

For one particularly great race, it would have to be Poland's Tomasz Gollob beating Australia's Jason Crump in the World Cup race-off at Poole in 2004. Although, ultimately, it was 'only' for second place, with lightning-trapping Peter Karlsson grabbing first for Sweden. With Australia trailing leaders Sweden by six points, but only one behind Poland going into the final race, Crump came in as a joker scoring double. It meant even if Gollob won Heat 25, Crump 'only' had to finish second to send Australia through to the final instead of the Poles. When Karlsson gated and emerged out of the second bend in front, the dynamic quickly changed. Whoever finished second between Gollob and Crump would now book their team's place in the final, alongside Sweden, who'd already qualified. It seemed tough on the Poles, who hadn't been able to use the joker (where have you heard that before?), but Gollob fabulously rose to the occasion and led Crump into the second lap. However, the Aussie drove hard inside Gollob on the second bend, second lap, and everyone inside Poole Stadium must have felt it was a done deal. Crump, who plundered his first individual world title that year, was almost unbeatable from the back. But the Pole pulled off a vintage Gollob move by roaring outside a stunned Crump on the third and fourth bends to force his way back into second. Then he somehow kept a hard-charging Crump at bay in an epic remaining two laps to send the Poles into raptures.

Chris Camp: Probably the finest moment for me as a Milton Keynes fan was beating Mildenhall at West Row, as we didn't often win away and the Fen Tigers were one of our fiercest rivals. That one meeting represented everything I loved about speedway at the time; a good track the riders could really race on, passing aplenty, the passion of the fans with lots of banter and the riders, Knights and Tigers, joining us in the bar after the meeting to celebrate the win. Andy Hines, Kevin Smart and the entire team gave their all that day, it meant as much to them as it did to us and the celebrations went on long into the evening. Riders like Chris Morton, Kevin Smart, Barry Thomas, Peter Collins and others were the lifeblood of the sport and always provided racing that was exciting and entertaining. Riders like them just don't seem to be around these days.

Glenn Collins: A meeting that will always stand out for me is Poole v Eastbourne in August 2000. Eagles had stormed into a 10-point lead after six races but Poole clawed it back with an incredible 5-1 from Mark Loram and Scott Nicholls in Heat 7, and then another from Lars Gunnestad and Loram in Heat 8. Two 4-2s for Pirates put them two ahead and from there they went on to win. It was an extraordinary turnaround in a fierce local derby.

Kevin Smart of Milton Keynes.

A race that will always stand out in my memory is the final of the British Grand Prix in 2002. The four riders in the final had never won a GP before, so whoever won, it would be their first Grand Prix win. Ryan Sullivan made a dreadful start and was last going down the back straight but then lined up Todd Wiltshire, Leigh Adams and Mikael Karlsson and passed all three in one go to win.

Matthew Lawrence: April 25, 2011, I watched a double-header at Scunthorpe in which the Scorpions faced Somerset and the Saints faced King's Lynn. The NL meeting, in particular, sticks in my mind as it had something of everything. James Cockle missed the two minutes and went off 15 metres, but his bike packed up straight away. As he was pushing it onto the centre green, it got going again. The other riders passed him going into lap two, but Cockle got back on the track, a whole lap behind, and completely ignored the official with the black flag stood in front of him!

Heat 14 in that meeting was possibly the best race I've ever seen. Greg Blair couldn't have gone any wider or through a smaller gap to round the Young Stars off bend four on the fourth lap for the win. If my memory is correct, he blew an engine prior to the Saints' next meeting and has never ridden competitively since.

5 THEN AND NOW

What do you miss most about speedway in the past? What, if anything, would you like to see reintroduced to speedway today?

Eric Marchment: What do I miss about speedway in the past? That's a polite way of asking what is wrong with speedway now. For me, it's the lack of expectation, excitement and entertainment.

The current promotional attitude is, 'give them (the paying public) 15 races and let them take it or leave it'. Then when we, the public, decide to leave it, they profess not to understand why.

What should be re-introduced? The list would be too long and complex to stand a chance. The easiest way is to give an example: it's to say that Cardiff is the last remaining example of what presentation and organisation for a meeting should be like.

The worst innovation was the four-valve engine: faster, easier to ride, but not easier to race and less controllable when things go wrong. Mostly, you get four riders doing four laps at a greater speed and just a few able to produce a good race.

Another ridiculous thing that is killing interest is the time wasted by the riders 'gardening' at the start, then an over-fussy referee calling the riders back for a restart. If you watch races from the 70s, with Mauger, Olsen, etc, as long as they didn't break the tapes, the race was allowed to continue. Nowadays, the race is stopped, the riders go back to the pits, which seems to take forever, while Joe Public is left in limbo. A whole lot of things could be brought in in place of the pathetic, disheartening state of affairs we are asked to pay for today.

I know we have to have point limits, but in the old days teams like Wembley and Wimbledon maintained the nucleus of their team season after season, and you looked

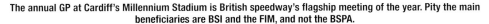

The annual GP at Cardiff's Millennium Stadium is British speedway's flagship meeting of the year. Pity the main beneficiaries are BSI and the FIM, and not the BSPA.

forward to supporting them year after year. The points limit is supposed to produce good racing by making the teams more equal, which it doesn't. Then, when that doesn't work, the ridiculous Joker is used. How do you introduce and encourage new spectators when things like that make the sport look stupid and unprofessional? What other sport would reward a losing team? Negativity has always been the downfall in speedway.

To attract serious investment, you need a good, branded, successful product, but speedway doesn't reward

One of the great leg-trailers, George Newton of New Cross.

success: a successful team is decimated at the end of a season and improving riders find themselves jobless.

The other thing from the past is that supporters could connect with the riders. You saw them as people. Now all you get is a walking advertising board topped with a full-face helmet or a baseball cap.

Bert Loader: There doesn't seem to be the same atmosphere at meetings these days as in the past between fans and riders. It seems to be all too clinical.

Maurice Plowright: In the early days, with track surfaces having bumps and dips, bikes having higher frames and longer wheel bases, the outcome of a race was so much more uncertain. The foot-forwards style, being more upright, also made the outcome of a race more predictable. For the bikes, longer wheelbases and higher frames would produce more spectacular speedway, but also more dangerous speedway, so it will never happen.

Ken Carpenter: What I miss most about speedway? The one-off World Final at Wembley. What would I re-introduce? The one-off World Final at Wembley.

John Hyam: The fact that we no longer have the whole club concept about the sport in which riders continued season on season with the same team. I would like speedway to return to the way things were run in the 40s (a continuation from the pre-war days format): 14-heat league matches, eight-rider teams, with six team men getting four races each and the reserves a minimum of two rides, plus an attractive four heats and a final second-half.

Wally Loak: The return of second-half racing has several advantages – most importantly, the opportunity for young, local talent to race, but also it gives an added interest for home supporters who, if we lost the main match, could still yell like blazes for our top rider of the night to beat the opposition.

We need to go back to the basic machinery of years ago (it's almost impossible, I know, but we sadly missed the opportunity a few years ago when Eric Boocock tried out the Honda bikes). It would cut the cost of speedway to everybody, most especially the youngsters.

Ron Byford: I miss the showmanship, the roar and the smell of the bikes (no silencers and Castrol R), the atmosphere and the value for money, with at least 18 heats. We need to bring back regular meetings – the fixtures are too spread out now and it can be a month between home meetings sometimes – and improve the presentation.

Dennis Hoppe: Unfortunately, I moved away from London in 1949 and was not able to attend any tracks for many years. However, I followed the sport through the *Speedway News* for a long time and read the daily results in the national press.

In more recent times, I went to meetings at the now defunct Smallmead track in Reading, but there was not quite the same thrill I experienced during my teenage years in the capital. The contemporary racing styles do not excite me as once they did and I regret the passing of the 'old-timers', bless them.

Ken Wrench: I miss the large crowds and what was a simple-to-understand sport which had a less complicated rulebook and no silencers (impossible now, of course). We need to return to less complex, less expensive and safer machinery with, in the light of the record of recent years, an accent on safety.

Keith Barraclough: I miss not having speedway at The Shay in my home town of Halifax, or at Odsal, Bradford. I can't see speedway ever returning to The Shay because of the new terraces and stands built for football in the last 10 years or so. There is talk of speedway returning to Odsal, so I'm hopeful that West Yorkshire will again have its own team in the near future.

I would very much like all teams to have body colours as I remember them. Who can forget the Coventry bee body colour (not the rather idiotic-looking bee of recent years); the Poole skull and crossbones; the Halifax elephant on red and blue halves; the Cradley Heath CH; the Belle Vue ace of clubs and triangle with straight sides (not curved)? I never felt that team leathers worked. Halifax tried them in the 70s but there was always a reserve/guest who had to be drafted in for an injured rider who didn't have the team leathers.

Cedric Read: We should cultivate the press' interest. One of my abiding memories is seeing *Birmingham Mail* reporter Rob Bishop at Cradley, typing his match report on a portable machine while sitting on the concrete terraces. No wonder there is little media attention!

Keith Walker: Most missed are decent-sized crowds making a noise. Most racing now seems to be greeted with total silence, apart from the occasional skilful move which generates moderate applause.

As for re-introduction, bring back true scoring. That is, do away with tactical rides and the nonsense of double points. If a team is behind, it is because their opponents are riding better, so why reward the poorer team? Is a guy going to

Super Swedes: Bernt Persson (Cradley Heath), Anders Michanek (Reading), Bengt Jansson (Hackney) and Christer Lofqvist (Poole) on parade prior to the 1972 BLRC at Belle Vue. Didn't we just love the simplicity of those uncomplicated racejackets bearing their distinctive club colours and emblems – and not a sponsor's logo in sight.

ride faster because he is wearing a black and white helmet? Do away with 'unsatisfactory starts' and the inevitable delays they cause. Perhaps consider a return to meaningful second-half races. In the past, even a dull league match could be revitalised by an entertaining rider of the night competition.

Ken Taylor: So, things I don't like about present day speedway? First, bikes have become advertising billboards; race-jackets similar, too much advertising. I do not like dirt deflectors and let's have a bit more dirt flying around. Better track preparation with more shale and proper (informed) watering. Yes, I still do go to speedway meetings anywhere I can.

John Chaplin: I miss full-blown, round-the-boards, devil-may-care spectacular leg-trailers. The 18-heat formula should be re-introduced, as in the old classic England v Australia Test matches, with eight-man teams – three pairs and two reserves. Each pair met their opposite numbers twice, once from the inside gates, and then from the outside gates. Reserves could be used at any time as necessary up to a maximum of six rides. The formula does away with guests, double points nonsense, tactical substitutes and handicapping. It also gives the paying customer more value for money.

I would eradicate gate 'gardening' at a stroke. Riders would be held at a line a bike's length from the tapes. When the green light went on, they would be under starter's orders and only then go forward to the tapes.

When I go to a speedway meeting, I don't want to hear pop groups, see silly people prancing about dressed in silly suits, hear microphone chat from ill-informed centre green presenters or see scantily clad young women twirling umbrellas – all I want to see is speedway racing. So, I'd like to see pure speedway racing re-introduced to speedway racing. And if modern speedway is on the skids – forgive the pun – modern promoters have only themselves to blame . . . for not promoting it.

Showman supreme John S. Hoskins, the granddaddy of speedway, and Trevor Redmond, another who really knew how to promote the sport.

Tony Webb: I miss the second-half, the races for juniors and the final of the night. I miss the clear, precise announcing of men like Ted Sear at Hackney. I miss the antics of Len Silver, John Berry, Dave Lanning, Johnnie Hoskins and all those larger-than-life characters. We get short changed now, the price goes up but the product gets smaller. I also miss the fun in the bar after the meeting.

Philip Dalling: The feeling of being part of a sizeable crowd. I do feel sorry on occasions for the riders, particularly on the pre-meeting and victory parades. At many venues, they are faced with virtually empty, or even partially demolished and disused, stands and terraces. Long Eaton never had particularly big crowds compared to some tracks, but photographs and film show spectators all around the arena. It made a huge difference to the atmosphere.

I would like to see a bit more showmanship re-introduced. Very few promoters take to the centre green microphone these days, leaving it all to the presenters, which is not at all the same thing. More Len Silvers are needed.

John Cross: The one thing that I consider is missing from speedway in our country today is loyalty to British riders for their team places, whereby they are so easily replaced with a rider from foreign countries. I would also like to see all riders wear definite helmet colours: red, blue, white and yellow/black, as sometimes it's a little difficult to see the difference between the white and yellow.

Tony Emmott: The only speedway I see these days is the Grand Prix at Cardiff, although I have been to one Polish GP at Wroclaw. I see a few matches on TV but the attendances seem abysmal. I agree with the view that second-half events should be re-introduced to encourage more local home-grown riders. In the old days, most of the Odsal riders were local to West Yorkshire and the team was the same year in, year out, which encouraged team-riding. Now, riders seem to move on every season, which is hardly conducive to team spirit with little continuity for the fans. There were supporters' clubs and coaches organised to away matches. Is that the case today?

The real problem seems to be the top 20 or so riders participating in two or three leagues throughout Europe. Speedway must be the only sport run on these lines and whilst it may be better financially for the riders, I'm not convinced it is best for speedway as a team sport long-term. It precludes any kind of European league or competition.

Oliver Chapman: I miss teams consisting of mainly British riders, who remained with their team for more than a single season; the large crowds consisting of the full age range; and second-half racing where you would follow the local youngster starting out on his speedway journey.

Ipswich with the 1975 British League championship trophy. Standing, left to right: Billy Sanders, Mick Hines, Ron Bagley (team manager), Tony Davey, Ted Howgego, Trevor Jones. Kneeling: Mike Lanham, John Louis, Dave Gooderham. With the exception of Sanders, an Aussie who joined the Witches at the age of 16 and quickly became an adopted son of Suffolk, the whole team was born and lived within a short distance of Foxhall Stadium.

Have bike, will travel. Halifax stars Eric Boocock and Dave Younghusband attach a two-valve Jawa-ESO to a rack on the back of a MkII Ford Cortina. Bottom: This time Eric gets a hand from brother Nigel as they lift the bike from the boot of a different Cortina. Opposite: A trailer also did the job in days gone by.

Barry Scowen: I think the older supporters miss the big stars, the 'greats' who made headlines on the front of the speedway papers when they lost a single race. People like Mauger and Moore drew extra crowds when they were due to appear at your track.

Tim Templeton: I miss the strong smell of Castrol R, straight-through exhaust pipes and track lighting only over the track when the racing is on. The lack of noise, in particular, has taken so much of the atmosphere away. It won't happen, but noisier engines would add so much more for me.

Bert Harkins: I think the racing is faster and closer nowadays, but I miss the second-half with a novice race, a reserves' race, plus four qualifying heats and a trophy final. Now, it doesn't seem like value-for-money for the fans anymore but it helped to bring on juniors and also gave team members a chance to experiment with equipment without losing points.

Mike King: The one thing I miss from the past is the smell of Castrol R and the roar of the JAPs, with their polished chrome frames, mudguards and fuel tanks glistening under the yellow glow of the County Ground's lights.

I believe the most important thing that needs to be re-introduced is second-half racing, starting with junior and reserves' races and culminating in a rider of the night final. This is where novices and juniors all had a go and stood a chance of meeting established team members, thereby boosting their experience and potential. In the event of an absentee in a main match, local reserves could, and often did, stand in and became useful assets with their track knowledge and enthusiasm.

David Walker: The first thing about the past era was consistency. You knew which night was the one for your team. Ronnie Greene of Wimbledon swore that if there was a lack of continuity, and a meeting night was missed, the attendance suffered. This, of course, is totally at odds with today's combination of demands made by television and international meetings, especially at the top level. Tracks are continually messed about to fit in with the television companies plus, effectively, the whole weekend, from Friday to Sunday, whenever there is a Grand Prix round.

The next aspect is that of cost. Promoters and riders are perpetually moaning about increasing costs, but no-one seems to grasp the point that the combination of continuous air fares, plus van-loads of bikes (frequently in several countries) is not cost effective.

I'm well aware that modern machinery is more complex. I designed and was responsible for supplying the valves used in GM engines that won a number of World Championships, so it's not totally strange territory and my youngest son also runs a car racing team, hence a wider interest in most forms of motorsport.

Whilst the 40s, 50s and 60s archetypal bike-on-a-rack on the back of a car, with a box of tools, a couple of extra sprockets and a couple of tyres, might be a bit too basic for today, there is no question that action is needed to reduce running costs and increase the length of engine life.

Respected promoter Ronnie Greene with top Brit in his day Nigel Boocock.

Interestingly, moto-cross engines have to last 45 minutes per race and most do a full season without attention. Also, Formula 1 engines, revving a great deal higher than a speedway engine, have to do an hour-and-a-half, thus proving that it *is* possible.

What else do I miss? The smell of Castrol R and, above all else, the proper noise of a race engine, which is becoming more and more strangled.

I would like to see the following re-introduced into speedway today. For league racing, a proper, structured meeting of 13 heats, with a full second-half, which enabled riders to try out machinery and add to the entertainment, plus giving youngsters a chance to find their way into the sport.

Banning all mechanics from coming on the track, to do perpetual 'roadside tuning', plus keeping the pit gate closed. In the event of a false start, make the riders go straight back round to the tapes.

Also, ban all the 'gardening' and hole-digging at the start. More than one ex-rider has pointed out that it does nothing to help provide extra grip and merely delays the start.

Ditch the idiotic tactical ride rule and bring back the old tac-sub system.

Bring back the one-shot World Final. By all means move it round, but the qualifying rounds, as used in the past, were just as hard as the present system and would make for just as good television.

Richard Tyrrell: After Oxford's demise, I miss seeing what I call ordinary people who I would see every week on the terraces, all bound by that one common interest. It was more than just the racing.

Several things should be brought back. One, if a rider anticipates the start and doesn't touch the tapes, let the race go on, providing they are level and stationary at the gate. Two, when a race has to be restarted, get the riders straight round to the start again, no messing about at the pits gate. Three, get the bikes pushed out onto the track and let's see the riders walking out of the pits fastening their helmets, pulling their gloves on, etc. It all adds to the build-up.

Four, get rid of lay-down engines and introduce some skill into riding on well-prepared tracks, instead of the bravery of riding a rocket for four laps.

James Easter: I miss the English riders. The problems being experienced now are exactly what Sweden went through in the 80s. So let every Elite League team race once a month at home, on a stipulated night, using anyone they wish. For the rest of the season, everyone runs in one big league with a low, low points limit, say 35, with five British-born riders. You then produce your own stars in a year and the costs come down by thousands. All engines are provided by the track and fitted on the night.

Without doubt, second-half racing should be re-introduced with six races – three for juniors and two heats and a final for the seniors.

Andy Wilkinson: What I miss most is just getting in the car on speedway night and driving to Plough Lane thinking, 'this is going to be a tough match' or 'we could knock up 60 in this one'.

We used to go early for the big meetings – Internationale, Laurels, Spring Classic – to make sure we got a 'box'. These were the sets of seats with a table type thing they used to have on the third and fourth bends. We once took my mum and dad to watch a match against Hackney. We treated them to a meal in the grandstand. As we were going in, Mum, bless her, was looking around and I asked her what she was looking for. She said she was looking for the boxes we came early to get on a normal night. We had always told her we were going early so we could get a box and she had envisaged a pile of boxes – orange boxes or tea crates, I think – which you could grab to sit on at the start of the meeting!

I'm not a great one for razzamatazz – loud music, fireworks, etc – but as has been said before, promoters promoting seems to have gone. Changing times, I suppose. I still live in the days of *Blaze Away*, the National Anthem and that damn *El Paso* country and western song which I swear they used to play at least three times a night.

I also think that clubs use too many riders in a season. There are less and less loyal servants of one club and I wonder if supporters today do not think 'will we win or will we lose?' but 'who will we have riding for us, how many of our own riders, how many guests and how many will be British?'

Paul Hiscock: One of the features that all tracks had was a signature tune played by a brass band – pre-recorded, of course. I think the West Ham tune was the RAF March Past and all the track staff came out, followed by the riders who were introduced to the crowd.

In terms of atmosphere, it always seemed more exciting when the lights in the stadium were dimmed and the only lighting was on the track. West Ham, like a number of other tracks, had a rather fancy hut by the starting gate where the start marshal kept the various flags and that was covered in coloured lights – it all made the event of a Tuesday night at the speedway seem a little bit more special.

Centre greens were also kept in pristine condition but crowds were good in those days and that always helps to create an atmosphere.

Programme notes were always interesting – not the banal rubbish we read today. Where did those good times go and what happened to the art of promotion? You never see any adverts in shops, etc, like there used to be.

The sport is one of the best-kept secrets but I think it is in terminal decline thanks to promoters who believe that 14 meetings a season is what the public want. Crazy!

Tony Lethbridge: It all seemed more free and easy in the past with far less silly bureaucracy. Life was simpler and fans were far less cynical, while there were fewer attractions for people

Howdy Byford sings a tune accompanied by guitarist Len Silver.

to spend their money on and draw them away from speedway. Crowds were good, even for a filler meeting, and promoters (who really promoted) gave them better value for money. They often put on extra attractions such as sidecars, scramble bikes and karts. At Exeter, Len Silver and Howdy Byford would often take the microphone and sing during the interval

Len was always the showman and once, after high diver Stanley Lindberg finished his act, Len was persuaded to climb halfway up the tower and jump into the tank of water. Apparently, he was paid an extra 75p for doing it but, unknown at the time, he hit his head on the tank and nearly drowned.

As regards the bikes, you cannot stop technical advancement. The top riders now also compete in the continental leagues, so it would be impossible to save money by making them all ride two-valve Jawas again. The rulebook is certainly in need of sorting out.

Jeff Davies: The racing in the past always seemed to be much closer than it is today, so I would like to see more evenly matched teams and riders. The points limit necessitates clubs bringing in riders on very low averages to fit into the limit, but they are not competitive and hence the field gets very spread.

Richard Bott: I would love to have been reporting and watching speedway when it was absolutely huge in the immediate post-war years. What do I miss? Tracks like Blackbird Road, always one of my favourites, Hackney's Waterden Road, Belle Vue's Hyde Road and, of course, Wembley and 'World Final night'.

What would I like to see reintroduced to speedway? The second-half heats and rider of the night final. Fans are short-changed these days.

Roly Clarke: I miss the glitter of the chrome on the bikes under floodlights, wide cow-horn handlebars, seeing cars displaying speedway stickers, the second-half, deeper tracks, upright engine bikes (the racing was better) and the characters that every track seemed to have.

Bryan Newbold: Where do I start? I know it's a cliche often rolled out by fans of a certain age like myself, but the fun seems to have gone out of speedway these days. Riders seem to flit from team to team and youngsters don't have the same riders to cheer on from one season to the next. When I started going to speedway, the top riders were synonymous with their tracks. Leicester had Ray Wilson, King's Lynn had Terry Betts, Swindon had Barry Briggs, Belle Vue had Ivan Mauger, etc. Not only that, but there were riders in those days who added an extra dimension to the evening's entertainment, such as Malcolm Brown, Jack Millen, Frank Auffret and Garry Middleton. Many a time I've seen riders paying a visit to the referee's box to 'put their own point of view across', ride through the tapes in a fit of pique, or exchange handbags at dawn with another rider. These days, the sport is far too serious and much of the fun has been diluted.

Other things I miss (and before anyone accuses me of being an old fart who's living in the past, I realise that speedway, like any other sport, has to move with the times and not be stuck in the dark ages) are chrome-plated bikes, leathers as opposed to baggy pyjamas, the smell of Castrol R, cow-horn handlebars, banana seats, straight-through exhausts, fans hanging over the safety fence, etc.

Paul Jeffries: What speedway needs, above all, is a presence in London. That's where the media is. Sad to say, most of the stadiums are just memories now. The BSPA should club together and buy Wimbledon, now, before it's too late. Because, aside from Belle Vue, London is where speedway's great history and tradition is centred. And the media doesn't really want to know about sports that don't happen in the capital.

We all hanker after the mythical 'good old days', but don't forget that speedway makes its

Garry Middleton, seen here holding aloft the KO Cup in 1971, was never afraid to ruffle feathers and cause a storm.

own rules. If speedway was really truly better with everyone on two-valve uprights, leg-trailing, on cinders, then that's what we would still have, because the powers-that-be would make the rules that way. There are reasons for changes, there must have been, or why would we have made them? It's their livelihoods, they must know what works best. But what I really crave above all is to go back to a simple league system of two points for a win, one point for a draw, and the team with most points are the champions.

Doug Nicolson: I really miss the quality of the racing; going to watch in decent stadiums, like White City (Glasgow), Hampden, Wimbledon, Wembley and Shawfield; showmen promoters like Hoskins, Redmond, Silver and Fearman; world class riders coming to Scotland for league meetings; seeing the sport through the eyes of a starry-eyed teenager.

I would like to see a limited second-half reintroduced, so that juniors – formerly number eights and nines – would race against both teams' reserves. This might re-establish a route into the team for juniors and might ultimately get more British riders riding in the Premier League.

Dennis Lindo: Speedway in the past always seemed to be more fun. The promoters tried very hard to entertain and bring in the crowds. I can remember at Middlesbrough seeing a stunt diver called Don Lindberg, who set himself on fire and dived off a platform into a large tank of flaming water. The Royal Signals White Helmets display team were interval attractions on more than one occasion. Celebrities such as Pat Phoenix would open the season. We also had the Sabrina Trophy – I don't know much about her career but I remember her being driven around the track. She was a beautiful girl.

I can remember Ivan Mauger winding the crowd up by jumping the safety fence and heading up to the referee's box to voice his complaints. I can also recall two riders, I think it was Exeter's Len Silver and Howdy Byford, coming onto the centre green at the interval and entertaining the crowd by singing and playing guitars.

The end-of-season would see a lot of high jinx with the promoter usually getting flour-

The 60s-style victory parade, this time featuring Wolverhampton and Norwich.

bagged by the riders. There was certainly a lot more fun in those days. Sadly, the fun aspect is missing today and there is very little atmosphere at some tracks I've visited of late.

I would like to see the promoters doing their jobs and actually promoting the sport rather than constantly trying to cut costs and devaluing the product. We're told that deep tracks provide the best racing but tracks are consistently prepared slick. We often hear on television riders saying: "It's slick out there and difficult to pass." Surely, if they can provide better racing, they should do so.

Two crowd-pleasers from the National League era of the 70s and 80s, Barney Kennett of Canterbury and Rye House's Kelvin Mullarkey.

I would also like all team members to wear the traditional race bibs. They looked much better than the current one-piece suits with the team insignia disappearing into the background. I think it looks so unprofessional when I see guests wearing baggy football shirts.

Ian Martin: I would like to see the tactical rides that try to contrive close meetings done away with. The Joker, too, in the Speedway World Cup. To me, it is nothing more than cheating the public. I also miss the yellow/black helmet cover. These days, under lights, I sometimes get mixed up between the yellow and the white.

Harry Ward: I miss the riders with character, like Jack Millen, Kelvin Mullarkey and Olle Nygren. It was an experience, an event to look forward to for the whole week, but now, sadly, it has become a habit really.

I also miss Frank Ebdon refereeing – he was swift on the two minutes and got meetings moving; bikes without silencers; West Ham beating Hackney; riders waiting on the track for the two minutes; the 13-heat formula with second-halves; the Golden Helmet and Silver Sash; tactical substitutes; the list is endless.

Steve Johnston: The variety of teams, colours, and souvenirs especially – where are the sellers with their photos and badges on a large board like at West Ham? The magazine sellers, who would walk around? The access to the pits area/approaches, where you could get an autograph/photo? The pits tea ladies – I'm biased here, as my daughter Jenna would help do this in the pits at Arena-Essex (sorry, Lakeside) with Rose until it was deemed 'unprofessional'. What better way to lose a willing helper and four regular fans!

Andrew Edwards: British riders in British teams. Unless we go back to basics and get more young British riders to fill our own teams, then British speedway is going nowhere. An Elite League match now seems to be filled to the brim with foreign riders, and not even the top foreign riders we used to have in the 70s and 80s, but quite often very forgettable riders who are average in ability. That's why I much prefer to support our National League (third tier) and the British youth meetings. That's the future where we can produce our own talent and get out of the era of Britain being in the international third division. Johnnie Hoskins must be spinning in his grave.

Bob Radford: Atmosphere, anticipation, tension, crowds, characters, presentation, promotion. Sorry, but to me, and clearly many others, it has all slowly disappeared. We need status and respect and the

Time for the fans – Coventry and England's Jim Lightfoot obliges his admirers.

sense of occasion – the sport has largely lost them all through several decades.

Derek Chalmers: I think the bikes of today are too specialised. I can only talk of the bikes in the 80s, but I think they seemed more versatile. You would get a rider finish last in his first race, who would change the rear sprocket and come out and win all the rest. I think we should get rid of the new exhausts and go back to the lower revving engines, with lower costs for riders and hopefully it will produce closer racing.

David Hoggart: The close camaraderie between riders, fans and promoters. It was always very social and I only remember a warm feeling about speedway in the past. Despite the onward journeys, everyone seemed to have so much time for each other.

I'm not a lover of the current tactical ride, I can see benefits but it's not for me. A return to a tactical sub would see all of a team's points earned on the race track and not through the rulebook.

Martin Rogers: The 60s and 70s were such optimistic and exciting times and the sport seemed to be moving forward in a sustainable way. It's hard to get the same vibe today. Of course, having been living here in Australia and away from the UK scene for so long, we don't have quite the same intimate knowledge of what's happening now, but I'd like to see an end to the nonsense of full-time doubling-up and the abolition of guests.

The trusty two-valve Jawa was easier than the JAP to ride and low on maintenance costs.

Pete Rout: Overtaking, team-riding, rider loyalty and consistent team line-ups from one season to the next, the riders' lap with no helmets at the start of the meeting, individual riding styles and distinctive leathers, Golden Helmet match-races, two-valve Jawas, straight-through exhaust pipes and the smell of Castrol R.

Steve Casey: I miss the smell of the old un-silenced JAPs and Jawas. Everyone who has ever been always mentions the smell. Castrol R and methanol is a unique aroma which the new engines don't quite seem to replicate. There was also nothing quite like the second-half scratch races as young upstarts had the odd chance to race against the senior riders. I remember a junior rider beating Alan Wilkinson, who was the Aces' captain at the time, in a scratch heat to qualify for the second-half final. The track was pretty slick by then and the lad made the gate and couldn't be caught. Wilkie was, how shall I say it, miffed! But it was a talking point for a while.

I know things progress but I miss the original body colours where the team logo was clearly visible and not just a list of sponsors. I just about 'get' team race-suits, but the emblem should always be crystal clear. The other big miss is Test matches. These could be pretty hard affairs with plenty of needle, but they would be too difficult to organise these days.

Geoff Theobald: Personalities. Now you have to be more professional, more PC, all health and safety. Youngsters are no longer allowed to ride round with their favourite. Whatever happened to wearing a rosette of your favourite? Riders get fined for anything, as do promoters if they say anything out of line. Len's too old to leap any longer, but when was the last time you saw a promoter actually promote? No-one is allowed to be different any longer, and the fans have little to react to.

I also miss individual meetings that mean something. The Laurels and the Internationale at Wimbledon were great traditional events that drew crowds from every track to support their star man. Now, even for the ELRC, top riders don't bother to turn up, so why should Joe Public?

What can be done?

1. Standardise the machinery in league racing to cut the basic cost of the sport for the riders, and thereby keep admission prices sensible.

2. Find a way to allow teams to pick the best seven they can, without having to select based upon averages. Too many riders are 'fillers' due to the system and that affects the quality of the product.

3. As the cost of going to meetings increases, so promoters have to find ways to give better value, without adding to the cost. They could use the resources they already have better.

When there is a delay between heats, why do not all tracks have an interview – in full view of everyone on the centre green, rather than tucked away in the pits – with riders, promoter, fans, mechanics or past riders?

Keep the public entertained. Promoters need to think outside the box. We have all been to meetings where there is a delay due to riders being sent to hospital and, unfortunately, we have to wait. Newcomers to the sport are immediately put off by having to sit/stand around with nothing to entertain them. Do they return after such an experience?

Riders love pulling wheelies and the crowd enjoy it, so why not have wheelie competitions, with the crowd to judge the winner by the most noise? Or the fastest one-lap competition?

Lakeside had a wheel-changing competition for mechanics and the crowd get involved, as do the riders, encouraging their man.

Intervals? Fine, if you want to go and get a drink, but otherwise it's another delay with nothing happening. Why not do something on the centre green to entertain those who are just standing there?

David Beresford: More settled teams, being able to see the bikes which are now hidden beneath a plethora of covers, old style race-jackets, yellow and black helmet covers, sensible tactical substitute rules, 13-heat format, the old Hyde Road stadium, the *Speedway Mail*, the list is endless really. Happiness is 40-38. A return to the old 13-heat programme formula and second-half. Why complicate something so simple?

Mark Wilkinson: I miss the one-off World Final but it will never make a return, and I miss the magic ingredient of the crop of top USA riders that speedway benefited hugely from in the 70s and 80s. The sport has been very much the poorer since.

I'd like to see tactical substitutes re-introduced. Its removal has taken away an important aspect of team matches which the double-points measure cannot replace. If re-introduced, it would need to be in a modified form, though. Perhaps permitted when a team is eight points behind, rather than six, and if a rider is used as a tac sub, then he's ineligible for Heat 15 – and safeguard the three rides minimum per rider.

Robert Wiles: The thing that I miss most about speedway in the past is passing. Modern machinery, tyres and track preparation all work against overtaking. Whilst the racing is faster

The Americans brought colour and razzmatazz to the British League in the late 70s and early 80s. Lining up before the England v USA Test at Wimbledon in 1983 we have (left to right): Shawn Moran, Mike Faria, Bobby Schwartz, Dennis Sigalos, Lance King, Kelly Moran, Rick Miller.

than it used to be, whoever makes the gate usually wins and that wasn't the case when tracks were deeper and motors more 'torquey'.

It's easy to yearn for a return to the 'good old days', but to someone from my era, it would be great to see upright engines and open exhausts make a comeback. Bring back the Rotrax JAP and the ESO!

Seriously, though, I really believe that something should be done to control the costs of machinery, and particularly engines. The new generation of high-revving lay-down units must be frighteningly expensive to maintain in even remotely competitive order. I would also like to see tracks being prepared with more dirt on them to make the racing more interesting again.

Alan Jones: To go back not too long ago in time, there was a full calendar of fixtures week in, week out. Nowadays there are far too many gaps and, as a consequence, the continuity is broken and momentum lost to keep the occasional supporter hooked.

I'd like to give team managers more scope within the rules to make a difference and so change the balance of a meeting if it is slipping away from their team.

John Farr: The machinery seemed to be more raw, and look meaner, than today's clinical bikes. It was louder and smellier in days gone by, which, in my book, made it more exciting. Also, the personality side of speedway is sadly lacking today. Of the current crop of top riders, only Chris Holder has that warm character which endears him more easily to the fans.

I also miss the one-off World Final, although I do acknowledge that the present system is a fairer way of finding the true World Champion,

I'd like to see a reduction in outright speed in speedway, with reduced equipment costs as a result. I've always said that speedway in an enclosed stadium shouldn't necessarily be all about 'million-miles-an-hour' speeds. It should be about sensible speeds where riders are

Poole's Colin 'Joe' Gooddy was one who liked a 'word' with the referee.

more confident of racing each other more closely. Closer racing equals more excitement, equals more spectators.

Ken Burnett: I miss the banter between riders/promoters and referees. They could make a boring meeting good and send you home with something to talk about.

I would also like to see riders not only trained to ride motorbikes, but also in the art of being interviewed. Some seem as if they have come straight out of Jeremy Kyle!

Food outlets are so out of date, too, the sport needs to get away from the burger and chips look and move with the times. Stadiums are out of the ark too, but it's difficult to improve them, I know, when most promoters don't own them.

Greg Unwin: The thing I miss most about speedway is the old World Championship where often well over 300 riders worldwide would set off at the start of the season to attempt to become the next World Champion. You never knew who would be the champion until the Final was virtually over. Under today's Grand Prix system, you know that one of 15 named riders is going to be the next champion before a wheel is turned.

I wish television text services would re-introduce the speedway results to their menus. This used to be provided but now that most people have a computer, the excuse would be that the service is no longer needed. They just log on to Speedway Updates. All other sports still seem to enjoy the services and latest results while speedway has just disappeared.

Clive Inwood: The loss of characters like Joe Gooddy and the excitement of riders storming up to the referee's box after a controversial decision. They probably had a quick cup of tea up there but it got the crowd going and released tension rather than the bland silence of the politically correct today where all fans can do is stand around looking at nothing whilst it all goes on elsewhere. Referees never changed their mind in those days either.

It will never happen, but I would like to see the re-introduction of standard equipment and grippy tracks. The bikes are too powerful for real grippy tracks these days.

Phil Rice: There was more real racing then and big stars were in our league. At Belle Vue, we might only see Fundin, Briggs and later on Ole Olsen and his ilk once or maybe twice a season. Now we see what stars are left here up to five times a season.

I'm not technical but those that are say the bikes are too powerful, but they certainly seem easier to ride. The tracks appear too slick. The riders seem to have taken so much out of the sport that there is nothing left and promotions are holding on, sometimes by a thread. Costs must be reduced. The sport is so badly run with so much self-interest and not for the greater good. If I was in the sport, doubtless I would have to do the same. We do need a supremo, but who? There is no-one who could transform the sport.

Steve Wilks: The fact that it was 'Make it a Date, Friday at Eight'. There was speedway every Friday at Hackney. Nowadays at Lakeside, it seems to be every other Friday at best. Also, there used to be some great individual meetings at Hackney – the Champions' Chase, Superama and the London Riders' Championship spring to mind. I'd like to see the Golden Helmet re-introduced. I enjoyed seeing Dave Morton, in particular, take on the best around Hackney.

Dave Ede: I would love to see more young British riders coming through; perhaps the Premier and National leagues haven't produced the home-grown talent hoped for and I think this problem needs to be addressed urgently. Should second-halves be brought back? As they were mostly 'split purses', it probably wouldn't have the desired effect of helping junior riders.

Backtrack reader Guy Keeley sent us this pic of his old King's Lynn programme board, complete with league sponsor Gulf Oil stickers.

Paul Kerry: Too few British riders. It was great to have a smattering of Europeans and Aussies to add colour and spice to meetings, but these days some teams are all foreign. Also, racing every night of the week somewhere, except Sunday.

Alan Thompsett: I miss free stickers! Such a silly thing, but a free sticker, stuck on a programme board, sums up the best days of speedway for me. You can't beat the good times, recalled by the sight of a 'Gulf British Speedway League' sticker on a dust-encrusted programme board.

Chris Gosling: The British League, in its heyday, was a fantastic product. There were 22 teams and you only got to see them once, so you really looked forward to seeing Barry Briggs when Swindon came, or Ivan Mauger or Ole Olsen. Having said that, all the No.1s were pretty good, like Ray Wilson, Ronnie Moore, Martin Ashby and John Louis, etc, and there were lots of other good riders and characters.

Racing was far less predictable back then. You occasionally saw a reserve rider have a good

Capital gains: Olle Nygren, Colin Pratt and Ken McKinlay, when Wimbledon, Hackney and West Ham enjoyed great rivalry in London.

night and produce an unexpected result, like Clive Featherby beating Mauger. I also enjoyed the second-half racing, which was often very competitive at King's Lynn.

Nowadays, I would like to see more dirt on tracks, closer racing and fewer team changes. Very few teams keep the same group of riders together like they used to.

Dick Partridge: The bikes are too quiet. Part of the spectacle is, or rather was, the sound of the bikes. I accept that we need to be good neighbours but it has gone too far. We need to stop doffing our caps at neighbours living in homes that were not even built when tracks were established, and we need neighbours to accept 15-20 one minute races, about 30 times per year, usually finishing before 10 pm.

The most important thing to re-introduce is second-half racing because there are so many advantages to an old style second-half. The junior leagues that, for a while, became a substitute for second-half racing were all well and good, but there was no real progression. One could become a big fish in a little pool, and sometimes stepping up to the next level proved too much. A well thought out second-half programme would allow ambitious raw talent to show us all what they could really do.

One other much-needed improvement is the selection of music between races. Speedway supporters range in age from toddlers to geriatrics, but the sounds played at most meetings that I attend (Ipswich and Mildenhall) are nearly all of the same genre, that is to say recent shrill-manufactured pop music. There is certainly a place for a percentage of this music, but having often spoken to others about it, I'm sure people would appreciate a far broader mix. The music is an area that requires much more thought and consideration to help make a night at the speedway the best possible value.

Peter Lush: What do I miss? Teams in London! When I started watching the sport, there were four major teams in London: Wembley, Wimbledon, Hackney and West Ham, which meant great local derbies and rivalry. Crayford, Rye House, Romford, Rayleigh and Canterbury were close as well. Now all we have are Lakeside and Rye House, neither of which are really in London. Unfortunately – and rugby league has the same problem – without a base in London, the sport's profile will always be lower than it should be for the quality of entertainment and endeavour provided.

What would I re-introduce? Apart from the Wembley Lions, some form of second-half. Looking back at old programmes, we usually got 18 races in the 'old days'. While I'm OK with 15-heat matches, if a match is one-sided, two or three extra races could make for a better evening's entertainment, and maybe give junior riders an opportunity. But there is an awful lot that I like about today's speedway.

Alan Johns: There is nothing I would like to see re-introduced from yesterday that has been tried and dropped. What is needed is a total rethink and marketing of the sport/entertainment package to appeal to young adrenalin junkies with cash to spend on excitement. I say 'young', because have you noticed how many supporters in the crowds are 'silverheads'? What happens when they can't get there to watch the sport they have loyally supported for years? There will only be riders, mechanics, team managers, track graders and, of course, the promoters left to watch, so it will be 'British Speedway, RIP'. It's time to think outside the box to generate a new generation of supporters.

John Brownhill: British speedway today is in dire straits. All the 'proper' promoters of yesteryear, who ran their tracks as a business, are gone and all we now have are the 'hobby' promoters, businessmen who do not promote the sport in the true sense of the word.

Having Grand Prix riders in the Elite League means that everyone has to spend huge amounts of money to race against them and the advent of doubling-up riders from the Premier League has

The way the pits used to be – Mike Broadbank with his bare essentials.

now passed these expenses down the rider chain, even into the National League, which now has a 'win-at-all costs' mentality for some tracks. These costs are passed on to the supporters and, quite honestly, some of the line-ups in the so-called Elite League this season bordered on farce – guests from the Premier League to cover for the non-availability of foreign riders for a multitude of reasons, but no reduction in admission prices.

The rulebook and all the various and varied calculations of riders' averages has become so complex that even the team managers and, in some cases, the referees are baffled. The speed of the bikes today has now forced the introduction of air-fences but these are not all foolproof, as we have seen.

My great memories of speedway are the large crowds that used to attend, the friendly rivalry of supporters, the occasional on-track dispute which was part and parcel of the evening's entertainment and the memories of the many brave young men who provided the thrills. We made many friends at speedway, but sadly some are no longer with us and many have stopped going over the years due to the poor racing, poor track maintenance and poor value for money.

Living, as I do, in Cornwall, my nearest track is Plymouth but I have never seen a meeting there. I did used to attend the Clay Country track at Nanpean where the Trelawny team rode and it really was a superb little track with many racing lines. We were fortunate to see the early days of Chris Harris, Matej Zagar and Ben Barker there, along with Steve Masters, whose style suited the venue.

On the rare occasions I visit my home city Sheffield, I do go to Owlerton and I have great respect for Neil Machin, who has run the operation there for 21 years as a proper business. Sadly, Neil has had enough; I hope that his efforts have been appreciated.

I really don't know where British speedway goes from here. There are so many problems and not enough British riders who the fans can associate with. How Len Silver can say the sport has never been better, I just cannot believe.

Richard Clark: What do I miss most about speedway past? My innocence.

What would I like to see re-introduced today? Hyde Road, Plough Lane, Powderhall, Smallmead, Cowley, Waterden Road, Dudley Wood, Odsal, Thornton Road, The Shay, the County Ground, Station Road, Craven Park, Cleveland Park . . .

Julia Wilson: What I miss most is the smell, the crowds and the atmosphere. I remember

Julia Wilson with her twin brothers Jonathan and Clive Read – all showing their allegiance to Coventry in the days when supporters collected badges and wore hats, scarves and rosettes.

we always had to queue in the car from Brandon village up to the stadium. Sometimes, we even abandoned the car in the village and walked, as we knew it would be quicker to get there on foot. I liked having lots of people all in together, with good-natured cheering and conversations. Unlike football, speedway supporters are united by their love of the sport, so it doesn't matter whether you stand by a home or away supporter, you can have a chat. I also miss the fact that you don't have the same riders riding for your team for a consecutive number of years. Today, it seems like the rider you cheered for on your team last week is riding for the opposition the next – and vice-versa.

Stephen Roberts: Where does one start? I miss the fact that you never know from one year to the next who'll be wearing your team's colours, which doesn't allow for familiarity with the team you support. There are too many foreigners of no real ability. The over-emphasising of averages and limits towards team-building and all the petty rule changes that, at the end of the day, doesn't actually bring any new fans to the sport. Why change a rule that works perfectly well and has for years?

Two things I would immediately change would be fixed gate positions and the make-up of the one-to-seven of a team. If a team manager wishes to place his star man at No.2 or No.4 for tactical purposes, then so be it. Also, choosing gate positions involved tactical moves and fixed gates is often unfair in that a team has successive inside and/or outside gates, which gives a disadvantage as dirt moves around during the meeting.

Richard Parsons: I miss the superstars of yesterday, like Collins, Mauger, Olsen, Lee, Michanek, Penhall and Gundersen. It was always a thrill when they were racing. I also miss the noise of the crowd, I miss England not being a world force, I miss a British Final that means something and I miss the World Final.

Gary Moore: On a personal level, I miss the buzz and excitement that I used to get when I was a kid. Waking up for school on a Friday morning, the first thing I would do was have a peek through the blinds to see what the weather was like. Also, I still miss regular night-time speedway. I know I'm stating the obvious but speedway, as a spectacle, is so much better under floodlights. I find Sunday afternoon meetings can be pretty soulless. Still, beggars can't be choosers and having speedway in Glasgow is the main thing.

Another thing sadly lacking is the old school promoters. Guys like Neil Macfarlane, who would stir things up a bit and get a bit of light hearted banter and controversy going. Nothing seems to happen at the speedway these days, it just seems to be 'get in, give us your money, get out again'.

Arnie Gibbons: I miss the crowds. It can feel very dispiriting being one of half-a-dozen souls standing on the third bend in a stadium devoid of atmosphere. I do miss the sudden spike in noise when something dramatic happens.

Also, tracks staging a regular meeting every week on the same day. It used to be a case of, 'it's Monday, the day I go to speedway, even if it's only some rubbishy pairs meeting'. Because I've not lived near a speedway track since Long Eaton closed, the only track I've attended on a regular basis was when I returned to my roots and became a Smallmead regular for its last three seasons. I still miss the racing at Long Eaton and the sense of belonging I felt on walking through the gates at Smallmead.

Mike Turner: In the past, it seemed there was always a meeting happening somewhere around the country and you need not look far for an evening's racing. Part and parcel of speedway was the individual and sponsored meeting. We used to enjoy many at Sheffield with mostly a guaranteed top rider(s) taking part. Many is the time the kids delayed their homework and we finished work early to drive off for a meeting. That is something missing today, the lack of those individual clashes, which had the fans flocking through the turnstiles. Let's hope speedway survives these hard times and has the resurgence it deserves with a healthy league system to bring back some thrilling competition.

Paul Rickett: Ooh, this one's going to upset a lot of people but I actually miss the shenanigans at the start of a race. The riders shoved the tapes almost to breaking point – Ivan Mauger was legendary at it – and refs must have gone home with headaches. Of course, the starts were ragged and things are much more disciplined these days, but it just added so much

The 1984 BLRC at Hyde Road and Chris Morton (outside) and Hans Nielsen sit still as Erik Gundersen nudges the tapes.

to the drama and excitement.

In team racing, which is the bread and butter of what we do, for starters I'd like to see tactical substitutes brought back. Ditched to cut rider costs, the tactical rule was brought in and, for me, it's a massive negative. Try explaining to a newbie that a rider who finishes second can earn more points than the bloke who's won; there's no wonder we're struggling to attract new fans. Tac-subs also cranked up the drama quotient and made team managers earn their corn.

We all talk about speedway's problems and I believe that when we harp on about bringing this back or that back to make it better, then it underlines the worrying situation the sport is in. Four blokes thundering around a track for four laps . . . why on earth have we made that so difficult?

Andy Povey: Big crowds and travelling on the supporters' coach to away meetings. I used to love that, feeling part of a group following your team up and down the country. Winning was always nice, but the camaraderie with our group of friends was brilliant.

Debbie Howland: I miss the drinks in the bar after meetings with the riders. Years ago,

John Louis and Don Godden on test day for the new Weslake four-valve engine at Hackney in December 1974.

there was no racing in the leagues of Poland, Sweden, etc, so the riders had more time. It was good to chat to them and get to know them a bit, which made the racing better to watch because you felt more a part of it.

Eddie Garvey: Monkey masks, open-face helmets, riders in their own leathers, Daytona boots, wide handlebars, Weslake engines, Elastoplast-laden throttles, Gulf Oil sponsorship and, most of all, race-jackets. I have been fascinated by race-jackets since the first night I went to Belle Vue, the old Aces race bib is a work of art on its own – classic design, fantastic colour combination and made by Astrapi Products in Stockport. It's a love affair that has transcended years and leads to a collection that has taken on a life of its own.

I would re-introduce the Weslake engine. There has never been a better looking machine than a Weslake-powered speedway bike, especially when it was adorned with Union Jack guards and a Shane Hearty Helmets fork cover!

John Davidson: Speedway seems a long way in my past now. For one thing, I've lived in the US since 1988. I've kept up with World Championship results in the loosest of ways and seen occasional meetings on TV. I always used to think that speedway died for me around 1981, because that's when Ivan stopped being truly competitive. In retrospect, the sport was changing and I was growing older. I was but one of many who found the sport less captivating during that decade, allowing it to drift away.

I'm too far removed from the sport now to say what should be re-introduced. It particularly saddens me that the sport in Britain is in such sorry shape, but there are too many alternative entertainments now. There's live sport on TV every night and we live in a culture where people are content to live virtually in an armchair. It amazes me that I used to take two buses and walk about a mile to get to Belle Vue from my home. I'm pretty certain I wouldn't do that now.

John Murphy: I loved the 70s. I was still at school and speedway was such a buzz, so new to me. I felt so lucky because all my mates were into football and thought me a bit weird. It was a time for so many possibilities.

Mark Sawbridge: I miss the old British and National leagues. I hanker for the days when both divisions contained 18-19 teams. There was a variety about the structure that is missing now, particularly in the Elite League. These were also the days when 60-70 per cent of British League riders were British. I have nothing whatsoever against foreign riders (see the earlier chapter for my favourite three), but there is something very remiss about having only one or two home-grown riders in each team.

I think the decision to scrap the Elite League KO Cup is a retrograde step, and I would like to see it re-introduced.

Clive Read: The crowds and electric atmosphere I remember as a kid are gone and that's a real shame. There was always a buzz as you arrived at the track, and there is something about being in a large crowd that heightens the senses, whether it's a big sporting or music event.

There's a tribal sense of belonging to a group of fans, cheering on your heroes and enjoying banter with the opposing team. Speedway is lucky in that the crowds are knowledgeable and will get on with each other (most of the time!) and will always applaud a great race, exemplified, too, by the riders themselves shaking hands at the end of a hard-fought four laps.

Travelling round the country and seeing different tracks for the first time was always a thrill. There were very few we didn't get to in those early years. At Coventry, we were lucky in having Ole Olsen at the top of his powers, so he could be relied upon to get a bagful of points. Even though I was very small, I had a good pair of lungs and would lead chants of "Ole, Ole, Ole", much to the amusement of other fans who couldn't quite believe a nine or 10-year-old could shout so loud!

Speedway is still a great sport but has a lot of problems in the UK, which reflect how badly it's been run for decades. There are all sorts of sociological and financial reasons behind this

Chris Holder was a popular winner of the 2012 British GP at Cardiff, where he was joined on the rostrum by Krzysztof Kasprzak and Antonio Lindback. Holder went on to win the World Championship that year – a great testament to the fact that he began his career in the third tier of the British league speedway at Isle of Wight.

but, overall, it has lost its marketing appeal to a mass audience, when there is so much else to compete for people's leisure time.

You only have to look on the continent to see that it is still a great sport with passionate fans. This year, I went to the Bydgoszcz GP with my brother and the atmosphere was electric, the presentation was great and the racing was brilliant – dish up that each week and fans will start to come back. Money is not solely the answer but you need to re-capture people's attention and give them a reason why they would want to go to speedway. People want close racing, a sense of excitement and entertainment where the result is in doubt to the end.

The riders, as entertainers, are still there, it's probably that with a generally lower profile for the Elite League compared with Poland and Scandinavia, the PR isn't ramped up in the way it was. This is ironic when we have so much more instant technology available – Twitter, Facebook and the web generally. I also follow ice hockey and the Coventry Blaze always send out an email to me as a season ticket holder before each match, reminding me who the opposition are, why it'll be a great game and that I should bring along friends. I have done so and they've loved it. Speedway can do so much more.

Brian Burford: What I miss most about the old days is the genuine stars that we had and the depth of talent. Away from the top eight in the world, and a few exceptions, the standard is low. I look at some of the 'world class' riders and think that many of them wouldn't have lived with the opposition that was around 20 years ago, never mind 30. The fact that riders like Hancock and Gollob are still competitive and at the top of their game is because the generation that followed are just not good enough to turn them over.

I am encouraged by the arrival of Emil Sayfutdinov, Darcy Ward and Chris Holder who are genuinely world class riders. Ward is the most talented rider I've seen since the early 90s but unless the promoters do what they're supposed to do, promote, they will only ever be stars in their own field. We haven't had a genuine superstar since Bruce Penhall quit. When I first started going, it was the young riders that interested me because that could have been me in a few years' time. The 30 or 40-plus riders don't interest the new generation of supporters because it's like watching your dad, it's your dad's era – and that's not cool. Hopefully Tai Woffinden's success can interest his and a new generation of fans.

Spreading the word, Exeter co-promoter Pete Lansdale in 1967.

Gary Miles: Speedway used to be an interactive sport for the fans. Today, Health and Safety laws have moved the spectator further from the action. I remember leaning on the boards at Canterbury feeling the draught of the bikes and the spray of the shale in my face. The secret to getting part of the action today is to get yourself a job on the centre-green.

I would like to see a re-introduction of a proper second-half. Nowadays, the meeting is run over 15 races and that's the end of the night. I remember, not so long ago, there used to be 20 races per meeting which included the main event, junior races and a rider of the night final. Now, with only 15 races at over a pound a race, speedway is an expensive night out. With travel costs, entrance fee, programme, food and drink, one person can easily spend £30, so bringing back a second-half will make it more cost effective.

Martin Smith: The lack of local, or at least British, riders within Elite and Premier League teams is a serious concern, as is rider continuity from season to season to establish a team identity that supporters can feel part of and relate to.

Fifteen heats is also too few for a modern night's entertainment but times have changed and I can't see the modern day Elite or Premier rider hanging around for an extra ride after the main meeting. Time for promoters to promote. Let's have a second-half with amateur or junior riders, handicap racing, endurance races, flying laps – be inventive.

Alex Mackenzie: Mostly, I miss the availability. I used to go every week and it only took 20 minutes to get there. Now it's Cardiff once a year and Lakeside, which is probably two hours away.

Also, of course, crowds, but more than that, the Castrol R smell. There must be a way to re-introduce that smell. It would be like the smell of baking bread or roasting coffee, the crowds would not be able to resist.

Craig Saul: The starting point for me is the role of the team manager. Ian Thomas was the absolute master of the rulebook, but his rivals also played their own part. Once the traditional tactical subs, extended choice of gate positions and total flexibility on the riding order for the main body of the team disappeared, so too did much of the role of the team manager. And, more importantly, so too did the role of the armchair team managers on the terraces. Take away a spectator's opportunity to strategise on what he or she would do in the next race if given the choice, and that spectator is left merely as just that, an onlooker.

I would bring back the old tac-sub rule. Speedway does need a means to balance out home advantage and keep matches meaningful whenever possible, but I don't believe the traditional rule is as artificial as some of its critics suggest. It requires tactical decision-making and not the lottery of programmed line-ups that the tactical ride relies on. And it's points earned on the track, not off it.

I appreciate that extra rides for leading lights have a cost implication. The compromise might be a 14-heat meeting that lops off the cost of the nominated race, but allows for two tactical subs during the night.

I would also welcome the re-introduction of

Ian Thomas was the master manipulator of the rulebook.

race-jackets and individual kevlars. Team suits certainly create a team feel, but they are hardly optimised when the team logo is hidden in amongst a myriad of sponsors – or occasionally invisible altogether. That's not good branding to me.

Chris Rowsell: What I miss most about speedway past is the quality of racing. Tracks were prepared better then. They bound due to the oil falling on-track and provided grip so that overtaking was more prominent. When I first went to speedway, I saw some meetings run in monsoons and whilst the racing wasn't always that great, the tracks were able to withstand such weather. Now, you only have to sniff rain in the air and the meeting is called off.

I know that it seems odd, but speedway also lost something when riders fighting on the track

became frowned upon and pretty much stopped, with the authorities clamping down on any miscreants. Riders got reputations as 'bad boys' and crowds would increase when they next came to town, if there had been an incident in the previous fixture. I remember a meeting at Reading in 1980, against Swindon, when Steve Gresham had Tony Briggs off in very dubious fashion and when the race was stopped, Barry Briggs came storming out looking to clock Mr. Gresham. The crowd loved it and you knew that they would be back for more the next time the two teams met.

Swindon's American 'hard man' Steve Gresham upset the Briggos at Reading in 1980.

When I first attended, the 70s boom was still going and the promoters probably didn't feel they had to go out

and sell the sport, but as the 80s came, attendances began dropping bit by bit and still they did nothing. By the time the 90s arrived, crowds had dropped to unacceptable levels, but I don't think the promoters remembered or knew how to promote any more.

Steve Wilkes: Speedway is so different now to what it was in the 70s. Teams are now built around averages and because of that, teams change year on year, so there is hardly any familiarity with the riders. The rulebook now seems so complicated, yet this is a sport with just four riders in a race for four laps. What can be simpler? One difference for the better, though, is the tape-touching rule – starts are much fairer without the 'rollers' so prevalent before 1984.

There is nothing wrong with the current 15-heat formula, but what needs to change is the double points from the gate. It could be allowed if a rider starts 15 metres back to earn his corn.

Steve Ridgway: Proper team colours, when your team was more important than the sponsors; crowds at the BLRC; not raining meetings off if it got a bit cloudy; seeing the same riders for the same teams for more than one year at a time, and feeling empathy with 'our' team because they were all locals.

I would re-introduce the one-off Golden Helmet. Not the over-hyped, over-blown, once-a-month 'nominated challenge' rubbish, but the one-off match-race that could suddenly pop up unexpectedly because one rider in tonight's match had beaten the previous holder the day before. There was real excitement about that, because it was so spontaneous and you only had one chance at it. It was a real shame when that went.

Oh, and a proper league, where the team that finishes top is the winner, something which would make the sport seem worthy of consideration as being serious again.

Rob Peasley: I think very little has changed regarding the past and now. If you read the *Speedway News* from 1953, people then were moaning about the same things as they are 60 years on. Apparently, in 1953, the racing wasn't half as good as 1928, etc!

There have been periods when speedway has been more popular with the general public, but the actual product, of four blokes sliding a bike for four laps, has never changed. And the presentation hasn't really either. Maybe that's the problem – speedway has never updated itself for a modern audience. People in 2013 demand more than they did in 1928.

I think you still have good meetings and bad meetings. That has never changed. However, what has changed are crowd sizes. And maybe that's what I miss most – the atmosphere. If there's an on-track incident, you need one set of supporters up in arms, and then the other set of fans joining in the verbal set-to on the terraces. It's not the same when there's only one man and his dog on the terraces. Oxford circa 1985 was real atmosphere.

And there are not as many confrontations on the track as there used to be. I remember a huge kerfuffle at Oxford in 1984, when Hans Nielsen was excluded after Sam Ermolenko took a tumble. It led to Ermolenko's mechanic, who'd gone potty, being manhandled out of the stadium.

A touch of glamour at the BLRC, where each team had a representative in the annual Miss Speedway competition.

Darcy Ward (above) and Emil Sayfutdinov, two of the modern Grand Prix stars who are both capable of going all the way to the top. But will they be part of British speedway in the future?

It made for great entertainment. Maybe British speedway is too sanitised these days.

I would keep the current 15-heat format, as I like having team meetings conclude with a nominated race (Heat 15). Happiness is not 40-38 for me.

However, I would go back to tactical substitutes as I detest the tactical ride with a vengeance. I don't agree with double points being handed out, unless that rider has a handicap at the starting tapes (such as the original Golden Double). It is really, really odd that a rider finishing second in a race can score four points, when the race winner only gets three.

I'd also like to see the restrictions lifted on where the No.1 can line-up. Give the team managers more to do, and bring team tactics back into it a little more. If someone wants their top rider to ride at No.2 or No.4, then let them.

Nick Nicklin: A proper second-half. I feel short-changed these days with just 15 heats all done and dusted in an hour-and-a-half. A 13-heat match followed by seven second-half races, including two or three junior heats, seems just about right to me. That said, I never felt that promoters made the most of second-halves and maybe a more concerted effort could have been made to organise something on a national basis with perhaps a big end-of-season final for riders who had made most appearances or scored most points in second-half racing. This may have discouraged more riders from pulling out of second-half racing or using it to test equipment.

I miss the coach trips. In the late 70s and early 80s when I was a teenager and following the Heathens all over the country, it was unheard of for the Cradley Heath Supporters' Club not to take at least one coach to away fixtures and, in fact, it was the norm to take two or three coaches in the week to places like Poole, Leicester and Sheffield, and up to five at the weekend to Halifax, Swindon, King's Lynn and Belle Vue. It is often quoted that Cradley took 32 coaches to the 1981 World Final. You soon built up a great social circle forging loads of lifelong friendships and created a host of shared memories.

These days the sport is far too expensive for riders, supporters and promoters alike, so I would like to re-introduce, dare I say, the level of amateurism that existed in the 70s. Riders regularly turned up with dirt still on the bike from the last meeting, with leathers to match and the bike precariously sticking out of the boot of the car, with the front wheel removed and stowed on the back seat. I say bike, rather than bikes, as most riders owned just one, although many promotions possessed a track spare to be used in times of emergency by any member of the team. Of course, all bikes had two-valve engines with most maintenance work simple enough to be carried out by the rider himself.

These days the sport is too professional and the level of income generated by the support on the terraces cannot sustain the amount of expenditure the riders require and demand.

Martin Neal: What I miss most about speedway from the past is a strong, well-populated top division featuring the world's top riders. The Elite League these days is a shadow of that. It's still a great sport, though.

Dean Felton: I miss the team aspect. With riders riding for different clubs and doubling up/down, plus guests, etc, the team aspect seems to have been lost. I never thought I would say this, but I would re-introduce the upright engine. It would bring back throttle control and, I believe, better racing.

Christian Weber: International matches. I used to love the Test matches, especially the winter tours of the British Lions or overseas teams to Australia, New Zealand and South Africa. I miss that most.

Re-introducing more variety would be good. League meetings are fine, but it lacks a bit of variety. International matches, or tours of foreign teams, would be good. And I'd like to see a return to a much simpler rulebook, a reduction of guest riders and the return to the old tactical substitute rule instead of the double points joker.

British league clubs should be forced to include more (a minimum number of) UK-based riders (ACU licence holders). There are simply way too many mediocre foreign riders in the leagues these days. To be honest, of the three leagues in the UK (Elite, Premier and National), I enjoy the National League most. It reminds me so much of the old (80s) National League. Clubs like the Kent Kings, or Dudley Heathens, for me represent the true spirit of British speedway.

Derek Barclay: Being a Londoner, I miss the sport being in the capital the most. Oh, for the days of Crayford on Tuesday, White City on Wednesday, Wimbledon on Thursday and Hackney on Friday. I was a teen then but could get to all the tracks by public transport quite simply. The fact that in many places, people can only get to speedway by car these days is a real problem for many youngsters who'd rely then on parents to take them.

I would bring back the 13-heat match format and a full second-half, including junior league racing at all tracks. Track-time in real meetings for people starting out is the thing most missing nowadays and is in danger of throttling the lifeblood of the sport. Something to make machinery less expensive would really help too.

Jez Coupland: The tactical double point ride should be abolished because it's a complete joke. There has to be increased value for money and also better prepared tracks with extra dirt for more racing lines, like you get at Scunthorpe. And somehow limit the engine power to give the rider more throttle control, rather than wringing its neck all the time.

Chris Young: I miss the variety of teams in all the leagues and the fact that British riders are constantly overlooked. I seem to remember that rider replacement didn't feature too often back when I first started watching the sport in the 80s, although it could be that my mind is playing tricks on me.

Chris Camp: We knew our riders and a fair number of the riders of the opposing teams. Almost without fail, they all took time to talk to us and share the emotions and experiences of what we had all just seen. In 1986 at the World Long-track Final, we were there to support Trevor Banks, but we spent a long time after the meeting talking to Peter and Phil Collins and Trevor in the pits, and they all made time to talk to us. It seems today that the riders are too busy to spend time with the supporters.

Over the years, too many tracks have closed, for a wide range of reasons, and speedway needs to be able to adapt to the changing needs of the public. Sadly, the governing bodies involved in running the sport seem to spend most of their time making it difficult for promoters to promote and riders to ride, a situation in which no-one wins.

Glenn Collins: The thing I miss about speedway from the past is the amount of Grand Prix riders who ride over here in the Elite League. A few years ago, if you went to an Elite League match as a neutral, there were top GP riders in every team, which led to more exciting racing. Although the racing is still good today, the GP riders are missed by the fans.

Matthew Lawrence: It has always struck me that the rules were simpler in the past. Nowadays, they are too complicated even for promoters, as I'm sure some of the issues around averages are genuine mistakes because there are rules to apply to other rules in specific circumstances.

I would introduce regional divisions to cut costs, as too many clubs are faced with going out of business due to the costs and it might also encourage more EL and PL teams to track NL teams.

6 MOMENTS TO TREASURE

What is your favourite memory you take from speedway?

Bert Loader: My favourite memory is the many friends I made going to speedway, many of whom I still keep in touch with. We were a jolly lot who went on all the World Final trips abroad all over Europe.

Maurice Plowright: The day Bluey Wilkinson looked through my scrapbook of speedway photos and signed one of himself in his real name, Arthur Wilkinson. Arlington was an unlicensed track then and most riders rode under false names.

Ken Carpenter: I shall always remember the sheer grit and determination of Shawn Moran struggling to mount his bike while on crutches to have an after-meeting practice at Owlerton before going on to win the 1983 World Long-track Final that weekend.

Hans Nielsen disguised as Mike Patrick, dressed in his famous Rupert Bear trousers, popping wheelies, much to the delight and surprise of the fans, during a match-race with the infield presenter Mike Bennett (or was it Peter York?). That still gives me a chuckle.

Wiggy's famous end-of-season fancy dress parties were always great fun and very memorable.

John Hyam: Meeting Ove Fundin in the lift at Wembley Stadium after his first world title victory in 1956, shaking his hand and ignoring the glares from the other people in the lift!

Wally Loak: Interviewing the great Johnnie Hoskins in 1968. That was just unbelievable and then, in 1987, the feeling inside me as I stood in the middle of the trotting track at West Maitland in Australia, where Johnnie had organised his first speedway meeting in 1923, was amazing. I won't forget the time I beat the television boys to interview Anders Michanek after he had just won the World Final in Gothenburg in 1974.

Simon Wigg organised a number of end-of-season fancy dress parties for the riders. Here we see Wiggy (disguised as 'Mr T' from TV's A-Team) with his former great long-track rival and friend Egon Müller, dressed up as a pirate.

Such a dominant force in the 50s, Wimbledon skipper Norman Parker holds the National Trophy after the Dons' success in 1951.

Ron Byford: Ronnie Moore and Briggo winning their world titles and Wimbledon collecting a number of National League titles in the 50s. On a personal note, winning the National Junior Cup at Ipswich as Exeter junior team manager in 1986, which led to me taking on the senior team manager's job at the County Ground.

Peter Jackson: The World Final in 1960, my first visit to the Empire Stadium. As I walked up to my seat, the great crescendo of noise from the crowd cheering and the rattles.

Ken Wrench: My first meeting as announcer at Hyde Road in 1975, Belle Vue v Sheffield. Interviewing Jack Parker, my first speedway hero many years before, at a fans' evening. Going onto the centre green at Wembley with Peter Arnold, a great speedway journalist, when I was helping a friend who was directing the TV coverage. At the presentation, we stood a few feet from Ove Fundin who had just won the world title, surrounded by about 90,000 spectators. Few things can beat that.

Keith Barraclough: The huge crowds at The Shay in the first season of the British League in 1965; seeing Halifax beat Sheffield at Owlerton; and seeing the Dukes win at Belle Vue in the 1966 season when Halifax did the treble – British League champions, KO Cup winners and Northern Cup winners.

Cedric Read: So many, but above all the rest is introducing my children to speedway – my boys aged eight and my daughter aged 11 – and witnessing their excitement on the terraces and the anticipation during the following week ahead of the next fixture.

John Chaplin: The men who used to be my heroes. They were glamorous, daring and I held them in awe. They were my idols and I envied them. But the closer I got to them over the decades, I realised my idols had feet of clay. They were human, just like me.

Tony Emmott: The speedway 'spirit', shown between fans of rival clubs which may be unique in the world of sport.

Cecil Rockey: Helping in the pits, starting up the bikes and having a good old laugh with the riders.

Oliver Chapman: When riders removed the front wheel from their JAP and transported it in the boot of their Cortina, they were much more approachable and mixed with the busloads of supporters when they met at the various service stations en route. In the 60s, we (Leicester) would run three or four 40-seater coaches to places like Hackney, Poole and Exeter, and 12-14 to Coventry.

Michael Mayo: The general respect that riders command, whether from their own followers or from away supporters, something that football supporters would do well to note.

Tony Webb: Lifetime friendships, the brotherhood of speedway fans worldwide. I am now involved in veterans' reunions and simple get-togethers. To me, it is an honour to be able to meet my boyhood heroes at a function or a barbecue, to have a chat and remember the good

Leicester supporters enjoying a visit to West Ham's Custom House track in the 60s.

times. I am always amazed to see old enemies chatting together, laughing about past battles.

In 1982, I returned to Australia and for 10 years, speedway was put on the back shelf. I did not want my sons to be speedway riders, so they became pro cyclists. This took up all my time as they travelled all over Australia but I found the injuries and the politics were even greater than in speedway.

John Cross: In 2006, I decided to treat myself to a Grand Prix in Bydgoszcz. Travelling with Travel Plus Tours and staying at a hotel in Torun, I was soon taken in by a group of

Ipswich supporters who insisted that I joined their company for the whole weekend, which included a league match the following day at Gniezno. It is so nice to still enjoy their friendship.

Philip Dalling: Warm summer evenings, 60s pop records issuing from the loudspeakers (usually a few months behind the current chart sounds), the roar of the bikes starting up in the

Scottish pair Bert Harkins and Jim McMillan after finishing shock runners-up to Kiwis Ivan Mauger and Barry Briggs, with England's Nigel and Eric Boocock third, in the 1970 World Pairs semi-final at Belle Vue.

pits, and the mingling smells of burning oil, freshly-mown grass on the greyhound track (not sand in those days) and the unmistakeable odours of hot dogs and hamburgers.

Tim Templeton: My first meeting at Southampton sowed the seeds and speedway has been such a large influence in my life. I've watched it all over the world, had a great collection of machines, met most of my heroes over the years, and made so many friends as a result.

Bert Harkins: There are so many memories but I suppose that captaining Wembley Lions and Scotland stand out. Also, Jimmy McMillan and I riding for Scotland and qualifying from Belle Vue to the 1970 World Pairs Final in Malmo, Sweden. We didn't win, but we gave the other countries a fright!

Mike King: The greatest memory I take from speedway is the 1962 Provincial League KO Cup Final. On Saturday, October 20 that year, I and many others had journeyed by coach to the Sun Street stadium in the smoky atmosphere of Stoke-on-Trent. Stoke were rampant that night and beat the Falcons by 60-36, with Colin Pratt racing to a faultless 15-point maximum and Pete Jarman and Ken Adams weighing in with 29 between them. For Exeter, only skipper Len Silver put up much resistance with 13 points.

Two days later, on the Monday, the tapes went up at the County Ground for the last meeting of the season, with the Falcons facing Stoke in the second leg and looking to claw back a seemingly impossible deficit of 24 points. And claw it back they did in the most amazing fashion. At the end of the night, Exeter were winners by 70-26, a margin of 44 points. Len Silver scored a 15-point maximum and four more Falcons were in double figures. For Stoke, Pete Jarman was top scorer with 10 and, amazingly, Colin Pratt failed to score. We didn't care, Exeter were KO Cup champions.

David Walker: Watching Ken McKinlay come round onto the back straight, from the pits gate: Small blip on the throttle of the JAP, hands off the handlebars, quick wobble of the helmet and final adjustment of the goggles, then hands back on the 'bars, just in time to turn into the third bend. Judged to perfection, every time.

Also, the 1978 World Final at Wembley. Walking down Wembley Way, amid a sea of black and yellow scarves and jackets, we bumped into Sheffield's Dougie Wyer who, with a look of wonder on his face, said: "Is there anybody left in Coventry today?" The icing on the cake for us was Ole Olsen's win, celebrated in the hired minibus on Edgware Road, with a KFC and champagne!

James Easter: Taking 2,200 fans to the Gothenburg World Final in 1991, chartering a whole ship, plus four planes, and it all working without the slightest hitch. I had absolute pride in the product and the team who worked so hard for us.

Rob McColl: One memory that sticks in my mind was when they held, I think, a World Championship qualifier at Rayleigh. At that time, Ivan Mauger was considered the faster gater in

Coventry track photographer Jeff Davies celebrates with Greg Hancock and his fellow American Billy Hamill minutes after Greg won his first world title in 1997.

the business. In one of his heats, one of the other riders was unable to take part and the reserve for the night, Pat McKenzie, a rider from South Africa and a Rayleigh reserve, was brought in. The tapes went up and McKenzie left Mauger for dead. We couldn't believe that the fastest gater could have been beaten by a reserve but McKenzie was actually a very talented rider.

Tony Lethbridge: Taking the stadium tour at Briggo's Wembley Banquet in 2000 and finding myself walking

Glasgow's Charlie Monk after winning the 1965 Wills Internationale at Wimbledon.

down to the pits with Ove Fundin. Ove recalled travelling to his first World Final by tube train and showed us his regular spot in the pits. One disappointment at Wembley was the dressing rooms. I always imagined they must be cavernous but, in reality, they were quite pokey.

Another moment to treasure must have been in about 1990 or '91, when a young lad with ginger hair approached me towards the end of a meeting and said very politely: "Please, Mr. Lethbridge, my granddad says can I have four laps after the meeting?" His granddad was my good friend and childhood hero Neil Street and the lad was, of course, Jason Crump. I didn't realise then that I was assisting the career, in a very small way, of a future multi-World Champion.

Jeff Davies: Being with my great friend Greg Hancock the night he won his first World Championship in Vojens in 1997 and Coventry's treble-winning year in 2007. Incredible.

Eddie Andrews: Having the honour of watching Tommy Jansson's rise to becoming a great rider in his short career.

Paul Ackroyd: Being with Erik Gundersen, minutes after he had won the World Championship at Bradford. I was the Drugs Testing Officer for the meeting and, being the winner, Erik was automatically selected to be drugs-tested. His adrenalin was in full flow and he and I were locked in a room together for 15 minutes. I was privileged to share some very personal moments with him.

Roly Clarke: Spectating from the back of the stand at Newport's Somerton Park while kids outside were pelting it with stones. It was no problem – until one large stone came straight through the rusty metal and then we moved!

Trying to find the Cradley Heath track for the first time. We saw a car displaying a Heathens sticker in the rear window. Sticking like a limpet to the rear bumper, I followed it . . . straight into the local crematorium!

Roy Blanchflower: Whenever I travelled to any away meeting with the Norwich team, I was always in the pits among such riders as Jack Parker, Tommy Price, Split Waterman, Jack

Young, Peter Craven, Ronnie Moore and many more. I look back now and think how very fortunate I was to be there in such famous company. The years from 1949 to 1956 were without a doubt the years of my young life.

Robert Rogers: World Championship finals at Wembley where fans from all over the world happily mixed – and I got a chance to swap speedway badges which, for a kid in the 60s, was VERY important!

Good night for Belle Vue fans at Wembley, where Ivan Mauger and Soren Sjosten finished first and second on the rostrum in the 1969 World Final, with Swindon's Barry Briggs second.

Bryan Newbold: Spending quality time with my late dad during many years of following our team. The endless hours talking about our favourite sport and, best of all, Dad always being there during the four or five years I desperately tried, and failed, to become the next Ivan Mauger. He was always there to pick me up, brush me down, spend endless hours at hospitals and just be there. Thanks, Dad, I didn't always show my appreciation but I couldn't have done it without you.

Paul Jeffries: Goodness, that's a tough question. Because, actually, what lingers longest in the memory can often be the bad things, like the serious accidents (thankfully, I've never witnessed a fatality), or the nights when you've driven miles and miles, only to find the match rained-off, or a lousy track surface with no decent races. Moments to treasure in a positive way, for me, tend to be associated with first visits to tracks, any tracks, that I haven't been to before.

Doug Nicolson: The magical first couple of months in the 1965 season when Glasgow went from being bottom of the old Provincial League the year before to top of the first published British League table, beating Coventry 56-22, a result that proved the old PL teams could make it in the newly-formed BL. Charlie Monk was carrying all before him and won the Internationale at Wimbledon, while Tigers were victorious at Edinburgh and Belle Vue in that golden summer. Almost predictably, it didn't last but it was a truly memorable time.

My son and daughter being mascots for the night at Shawfield, something they both loved. Also, Robbie Nagy speaking to them at a service area on the way back from a meeting at Berwick. It really made their night.

Mike Keir: What speedway gave back to me: 13 consecutive World Finals (1978-90) and the chance to go to California, Russia, Poland and Scandinavia, places I would never have gone but for speedway.

Rod Haynes: Too many to properly remember but seeing Peter Craven at Sheffield barely a couple of weeks before his fatal accident and getting his autograph. I was a 12-year-old, but he stood only a few inches taller than me.

Steve Casey: So many memories to treasure, some good, some bad. I suppose my first

Wembley World Final, in 1969, was the good. I travelled overnight by coach from Manchester with some cycle speedway buddies. It wasn't an organised trip either, just a scheduled coach to London's Victoria coach station and then by bus to Wembley. We got to Wembley at about 10 in the morning and sat about around the stadium all day. We must have been nuts. It was quite an adventure for a 14-year-old. But Ivan made it all worthwhile with a faultless display and, with Soren Sjosten third, it was a great night to be an Aces fan.

The bad was watching as the Hyde Road stadium was gradually isolated from the development around it, as rumours of closure became a reality. I remember coming away from the last match at the end of October and feeling so sad at the thought of never going back. Within a matter of months, it was all gone. Such a shame.

Dennis Lindo: My favourite memory doesn't actually relate to an on-track incident. One Sunday morning, I was riding my bike to the local park when I glanced into a side road and saw a trailer with two speedway bikes on it. I had to investigate. This was the closest I'd been to an actual speedway bike and I can remember thinking that these bikes, like the pushbike I was riding, had been made up from spare parts with insulating tape acting as handle grips. They were nothing like the sparkling bikes we see today. I'd never seen the bikes in this area before, so had no idea who they belonged to.

I went into the park and my curiosity was satisfied, the bikes belonged to Roy Trigg who, at the time, rode for Hackney. He was playing football with a couple of kids. I couldn't resist bombarding him with questions. He'd been riding at Edinburgh the previous night and I wanted to know everything about the meeting and, in fairness to Roy, he answered the questions while still trying to play football. I'm sure it was 10 minutes of torture for him. I

Opening night at Leicester's purpose-built Beaumont Park track in 2011.

was straight to Uncle Tom's house to tell him Roy Trigg was in the park. I thought Tom would be as excited as me and come to the park to see him, but he declined.

Stephen Quinsey: I would have to say the whole package because, for me, there is no other sport like it. Speedway has given me so much pleasure, the noise, the smell and the anticipation is something you can never forget.

Steve Johnston: My favourite memory is of looking forward to the Tuesday night at West Ham. Going through the turnstile and getting my programme, wondering which rider would be featured on the front that week. The music over the tannoy in the stand, waiting for the photo/badge seller to make his way around and seeing what new pictures he had of the Hammers' riders. Waiting for the riders to come out of the dressing rooms to get their autographs. The racing, of course, but the whole evening was magic in a lovely stadium that was sold far too soon – just think what a redevelopment of it would have brought.

Andrew Edwards: The whole fun of the thing. Before 1974 and MCN, my friends and I would regularly take in away meetings to watch Cradley Heath. Exeter was always special, I loved our annual visit. Swindon too, Sheffield as well, fantastic Leicester, deadly rivals Wolverhampton.

Bob Radford: The people – riders, promoters, managers, announcers, track staff and even most referees. And the places, both home and abroad, the sport took me to.

Bill Halliwell: It has to be the fans, and not just those in the UK. I have been lucky enough to travel to the 1976 and 1977 World Finals, GPs in Prague, Copenhagen and, of course, Cardiff and all the World Finals at Wembley in the 70s, as well as the 1981 final. The supporters are just amazing and being on a tram after the Prague GP with the Polish fans was just fantastic.

Commentator Dave Lanning (right) and studio presenter Dickie Davies were familiar figures throughout the 70s as ITV's Saturday afternoon *World of Sport* show brought speedway to millions of homes.

Mark Wilkinson: The culmination of the re-birth of Leicester Speedway at Beaumont Park on a balmy April evening in 2011. I still think it was all a dream, and that Martin Rogers wasn't really there, talking to the 4-5,000 of us from the centre green, 28 years after he was rudely interrupted.

Alan Jones: My favourite memory is more recent and the return of speedway to Leicester. It was too long dead and buried to think that it would ever return. Twenty-eight years is a large chunk of time out of anyone's lifetime and, for the older generation, to witness the Lions back on track was a dream come true. All the hard work that went on by so many people to not only build the stadium but to organise the opening was a colossus mountain to climb. But we did it and the sight of 5,000 smiling faces walking up the path from the car park to the stadium on that opening night was a scene that will never leave me or my colleagues.

Robert Wiles: My favourite memory is an unusual one. A family friend who ran a local motorcycle business and who was a keen grass-track racer took over the contract to supply the fuel to Canterbury Speedway. He asked me if I wanted to go along and help and, of course, I accepted like a shot. Once he decided that I could be trusted to accurately measure the dope into the riders' cans and record in the book how much each of them used, he would wander off and talk to his friends, leaving me to manage in the pits. I was around 15 at the time and I thought it was fantastic. I got to meet all the Division Two riders of the time (early-mid 70s). It's my best memory of the sport. Oh, that and the smell of methanol and Castrol R, of course.

Pete Rout: The coverage of all the big meetings on terrestrial television, including the 'high, wide and handsome' commentaries of Dave Lanning. And in more recent times, meeting many of my heroes from my involvement in vintage speedway, including Peter Collins, Briggo, Ivan Mauger, Ole Olsen, John Louis, Tony Davey, Olle Nygren and many others.

Pete Butler: To see a Reading rider win a World Final was always a wish and the fact that Bradford 1990 had such great racing, surpassing anything I'd seen at Wembley, including the 'Penhall Final', or any of the Inter-Continental Finals I'd seen, just added to the night's glory. I was a big fan of the Moran brothers and I made myself a Kelly and Shawn programme board for my trip to Gothenberg in 1984, but I was desperate that Per would prevail over Shooey in the run-off at Odsal in '90.

The 1990 final is the only time I've entered a stadium, on Thursday's practice day, seeing the yellow fence with the deep, pink kickboards and thinking, 'what a great fence'! It was the high point of a great eight-day speedway holiday: Reading, Monday; Long Eaton, Wednesday; World Final practice and Middlesbrough, Thursday; Belle Vue, Friday; Bradford, Saturday; Stoke, Sunday; and, to end, Wolves v Reading with the new World Champion on the Monday.

Greg Unwin: My favourite memory comes from the first meeting I ever saw between Plymouth and Weymouth. In Heat 9, both Weymouth riders, Roy Carter and Chris Yeatman, had crashed into the safety fence. Plymouth's Tony George was leading Devils skipper Mike Cake when he fell and only quick avoiding action by Cake averted a collision. Cake crossed the line for three points while George picked himself up and, still between bends three and four, proceeded to push his damaged bike to the finish line. The rear end of the machine locked up and still over 100 yards from the line, George hauled his wrecked machine to the finish. As he did so, the crowd cried, 'heave, heave, heave', in unison all the way to two hard-earned points.

David Ede and fellow Wimbledon fans show their colours on the packed terraces.

Whilst all this was going on, some track staff had to be prevented from helping him, as outside aid would have led to disqualification by the referee. It was a remarkable sight to witness in your very first meeting and a memory that has always stayed with me.

Glen Norton: As a kid, I would run home from school, run up to The Firs stadium in Norwich and get into the pits to watch practice.

Steve Wilks: The whole Hackney experience. Len Silver was a great showman, the racing was excellent and the Hawks had a number of riders who seemed to be poor starters and earned their points the hard way. Hackney was a good stadium and gave you a good view of the action.

John Vine: Being able to go to meetings almost anywhere in the country and know that it would be possible to find up to three generations of families and there would be no trouble amongst the fans, which was a pleasant change from football.

Ian Glover: Watching dear old Johnnie S. Hoskins MBE marching down to the pits at Kingsmead to 'kick arse' with Canterbury's strict 9.00pm curfew in mind. After that, giving

Michael Lee and Dave Jessup gave King's Lynn a World Championship one-two in 1980.

me a sweet as I used to sit three seats away from Johnnie in the stand, and him saying: "It's nearly 7.00pm and they should be out, son!"

Dave Ede: Opening issue 22 of *Classic Speedway* magazine and seeing myself staring out from the 'Welcome' page. I'm the biker with the pudding basin crash helmet holding my Dons board next to my then girlfriend Pam, now my wife of 42 years. John (on my right) was a schoolfriend who I still go to speedway with. I think this photo was taken at Hackney or West Ham around 1968 or '69. We all loved our sport and a good laugh was always guaranteed.

I suppose some away trips were real adventures, like running out of fuel on John's bike on our return from Swindon and the owner of a Wallingford chip shop giving us petrol from his motor mower. Despite our pleas, he would not accept any money in return and we got home OK.

I once went to the BLRC at Belle Vue with a work colleague in his Cortina Mark II and on the return journey we hit some debris on the M1, which holed his fuel tank. It was obvious the car was going no further, so we accepted a lift into Nottingham with a police patrolman and, after sleeping in the railway station, caught the first train to London in the morning. I can assure you the trip was worth it because of the superb racing.

Richard Mason: Holding PC's bag while he signed my autograph book. I still clearly remember it about 40 years later, so that must have made a good impression.

Paul Watson: The night Michael Lee returned to King's Lynn as 1980 World Champion. Another Stars rider, Dave Jessup, had finished second.

Chris Gosling: The excitement of going to King's Lynn when we had a good team, such as the early 70s with Betts, Simmons and Cole, the mid 70s of Betts, Lee and Turner and the 'Team Australia' side of 2000, when we didn't win the league but could give any team a good match, home or away. The camaraderie on the terraces was always good too. You could chat with the away fans and it was the best of times when good racing was the norm, not the rarity it seems to be now.

Dick Partridge: There have been so many over the last 44 years. It is always good to see guys get up after a nasty-looking crash, and infinitely sad that sometimes they don't. As I sit here at my keyboard, I easily become tearful at the thought of John Simmons, Marcus Williams, Pip Lamb, Vic Harding, Steve Weatherley, Kevin Holden, Alan Wilkinson, Lawrence Hare, Lee Richardson and many others who have paid such a heavy price for their love of speedway racing. On a personal level, although the project did not end well for me, it was good to see the tapes go up for Heat 1 of the Autovalet Trophy at Mildenhall in 1992. There is too much to say about that venture for here, but that moment felt good!

Doug Wyer: My favourite memory is going around this big world of ours many times,

Peter Collins could afford to finish behind Ivan Mauger in his last ride in front of around 100,000 at Katowice and still clinch the world title in 1976. Below: PC was joined on the rostrum by fellow Brit Malcolm Simmons and Australian Phil Crump.

visiting every country where speedway racing takes place, entertaining and meeting lots of great people who were involved in our sport.

Carol Stock: My friendship with Kelly Moran for one. We were friends for 32 years and I miss him. And Peter Collins winning the 1976 World Final. I was, and still am, a huge PC fan. I didn't go to Poland but was at Rye House that day with my mum. She had a small radio with her and she listened to Sunday Sport to get the result. When she told me Peter had won, I ran down to the pits to tell Les Collins, who was riding for Stoke that day. I'll never forget the feeling that my favourite rider, my hero, had won the World Final. Just wish I could have been in Katowice that day.

Richard Bott: I know I'm in danger of repeating myself but it has to be the 1976 World Final in Katowice and the moment PC crossed the finishing line in his fifth race to become champion.

John Brownhill: The large crowds that used to attend, the friendly rivalry of supporters, the occasional on-track dispute which was part and parcel of the evening's entertainment and the memories of the many brave, young men who provided the thrills.

Adrian Stockwell: There are so many but if I have to pick one it has to be the time when I was standing in my usual pre-meeting haunt, the crash barrier at the entrance to the pits gate at Wimbledon. I was 14-years-old and, as always, gazing in reverence at my hero Ronnie Moore, who was puffing on his fag and warming-up his trusty JAP. It was then that he looked up, smiled and unbelievably strolled over to say hello. I was completely awestruck and stared at him blankly for a few seconds before blurting out in panic: "Hello, Ronnie, erm, ah, my mum fancies you!" He laughed out loud, as did most of the people standing around me, and asked me if I'd like his autograph. I thrust my programme at him gratefully, which he signed and then said: "Say hi to your mum" before smiling again and returning to his mighty steed. What a man, a proper hero. It was a pseudo-religious experience for me but my mum was horrified when I told her!

Wimbledon favourites Ronnie Moore and Tommy Jansson in 1972.

John Earrey, who saw mic duty at Ipswich and White City in the 70s, was widely regarded as one of the best in the business So long as you know . . .

Julia Wilson: The indoor meeting at the NEC Birmingham at the start of 1980. The racing was not particularly memorable but it was just great to be able to see speedway in January. I also remember seeing a junior match at Coventry one sunny Saturday morning in February (possibly 1976) and we sat in the grandstand (normally it was the back straight), and again, I think I remember this because it was unexpected.

I remember the pre-season practice at Coventry in 1976 when everyone wanted to see our new signing Ole Olsen, especially after all the business with Hull in the close season.

The 1983 World Final at Norden, where a German in front of us turned round at the end and said, smiling: "We have a new German champion!" I think my dad, brother Clive and I all wanted to deck the man!

Stephen Williams: The feeling of delight and my increased heart rate as Ole won another race, won another individual trophy or inspired his team, be it Coventry or Denmark, to victory.

Alan Thompsett: A day slowly lapping King's Lynn at Olle Nygren's training school. Rushing to save our favourite seats, before walking round to the used programme stall at Plough Lane. The unique speedway smell (under lights at Wimbledon or the blazing sun at Arlington).

Richard Parsons: August 1977, when White City did the double over Wimbledon on the Bank Holiday Monday. It was just one of those days, the sun was shining, we rode brilliantly and to do the Dons on their own track . . . great stuff! 'R-E-B-E-L-S . . . as long as we know' (John Earrey, the best mike man in the sport).

Keith Wiggins: Meeting my wife; my daughter being the only voice still cheering Peter Ravn on when a race had been stopped at a packed Peterborough during the 1991 Four Team finals; and my son bursting into tears and shouting "why don't their bikes break down?" as Peterborough suffered their third engine failure in the first six heats against Middlesbrough in 1995 or '96.

Rob Scrutton: My first visit to the electric atmosphere of Wembley and Belle Vue. I found

Wembley Lions of 1971, their last season of league racing. Left to right: Dave Jessup, Tony Clarke, Brian Leonard, Gote Nordin, Sverre Harrfeldt, Brian Collins, Peter Prinsloo. On bike: Bert Harkins and Freddie Williams

Martin Rogers, his wife Lin and their son Martin junior bid farewell to England at the 1988 NL Fours Team Finals at Peterborough, where they last promoted before emigrating to Australia's Gold Coast.

that an amazing place with the fairground and rollercoaster in the background.

It was there, in 1973 or '74, that I saw my only streaker at speedway during the BLRC when this was a meeting worth winning. There was a huge cheer when a naked man jumped over the fence on the back straight. He calmly walked onto the centre green before bowing to the four corners of the track and returning to where he came from. There was a steward who looked like he wasn't sure whether he wanted to apprehend him or not, but he made a token gesture just as the man was hopping over the fence.

Peter Lush: The 1971 Wembley Lions. After Fundin left, the 1970 team were not very strong. But in 1971 it was a real team, not dominated by one or two stars. A nice mix of experienced riders and rising stars, such as Dave Jessup. Even after Gote Nordin left, they were still very competitive. And I understood a bit more about the sport, so could appreciate what was going on.

Gary Moore: My most treasured moment from speedway has to be the time I've spent with my dad for the best part of 40 years. I played football all over the place when I was younger and Dad never got to see me play much due to work or one thing or another, and it was my grandpa who would follow me. So having speedway gave Dad and I a connection and bond that was our own special thing.

Martin Rogers: When we finished up in speedway and emigrated to Australia in 1988, it was pretty much without regrets. There were tough times and great times but, bottom line, we achieved some decent successes at all the tracks we operated, made so many great friends and enjoyed such loyal support from so many directions. The interaction with those people (supporters, riders, etc, especially the young up and comers) was always a huge buzz.

Arnie Gibbons: Per Jonsson's world title win at Odsal in 1990. In the days when top riders changed clubs less often, their success at individual level on the world stage mattered much more to devoted fans. Jonsson, a superb all-round stylist, spent his 11-year British career entirely at Reading and we idolised him.

My speedway travels extend far and wide, including 45 tracks outside the UK in 12 different countries. These have produced plenty of unforgettable experiences, including: the Czech Golden Helmet weekend in Pardubice (a city best known for the manufacture of semtex), my number one recommendation for anyone who wishes to see our sport overseas; my first trip to Poland when British Airways lost my luggage and I had to shop for replacement clothes in a country still emerging from the socialist-style planned economy of the communist era; returning from the 1991 World Final in Sweden with a clean-cut young man who needed 'subbing' after blowing all his money on a phone call home from his hotel room; ice speedway in Saransk, where the statues of Stalin were still standing and (much against my abstemious nature) I consumed copious quantities of vodka; driving on the Sturt highway through the Australian desert from Adelaide to Mildura; the 2001 World Cup in

Denny Pyeatt was proving a match-winner for Reading before fate intervened at Hackney in 1982.

Poland featuring a thunderstorm of epic proportions in Gdansk and two fantastic meetings in Wroclaw; a shared speedway/heavy metal 'music' festival at Champion Speedway in upstate New York. What a racket!

But one event has left a much stronger impression than all of those happy times. On July 16, 1982, I started my evening anticipating a lively night's racing at Hackney. It ended in despair, sitting on the steps of Hackney Hospital. There was a lot of rivalry between the Racers and the Hawks (Hawks promoter Len Silver had been part of the consortium that built Reading's Smallmead home). The evening was going well. Without an away win for over a year, Racers were 27-21 up thanks to two race wins from Denny Pyeatt. Our American hero came out again in Heat 9 but was clipped by Hawks' 18-year-old debutant Marvyn Cox. From the moment of impact, everyone could see the situation was serious. The ambulance rushed Denny to Hackney Hospital (a former Victorian workhouse less than a mile from the stadium) and after half an hour, a clearly distressed Len Silver announced the abandonment of the meeting. The Reading team gathered at the hospital, with Denny in a coma and on a life-support machine. At 8.45am on the Saturday, Denny passed away.

Mike Turner: Speedway has given our family a legacy which continues through to today, starting with my wife attending the early British League years and my introduction to speedway, and then our children taking up the interest. This has now passed onto our grandchildren, with our grandson helping at the Cardiff GP in Emil Sayfutdinov's corner. Not many sports are truly that family-orientated.

Paul Rickett: Believe it or not, my biggest memory dates back to 1975 and it was a rain-off. Tigers were at home to the old enemy Belle Vue and, despite it having rained most of the day and there being a bus strike, I wasn't going to miss it. So, with meticulous planning, I got

Anders Michanek and former Reading press officer Andy Povey at the final Smallmead meeting in 2009.

a lift from where I lived into Rotherham, took the train to the city centre and then walked the three miles to Owlerton, optimism abounding with the fact that the monsoon had slowed up and the Speedway Office had told me that they were all walking around in Bermuda shorts and flip-flops at the stadium (how many times have you heard that?). But turning the corner from Penistone Road into the stadium, there was the sight no speedway fan wants to see – cars funnelling out and the rain-off signs going up. I think that was the first time I swore. Too young to go to the bar, it was a case of walking back to the station, catching another train and then walking the extra few miles home because my dad had just gone out. Oh, how I laughed.

Andy Povey: As a young boy watching the likes of Reading at Tilehurst, idolising Anders Michanek. So it was a dream job when, years later, I was appointed press officer of the club. That was the proudest and most enjoyable period of my life.

Paula Peirce: My moment to treasure is getting Mitch Shirra's autograph EVERY week at Coventry and walking round the pits with him to his car. The riders always had time for the young fans.

Paul Minns: For a King's Lynn supporter, October 27, 2006 is a date that will always live long in the memory. That was the night the Stars completed their first treble and at the same time won the league title for the first time since they were formed.

The season had started with a big cloud hanging over the Norfolk Arena. The previous

Eddie Garvey with the leathers and racejacket Chris Morton wore in the 1976 World Final – just part of photographer Eddie's impressive collection.

November, just after the British season had ended, King's Lynn lost one of their shining stars when Ashley Jones was tragically killed in a track crash Down Under. At the 2006 press and practice day, the riders had said they wanted to win the league for Ashley and no-one wanted that more than his childhood friend and fellow King's Lynn rider Kevin Doolan. Above the second bend, hung high on the fencing, was a banner with Ashley looking out across the Norfolk Arena.

The atmosphere was highly charged that Friday night for what was the second leg and the Stars had a 15-point deficit to make up from the previous night's first leg.

Anybody who saw the riders as they arrived and prepared was left in no doubt how badly they wanted that title and that third trophy, not just for themselves but for Ashley. King's Lynn chipped away at the 15-point deficit all night and it all came to the boil in Heat 14 when

Doolan and Chris Mills took a 5-1 and, with it, the league and the treble. How apt it was that Ashley's long-time friend Doolan won the heat that brought the league title to Norfolk.

The whole night produced many wonderful images and memories but the scenes after Heat 14 will stay with me for a very long time. I've never seen any rider express such sheer joy as that expressed by Doolan as he and Mills enjoyed their lap of honour.

As they approached their team-mates who had gathered by the finishing line, Kevin acknowledged them but carried on and rode straight past, coming to a stop on the second bend facing the banner which had his best mate Ashley Jones on. He stood, raised both arms and punched the air. It's difficult to imagine the emotions that must have been going on inside that helmet.

Eddie Garvey: My fascination with photography and racejackets. I don't like team suits, never have, because they take away a rider's individuality and, for me, as a kid growing up and new to the sport, that individuality gave me something to latch onto and follow.

I can look back even now and identify riders from their leathers and riding styles and then those magnificent racejackets that topped everything off. The photographers of the 70s also left a big impression on me. Mike Patrick, Alf Weedon and Trevor Meeks produced some jaw-dropping stuff at a time when it was an awful lot harder to take a good sports picture than it is now.

John Davidson: I especially cherish the first time I had my photograph taken with Ivan Mauger at a benefit for Alan Wilkinson. He was so kind and sincere in our interaction, confirming to me, in retrospect, that I wasn't worshipping a false idol.

More randomly, perhaps, I'll never forget staying up late into the night in September 1977, listening to the radio reports (after every four heats) from the World Final in Gothenburg. The meeting was delayed because of the conditions, and I was still glued to the radio at midnight when the announcer finally reported that Mauger had

John Davidson with his boyhood hero.

won his record-equalling fifth title. I could scarcely have been more excited if I'd been there.

For a decade I ate, drank and breathed speedway. I loved getting up each Wednesday morning to read *Speedway Star,* which I had delivered. If it was late, delayed by a day, I frequently sulked about it all morning. I collected every copy of the *Star* 1968-82 (and more), every World Final programme from the era and programmes from as many Mauger landmark meetings as I could.

Speedway has been far removed from my day-to-day life for years now, but it was a defining part of my childhood and youth. Even today, it still comes to mind and I fondly remember so very much of it.

Vitek Formanek: The excitement of seeing friends and riders once a year, since it was a Red Letter Day for me during Communism. There was a friendly atmosphere too, unlike at football matches. Then came England, which was the 'promised land' for me in those years.

After the Czech Golden Helmet meeting in 1990, my then wife and I stayed, as all the riders did, in the Hotel Labe. I left the room to go and congratulate winner Jeremy Doncaster on his triumph but when I returned, I found my wife standing in her knickers in the corridor shouting that we had a burglar in our room. I shouted for help and, in no time, Gary Havelock appeared holding a bottle of champagne as a weapon! When we got into the room, we realised the villain had run away via a window but had stolen our money.

When we went to the gala night, Gary, Paul Thorp and Kelly and Shawn Moran took us to their table and looked after us. The next night in Prague, we were given money, which was the proceeds of a collection organised by some Birmingham fans who were known as the BSPA (Birmingham Speedway P***head Association!). That was a very nice gesture. It is now 23 years ago but it still lives in my memory and I have always respected Havvy since then too.

Richard Gilson: My favourite memory is the old World Championship, how it progressed each season via the British semi-finals, British Final, Commonwealth Final, Overseas Final, Inter-Continental Final and World Final. The drama, the excitement, the worry . . . three bad rides and your favourite was out. I like the Grand Prix but you can have a bad meeting and still be World Champion, unlike the old days.

Ian Shelton: The moment Erik Gundersen crossed the line punching the air in October 1983 to confirm the sport's greatest team had won the British League. Although we won the league at Eastbourne in 1981, it seemed appropriate that 10,000 people who had supported the Heathens and speedway over five decades, and watched many inferior Heathens teams and performances over the years, should celebrate the club's league title win at Dudley Wood against Ipswich. It was an emotional night and those Black Country folk deserved the moment.

The other moment is a little personal but, as Heathens supporters who had not seen our club ride for three seasons, I helped to put a team on track as Club Cradley Heath in 1999 to race at various Conference League tracks. There was no prouder person than me to see our racejacket reappear in action at Buxton that May afternoon with 300 travelling Cradley fans and I hope the project helped keep the name alive.

John Murphy: A simple moment to treasure was after an England v Denmark Test at The Shay. Somehow I ended up walking up the track banking with Peter Collins! I remarked to him "crikey, this is steep" and he laughed. We had a lovely chat.

Mark Sawbridge: Every year, I used to take my holiday form to my boss in the hope that he would sign it off and I could then spend the time watching my favourite sport. "Where is it this year, Sawbridge?" I well remember him asking me in early 1986. "Er, Poland," I replied. Having accepted the usual rounds of holiday requests from office staff jetting off to some plastic resort on the Costa Brava or Ibiza, this was a somewhat novel proposal I was giving to

Alan Wilkinson paid a visit to the ref's box at King's Lynn.

him. He signed my form with a shake of the head, and in August I headed east to watch that year's World Final.

When I tell young people that I went behind the Iron Curtain, they look at me as if I'd been to watch the Crusades or the building of the Pyramids or something. The whole trip was an incredible experience, which remains etched in my mind. It was scary, exciting and fun in equal measures and I wouldn't have missed it for the world. In fact, I went back to Poland the following year, to Gdansk and Torun, and again had a wonderful time.

Being a speedway fan has allowed me to go to countries all over the world to places that most people would never visit in a month of Sundays. I feel, strangely, that this has helped to shape my view of the world, and I feel very lucky that I have been able to do so. And I've still never visited the Costa Brava or Ibiza.

Clive Read: I remember it as a great family time, travelling to meetings home and away, and attending bigger, more important meetings such as the World Championship rounds and many World Finals. I had my first taste of travelling abroad and seeing new countries such as Sweden, Denmark and Germany and the tension, sometimes unbearable, as a result hung on four laps to decide whether your favourite rider would go through to the next round or win a meeting. We went to some pretty unusual places I wouldn't ordinarily have gone to – Reading, Peterborough, Boston, White City and Stoke (where, having stopped for fish and chips, we were invited to join a Stoke Hospital Radio broadcast after seeing Frank Smith make his home debut there in September 1978). Going on national TV on Noel Edmunds' Swap Shop in December 1977 was pretty amazing, too, after our sister, Julia, had written in to say how nuts we were about speedway.

Most of all, I remember the racing, the excitement of large crowds cheering on their favourites, four laps in which the riders went for it, and the thrill when your man won or the team had ridden well, especially away from home.

Gary Miles: In over 40 years of watching speedway, it is very difficult to pick a favourite memory. But being 10-years-old and seeing Canterbury win the 1978 National League title will always stay with me. More recently, it was seeing my son take his first ride around the Sittingbourne junior track.

Martin Smith: My moments to treasure are supporting the magnificent Ipswich Witches team of the 70s as a schoolboy. A team of local lads (and Billy Sanders) blended over time into a formidable team through a combination of wonderful and committed riders – magnificently led by John Louis, brilliant management, superb team spirit and an unforgettable atmosphere at Foxhall Heath on race-nights.

Alex Mackenzie: Thursday nights. CSA were South London's finest rock and roll band and they played in The Fountain on a Thursday night to an audience which looked like they were still living in the 50s. So, come home from work, have a quick tea and off to the speedway, then round the corner for an injection of rock and roll. The perfect evening's entertainment and it happened every week.

Garry Robinson: Watching Alan Wilkinson run across the centre green at King's Lynn and climb the ladder to the referee's box to debate a decision. The look on the Belle Vue manager's face when he saw what he was doing was priceless. We feared a body being tossed out of the window!

Chris Rowsell: The thing that has always stayed with me about speedway is the smell of methanol. When I first walked into Smallmead in 1978, it was the first thing to hit me. It

Paul Muchene lost his life in a crash at Hackney in July 1989.

provided the anticipation of what was about to happen. Whilst many races are pedestrian, there is always something to watch and, at its best, speedway has the ability to set so many emotions racing for a whole minute. Other sports can take you to the heights for a few seconds, but speedway can do it for a whole race lasting up to and beyond a minute.

Andrew Gallon: The first, in summer 1990, of three speedway holidays I had. After graduating and starting work, I finally had the money to contemplate such a venture. Eight meetings in eight nights, going to tracks I'd only ever read about. Wonderful. I travelled by train and stayed in B&Bs or youth hostels. My itinerary for the first was: Coventry, Rye House, Exeter, Milton Keynes, Long Eaton, Ipswich, Hackney and Arena-Essex.

Steve Ridgway: The smell, the noise, shaking my head in the kitchen and listening to the patter of shale bits on the lino, the looking forward to next week's match. I can still remember the records that were played the first time I went, as well. I suppose it's a bit like wishing you could regain your lost youth.

Tim Allan: After a winter break, the smell of methanol in the air at the press and practice always said to me, 'here we go again'! Opening night at Weymouth in 2003 was one I'll treasure. I was presenting the meeting after being out of hospital just a few days following multiple blood clots on my lungs. I was tired after that one! Plus, seeing Mark Loram parade around the Poole track with his World Championship trophy in 2000.

Rob Peasley: I think it's the 2005 Oxford Academy team winning the Conference League. I was lucky enough to be in the pits helping out in the away meetings, plus a few of the home meetings.

I'd been a bit wary about becoming too friendly with riders after the death of Paul Muchene in 1989. I spoke to Paul and his father, John, after the conclusion of every British Junior League match, which used to take place in the second-half. One week, I was wishing Paul good luck for the next week, because he'd got a National League place with Arena-Essex. The following Friday, while down in the pits, we heard he'd had an accident at Hackney. Four days later, Paul was dead.

In 2003, I started covering the Oxford Academy for *Speedway Star,* which brought me into regular contact with the riders. One thing led to another and for 2005, I ended up as assistant team manager to Bryn Williams for the Academy away meetings. Bryn eats, drinks and sleeps speedway and I gained so much knowledge from him. I really enjoyed it. The Academy were a great bunch of lads, and there was a genuinely great team spirit in the camp.

What proved to be the key match was an away fixture at Rye House in early September. We

Cradley Heath's first British League championship-winning team of 1981. Lrft to right: Alan Grahame, Erik Gundersen, Phil Collins, Peter Adams (team manager), Bruce Penhall, Bent Rasmussen, David Shields, Arnold Haley.

were without three riders and looked up against it. In turn, Rye House were missing their No.1 Steve Boxall.

Bryn wasn't feeling great, so he stayed by the pit gate, while I was in the pits with the riders. It was time for me to put into practice all I had learnt from Bryn, to help the riders get the best possible result from the meeting.

The Rye House riders threw away a few points and at the halfway point, I started to realise our depleted team was not only in the hunt for the bonus point, but the win as well. Our fixtures were skewed, so that we had seven home meetings to come but only more away (at rivals Wimbledon) and I fully realised the difference it would make if we won at Rye

We made countless programme changes that day because Kyle Hughes was out injured, so Sam Martin (at No.6) became our stronger reserve. Sam took seven rides, only two of which were his own.

Sam passed Gary Cottham for a priceless third place in Heat 14 and Craig Branney and Chris Mills won the meeting with a 5-1 in the last race. The Raiders' proud record of 50 consecutive wins had been ended, while the Academy were now in a position to win the league with wins in our remaining seven home league matches.

Peter Morrish, the CL league co-ordinator, wasn't sure he was going to be at the final double-header at Oxford and I was handed the Conference League trophy to keep safe for four days. I would only touch it by the base; I wouldn't touch the actual trophy because it wasn't ours yet – we still had to win two meetings!

Oxford promoter Nigel Wagstaff was also superstitious. He didn't want to get anything to hand to our riders on the night, in case it was tempting fate the other way. On the day of the meeting, I made a decision and went out and bought seven bottles of champagne for around £90.

After one or two nervous moments, we secured the title with a 54-39 win over Newport. At which point, I was able to grab the trophy by its handles for the first time, to take it out to the centre green to give it to Peter Morrish (who was there after all) to present to skipper Craig Branney.

And the champagne turned out to be the best £90 I've ever wasted, because it gave the lads something to celebrate with on the night (and soak Bryn with!), and it looked great in all the photos. I found out that Sam Martin took the empty bottle back to Australia as a memento of the night.

One of the nicest gestures at the end of that year was being presented with a photo and tankard by the team at the end-of-season celebration party. It was great to have been a small part of that team.

Nick Nicklin: I was lucky enough to see Cradley Heath rise from being a Cinderella club to one of the top teams in the country. The success of the team in the late 70s and early 80s, with league titles, Knockout and Inter-League cups, as well as individual rider successes, has left me with dozens of great memories. I would, however, say my favourite would be of the cold October day in 1981, when Cradley travelled to Eastbourne and finally secured their first British League title.

After a false start three nights earlier when Wimbledon held the Heathens to an unlikely draw to prevent them from getting the two points they required, Cradley made no mistake at Arlington. Hundreds of fans made the trip down to the South Coast and saw the Heathens turn in a clinical performance, gathering around the safety fence en-mass to congratulate the team as they made their lap of honour on the Eastbourne tractor. The coach trip home, as I recall, was a truly memorable affair.

Martin Neal: It has to be Havvy winning the world title in 1992. The hairs on the back of my neck stood up when they played the national anthem as Havvy stood on the rostrum. I believe Tony Mac and I stopped some good Polish beer going bad that night!

Derek Barclay: The friendship among speedway fans and the sheer excitement of a great race and great racers (we have another in Stevie Boxall at Kent at the moment) are constant moments to treasure. I actually think the sport is still great. Seeing new tracks open or re-open is a great thrill. When Wimbledon re-opened and I was so involved in that – though there were many issues that rain-ruined opening night – to feel the goodwill among people coming back after years and the old place full to the rafters? Well, you can't beat that feeling.

Graham Goodwin: Working with Belle Vue Colts for the last 13 years has been a thrill. Co-managing the Colts with my cousin Stephen Williams in the 2011 National League was something special. Although Belle Vue have an unbroken history of over 85 years of racing, there aren't a massive number of people who can claim to have managed a Belle Vue team in an official league season. To be one of them is an honour. Working in the Belle Vue pits alongside a childhood hero like Chris Morton is something I could never have imagined when I started watching the Aces.

Chris Young: Finding out my uncle, Alan Armstrong, was a former rider. Alan was ex-Middlesbrough, Workington and Castleford and listening to his tales from the track was simply wonderful.

Glenn Collins: If I had to pick one, it would be being at the first Cardiff Grand Prix in 2001. Mark Loram was reigning World Champion, the whole atmosphere of the city was amazing and even at the Newport v Glasgow match the night before, everyone knew that at Cardiff the next day, they were going to be part of something a little bit special. It surpassed all expectations and has grown from that.

7 WHY SPEEDWAY IS SO SPECIAL

Whether you used to attend speedway meetings or still do so today, describe what makes the sport so special to you.

Mick Brown: Speedway people are special. It's a sport where you can get involved with the riders, as my daughter and nephew did when they ran Christer Lofqvist's fan club. My daughter is still in touch with his daughter, even though Chris passed away all those years ago.

Eric Marchment: Speedway has always been a uniquely family sport. We have been to many tracks and have always been made to feel welcome and at home. Speedway is now out of reach for us since the demise of Reading, we don't have a track within a reasonable distance, so we have to rely on the television and magazines.

Maurice Plowright: Seeing four riders shoulder-to-shoulder on a loose surface approaching a U-bend at speeds of around 60mph will always be something of a thrill.

Lucy Burton: I met my husband Bill through the West Ham Speedway Supporters' Club in 1952. We were married in 1955 (we celebrated our 58th wedding anniversary this year) but we had to save for our home and we started our family, so speedway had to take a back seat because money was very tight. By the time we were in a position to pursue our hobby again, West Ham Speedway was no longer with us. We both still cherish those memories of the great

The main stand at West Ham Speedway, where so many happy memories were shared.

times watching speedway at West Ham and various other venues, and this is what makes speedway so very special to me.

Ken Carpenter: I have worked professionally in many sports but speedway is my favourite. The fans are loyal, passionate, long-suffering (often taken for granted and let down by the promoters, the governing bodies and the referees) but they never need to be segregated and it remains a safe sport for all the family to enjoy. The noise, smell, colour, personalities, danger, courage, skill and the fact that the entire race can be seen from the terraces all make speedway attractive to me. But it's the good-natured sense of being a member of the big speedway family that makes the sport so special.

Wally Loak: We can see all the race from beginning to end and never know what is going to happen from one fraction of a second to the next.

Ken Wrench: It is still a family sport. Fans are passionate, will argue, occasionally heatedly, but it virtually never goes beyond that.

Cedric Read: From the arrival at the track, mingling with the crowd, the noise of the revving engines and the intoxicating smell. The friendliness of the fans, family atmosphere and the approachability of riders after the meeting.

Keith Walker: It has an unexplained, and unexplainable, hold on the diehard supporter like me. Even after a frankly boring match, I still believe it will be better next week, and it always is. Who knows for how many years speedway will continue, but grateful thanks to all involved in giving us this unique form of entertainment today.

John Chaplin: It is without doubt the world's most exciting sport – and anyone who dares to decry it to me will, to their cost, find I defend it like a trapped rat. It has been the means by which I have travelled the world and the speedway friends I have made along the way have remained constant. And that is priceless.

Oxford team manager Bernard Crapper with Cheetahs' Hans Nielsen and Jens Rasmussen.

Glynn Shailes: I still get a thrill from speedway, even if I'm just watching it on television. Years ago, I used to marvel at the natural ability of Ronnie Moore, and these days it's the natural ability of Darcy Ward.

I should tell you that my happiest days at speedway in recent years were as press officer at Oxford, working for Bernard Crapper and John Payne. They gave me the job, and I was allowed to just get on with it. If they wanted the media to know anything, they would let me know for my press release (I have to say, however, that I had to sometimes act as censor when it came to Bernard and referees!).

I was always impressed, too, on visits to Poole to hear their supporters cheer and clap the opposition. It first happened at their opening meeting on April 26, 1948, and it's still happening today.

I have many, many happy memories and my Swindon project is a reminder of many hours spent at the Abbey Stadium. I took my autograph book to Bristol in the hope of obtaining the autographs of the famous twosome of Laurel and Hardy, but actually left with the autographs of Fred Tuck and Billy Hole, the Bristol riders. I began speedway autograph-collecting after that and, with the help of good friends, I'm still collecting today. I really do have hundreds of speedway autographs in books, on photographs and programmes and on postcards.

Oliver Chapman: The sport was a very large part of my life. I met my wife at speedway and our daughters learned their geography of the British Isles by relating to the various speedway tracks. From the age of 17 or 18 until the children came along, we went to speedway on four or five nights a week, which was easy from Leicester after the M1 opened. I was lucky that my work took me all round England and I could arrange meetings to coincide with the nearest speedway track's operating night. Camping holidays were arranged to take the children to new tracks, hopefully two or three per holiday. Exeter, Weymouth and Poole or Edinburgh, Glasgow and Berwick were favourites.

Tony Webb: The sheer spectacle of speedway has never changed. It may be packaged differently but it still has the same elements. Someone once said: "The glare of the lights, the vast stadium, lit brightly at the rim and the sea of shadow in the centre. Then the gladiators do battle, hectic, shoulder-to-shoulder, dive into the first bend, men and bikes locked together in a seething mass of limbs and wheels. Then that last dash to the finish. A crash that sends the heart to the mouth, followed by a sense of relief as the rider stumbles to his feet unhurt. The roar of the crowd, the instant hush when a rider falls. Yes, that is speedway."

I came back into speedway in 1996. I had an antiquarian bookshop in Western Australia with a few racejackets on display. I would often get asked for speedway books because there were not many around. Eddie Toogood helped me out with a starter stock, then I started writing a few biographies. This snowballed into a full-time interest and I then got permission to print the JAP manual and wrote the history of Davies Park. The latter got me introduced to the family of A.J. Hunting who commissioned me to research the early speedway history. This, we hope, will be published later this year. I was supplied with 3,000 documents from 1926, so we know the facts! The icing on the cake was the unveiling of a plaque at Davies Park in May 2013 by Scott Hunting, the grandson of A.J.

Bert Harkins: I guess it is the people involved, from the fans who support their teams to the riders who serve up the thrills. Present and past riders still keep in touch through the World Speedway Riders' Association with get-together lunches all around the country, from Scotland to Bournemouth, culminating in the annual pre-season Dinner Dance at the Leicester Marriott.

Philip Dalling: I still attend live speedway today, whenever I can. Obviously there have been huge changes to the way the riders dress, to the machines they ride, and to techniques. At root level, nevertheless, it is still the same sport and the fans are still friendly, enthusiastic, generally fair-minded and knowledgeable. A pity there aren't a few more of them, particularly in the younger age groups.

James Easter: Without doubt, the people in the sport: the riders, (most) promoters but, above all, the friendship and trust that supporters place in you. I have run my Travel Plus Tours business since 1980, we are the longest-running speedway tours company and now the biggest in the world. Some achievement! The business is based on honesty, long travel experience, knowledge of the sport, contacts and a great team behind me. I have always insisted that, whatever happens, you must deal with people honestly and in a manner you would wish to be treated by others.

Tim Templeton: Speedway has always been so special to me, at all levels. Although Poole take a lot of stick from some quarters, we are fortunate to have had a lot of the sport's superstars in our ranks throughout recent times. And it's only a mile-and-a-half away for me. It doesn't get better than that!

David Brassington: It has always been such a friendly sport to attend, thankfully very free of some of the crass and stupid behaviour I have seen in many other sports, especially football. It is so exciting when the engines are revving up and the pre-match parade is on and if you are near enough to the fence, you get that special aroma of speedway fuel.

Mike King: Speedway is so special to me because I'm able to say that, in nearly 60 years of watching our great sport, I have never witnessed any of the crowd violence that has sadly plagued football. On the contrary, it has been heart-warming to have visited many tracks, past and present, and enjoyed good-natured banter with other fans. Fans with opposing opinions

The Australia team that drew 47-47 with the National League at Wimbledon in 1989. Standing, left to right: Craig Boyce, James Easter (team manager), Todd Wiltshire, mascot, Glen Baxter, Craig Hodgson. Front: Leigh Adams, Mick Poole, Troy Butler.

and views, yet people who are more than willing to share their thoughts and memories with you and still end the evening with a 'nice to see you, have a safe journey home', and you know they mean it. This is something that always has me going home with a feeling of warm and pleasant satisfaction.

Richard Tyrrell: Speedway, for me, was very often a release from the pressures and stress of everyday life. For two to two-and-a-half hours, I could submerge my thoughts into what I saw in front of me. If I wasn't standing on the terraces, I could almost be out there on the track with the riders! It has given me a lifetime of joy and pleasure.

Andy Wilkinson: The overall package which is still there – obviously the racing and the personalities, but also the general atmosphere at a meeting. There are no tracks within easy reach of my south-west London home, so I only get to a few meetings each season, but there still seem to be mostly friendly vibes amongst supporters of different clubs, unlike some other sports – well, football anyway – where 'fans' seem to be at it hammer and tongs from the start.

Tony Lethbridge: After 60 years of watching speedway, the sound of the bikes warming up still sets the adrenalin pumping, although I miss that wonderful smell of Castrol R and the straight-through exhausts. The racing is probably as good as ever it was and the bikes are much more reliable. But what really makes speedway special for me are the people. I was extremely fortunate that Peter Oakes and then Colin Hill gave me the opportunity to get involved on the inside, as a result of which I have made a great many friends among which are some of the truly greats.

Jeff Davies: I was spellbound by the sport from a very young age – the noise of the bikes, the smell of methanol and the fact that it's a family sport with riders being very approachable. I admire the riders tremendously for their skill in controlling the bike, the risks they take (for relatively little reward). Contrast them to footballers.

Richard Bott: Amazingly, I have never been interested in other forms of motorcycle racing and never even owned a motorbike, only a Lambretta scooter. But I still go to Belle Vue on a

Reducing the power of engines may be one way of saving costs and improving the standard of racing, but these four took the idea to the extreme when they came out on cycles to entertain the crowd at Exeter in 1982. Left to right: Mark Reeve, Bob Coles, starting marshal Les Sawyer, Keith Millard and Andy Campbell.

regular basis and loved this year's British Grand Prix in Cardiff. People knock speedway and say it is boring and that the first out of the first corner generally wins. Unfortunately, that is often the case. But when the racing is top drawer, like in the Grands Prix, or in a really competitive team match, it is the greatest spectator sport in the world.

Robert Rogers: The lights, the sounds, the smell, the fans and finally the riders. Most are unlike footballers and are quite happy to chat to the fans, an example being the PL Fours at Peterborough last year when the winning Berwick riders walked alongside the fence shaking hands with the fans.

Bryan Newbold: Speedway has been a massive part of my life for over 40 years and I still love it just as much today as I did when I first stood on the Blackbird Road terracing on April 1, 1969. I've witnessed success, disappointment and heartache. I've laughed, cried and been completely frustrated with the sport at various times, but at the end of the day I really can't imagine life without speedway.

Paul Jeffries: Once speedway is in your blood, you keep on coming. The sport generates so much emotion, and you always have to expect the unexpected. Sometimes off the track, even. What an incredible story it's been this last (2012-13) winter about that brave woman Laura Morgan who has taken over Workington when all seemed lost (and my heart, after losing Newport the year before, was bleeding for Comets fans). Let's finish on that high note. I don't suppose I'll ever get there but that story somehow symbolises what speedway is, what speedway means.

Doug Nicolson: A unique motorcycle sport where you can see the entire race; the smell of methanol; the theatre of it all, particularly under floodlights; the friends I've made at the speedway; the friendly atmosphere among home and visiting fans – something that, sadly, has declined over the years.

Mike Keir: Following Wimbledon from the age of nine, it's in the blood. I always tell people it isn't about the bikes (I actually don't like motorbikes) – if they raced on lawnmowers it would still have the same appeal. What matters is getting behind your team. And when Todd (Wiltshire) came along, it was about following one rider, rather than a team. Now there's no Wimbledon and Todd's racing days are over, I don't get to speedway so much, but I have some wonderful memories to look back on.

Todd Wiltshire soon after he burst on the scene at Wimbledon.

Rod Haynes: Speedway is a special sport to me simply for its raw competitiveness and because it's not nearly as corrupt as some would have us believe. A simple joust between many a hard rider. I get to very few meetings today for a variety of reasons, the main ones being too many dud foreigners stuffing our sides, many unwilling to compete without resorting to foul tactics, riders pulling out of races at the drop of a hat, promotions who should never have passed the 'fit and proper' test procedure, if indeed it even exists. And for those with families, the prohibitive cost of attending meetings, due in part to the exorbitant cost of equipment, which will eventually lead to the demise of the fully professional riders and teams here in Britain.

Dennis Lindo: From the first meeting I attended, everything seemed right about speedway – the atmosphere of the crowd, the smell, the whole presentation and, of course, the racing. Over the years, I've been to many big meetings, including the Cardiff GP, and I'm pleased to say that the crowds are usually very well behaved. I have a friend who is an avid Manchester United fan. I asked him which is the most important to him. Would he prefer to see a United win or a good, close match? He answered by saying a United win. I think the mentality of most speedway supporters is just the opposite, they would prefer to see a good, close meeting with tight racing no matter who wins.

Ian Martin: Throughout my life, I have had a love affair with speedway and I can't see me changing now. I do think the sport was better in the 'old days' and that there were more characters around then. I can honestly say I have no regrets following speedway, despite some of its more stupid rules (double points) that seem to have been designed just to put me off. I very much hope the sport I love will have a great future and that it will delight (and occasionally frustrate) people as much as it has me.

Stephen Quinsey: Speedway is the only sport that gives me butterflies in my stomach, and the riders are worth every penny they get. I have seen the sport develop over the years, but at the same time it is unmistakably unique, which is what makes speedway so special.

Harry Ward: The simplicity of four riders on a track for four laps. It's such a simple sport made so difficult by those organising it today. Back-to-basics speedway is a dream that one day I hope may materialise.

Andrew Edwards: It is a lifetime of wonderful sporting memories, meeting such wonderful people, going to so many, many tracks, both here and abroad, visiting America twice, regular jaunts to Holland for the brilliant ice racing, Scandinavia, going behind the Iron Curtain to see Ivan Mauger win a World Final there, Germany for the long-tracks. All wonderful memories.

Bob Radford: I still have the utmost respect for the riders and the risks they take, if not often the loyalty (or lack of it) from so many today. Also, I love the team aspect of speedway, which is not evident in other motorsports.

Bill Halliwell: Having followed speedway through the glory years of the 70s, the downturn in the 80s and 90s and now the era of the GP superstar, I think it's the riders themselves. They are still as easy to access as they have always been. There are no prima donnas, just guys with great skill and courage, producing a fantastic motorsport spectacle.

Ivan Mauger won two of his six world titles in Poland. Above: Action from the 1970 final at Wroclaw, where the mighty Kiwi is seen holding the inside line against Russia's Valeri Gordeev and Pole Henryk Glucklich.

David Hoggart: I'm very privileged to be in a position of trust within the sport. I don't take that responsibility lightly and always want to be in a position of making a valuable contribution. It was Graham Drury who brought me back into the sport from my career sabbatical and, of course, Neil Machin who has been so good to me at Sheffield over the last 15 years. Both have encouraged and pushed me into the position I hold today.

My time in the commercial world has taught me to work and do business with people I don't necessarily like and I've brought that ethos into my relationships in speedway. I can fall out with anybody between the start and end of a meeting but once that meeting is over, so is the grief that goes with it.

We all need each other and for me it is a pride point to be able to work with respect for and from the personalities in every league, the SCB, the referees and the BSPA team based at the Rugby offices.

Martin Rogers: Look, at its best, it's fast and furious, still fantastic fun and great entertainment. When I come back to the UK and see maybe two or three meetings, I'm reminded of the qualities that attracted me in the first place. It was a privilege and a huge life experience to be so involved for so long.

Steve Casey: Speedway IS special. We should never forget that. I watch a number of other motorsports (I hate football) and it drives me crazy when most of the racing takes place out of sight in another part of the circuit. Few other sports take place in full view of everyone with the action there for all to see. It is also diverse, with a variety of options such as true team racing for club or country, right up to World Championship level where the Grand Prix can be absolutely fearsome. I find it incredible that our sport isn't given the credit it deserves when compared to some others.

Mark Wilkinson: Speedway is special on so many levels. At a sensorial level, there's the heady aroma of the fuel, the sudden and violent explosion of coiled-up power into noise and action. There's the easily visible interaction between man and machine, an interaction that takes various forms during the course of a race including the sudden occurrence of unexpected events and the unpredictability of their outcome. The unbridled elation released by a last-heat 5-1 that pulls from the fire a match seemingly lost.

It also appeals to the intellect, because it is based around numbers and formulas – a real

Leicester legend Ray Wilson (right) before the reopening of Leicester in 2011 with owner/promoter David Hemsley (left) and co-promoter Alan Jones.

statto's dream, producing endless debate and speculation both during the actual meeting and at the team-building level. Last but not least, speedway provides a brilliant and dynamic blend of individual and team endeavours and causes, which are ever-changing from race to race and from meeting to meeting, season to season and country to country. It is unique in terms of the sheer quantity of its dimensions and variables.

Robert Wiles: Speedway (and grass-track) was a major part of my youth and I made some good friends during that time. It is, or was when I was involved, a friendly, family-orientated sport and many clubs were very well supported. I don't think it's like that now. I read a comment somewhere that speedway is the "sport of the 500s - 500cc bikes racing in front of 500 people". That's a sad indictment of the way the sport has gone.

Alan Jones: Having spent a fair proportion of my time working within the sport, either through journalism or nowadays as co-promoter of Leicester, I have met and kept in contact with so many people who I now count as friends. The togetherness of speedway fans is enduring and that is what makes the sport so special to me.

John Farr: Speedway will always be a special sport, whether the people are at the top (riders and officials) or not (the regular supporters). But most of all, the sheer spectacle of riders on motorcycles with no brakes going sideways is really something else. And having tried it myself over a period of five years (I got nowhere), I take my hat off to the lot of them.

Ken Burnett: The thrill of speed and the thought of a rider daring to manoeuvre, last heat deciders and a 46-44 win. Mainly the friendship of many fans, it is still a great family sport. And the thought that I was the first person to interview Chris Holder on these shores, well before he became 2012 World Champion, is something I'm proud of.

Pete Butler: A great speedway race is one of the most exciting, adrenalin-pumping sporting spectacles you can witness. Unfortunately, many UK tracks are not wide enough and the shape, determined by the stadiums they have to fit into, does not provide the quality product that could be possible. The present speedway bike has outgrown many of the British tracks. The best race tracks in this country are stand-alone venues where the track shape is not determined by the sports pitch in the centre or another track on the outside. The relatively poor rewards compared to other sports means that the riders still live in the real world and, generally speaking, remain approachable.

Gary Peterson was killed at Wolverhampton in 1975. Below: Wolves legend Sam Ermolenko.

Greg Unwin: It's special because of the atmosphere and anticipation of what lies ahead in the meeting. Your weekly fix with like-minded friends all makes for a great night out with the entertainment starting from the sound of the engines warming in the pits. Once you have the speedway bug, it may go dormant for a while if you lose your local track but, overall and generally speaking, your love of the sport never goes away.

Steve Wilks: I still go to Lakeside occasionally and enjoy the meetings. I also think there is some excellent coverage on Sky. What makes speedway so enjoyable is that there is always a family atmosphere at meetings, never any need to segregate spectators. You also have riders who generally give their all in what is a very dangerous sport. It amazes me that you see a rider have what looks like a very serious crash and two minutes later, they are out in the rerun.

John Vine: Having become hooked on speedway in 1969, I look forward to the middle of March each year and the thought of another season of speedway. There have been very sad occasions – for example, when Gary Peterson died racing at Wolverhampton in 1975 – and good times, when Wolves riders Ole Olsen and Sam Ermolenko became World Champions. After each meeting, the thrill of another meeting the following week has not gone away and long may it continue.

Ian Glover: The friendship between fans and riders alike of all tracks. It's a dangerous sport and the vast majority of fans appreciate this fact and stick together as one to applaud the skill and bravery shown on track.

Dave Ede: Speedway is special because of the racing, the bikes, the riders and the camaraderie of the fans. Even today, whether it is the atmosphere in Cardiff, or Poole for the fantastic balance of Darcy Ward and Chris Holder, I love to see good sportsmanship and friendly rivalry.

Richard Mason: I rode moto-cross, I'm a massive football, Moto GP, road-racing and F1 fan and have attended many high level sporting events, but I still feel a special bond with speedway that no other sport has. The smell, the sound, the atmosphere which seems to surround any event whatever the level . . . I think they'd call it the chemistry.

Kay Walker: Speedway was special to me because it was the kind of place where you felt safe. Everyone spoke to each other. There was friendly rivalry between home and away teams. As I have said before, we ran Christer Lofqvist's fan club and used to ring him in Sweden during the close season. I am still in touch with his daughter in Sweden. My cousin and I used to wait outside the dressing rooms and go to the pits after matches to ask for autographs. I collected loads, still have them and look at them often. Every signature is a treasured memory.

Christer Lofqvist with some of his adoring fans.

Paul Tadman: Speedway is a great sport and is extremely special to me.

Most riders will tell you it costs them money to race and the rewards are few and far between, except for the ultra-gifted elite. Some, of course, have paid dearly with life-changing injuries and unfortunately too many have lost their life to entertain us. In today's digital age, we have a far bigger speedway family than ever before and, like families, we don't always agree. But we are one family and long may it continue.

Paul Kerry: The colour, the noise, the smell, the speed. I like most motorsports but they are individual events and, although speedway has these, it is best as a team sport. Plus, you can see the whole race and the closeness of some races and finishes is fantastic. My son is a season ticket holder at Huddersfield Town FC and, like me, is rugby and soccer mad as well. But he often says the best spectator sport of the lot is speedway and simply cannot understand why every league match is not packed to the rafters.

Chris Gosling: Speedway is special to me because I still enjoy the spectacle, the excitement and the danger that still makes the hairs stand up on the back of my neck. I remain hopeful that SpeedwayGB, the BSPA, ACU and Speedway Control Bureau will one day find a way to better promote and organise the sport, which still has the potential to have a much higher profile.

Dick Partridge: I don't know! On the face of it, the sport is as daft as my mum always told me. A shed-load of work, expense and massive risk to see who gets around a squashed circle four times fastest. But, of course, it is more than that. Whilst, after all these years, I still cannot define it, I just know that despite its many massive shortcomings, it is a great sport, with mostly great people. Outside family, it is probably the single most influential factor in my life, and I thank and love it for that.

Carol Stock: Speedway is a big part of my life. Apart from the racing, which I love, I also love the excitement of going to a meeting, the anticipation of what will happen. I love the friendships you make. I have friends from around the country, including the United States, thanks to speedway.

Stephen Hawthorne: It is special for me because of the family involvement, both male and female members attend. Since Cradley's last season at Stoke, me and Dad have not had anything to attend together. However, the birth of Dudley Heathens has given us an interest again and younger members of our family now attend too. I'm 54-years-old and he is 76, so neither of us are spring chickens!

Richard Clark: You can't beat a great race, it remains one of the finest spectacles. From a personal point of view, the riders, in general, are a dream to deal with. I can't help sniggering at the self-importance, wholly unjustified in my humble opinion, displayed by so many

The all-conquering Dudley Heathens who dominated the National League in 2013.

monosyllabic Premier League footballers – will someone please point out to them that they ain't Bob Dylan so, therefore, add up to diddly-squat in the grand scheme of things. The down-to-earth attitude of most riders is truly something the sport can be proud of.

Robert Gray: Not sure how to answer this but it was special to me in that I could follow my own team amongst the elite at that time. All supporters were knowledgeable and friendly. Sometimes, Hull, Belle Vue and Cradley fans got a bit hot under the collar but, on the whole, it was just good banter, particularly if we won!

I miss those days terribly, speedway nights were magical. I don't think today's sport has the same passion, or was I just fortunate to be young at the time when speedway was at a golden age?

Adrian Stockwell: It's the sheer assault on the senses. From the simple things like the satisfying 'plop' of the *Speedway Star* on the doormat on the morning of race-day; the comforting feel of hallowed accessories like Dad-made programme holder and 'Ronnie Moore' banner and precious badge-laden scarf; the heady aroma of burning methanol, hamburgers, onions, shale dust and cigarette smoke; the reverential marking of programmes with the mysterious lexicon of speedway - EF, RR, DNF, F, EXC/T, EXC/F, EXC/2; the strains of *Blaze Away* heralding the arrival of the riders at Wimbledon; raucous crowds cheering local heroes and booing pantomime villains; the unique thrill of the moment just before the tapes fly up; the deafening roar and speed of powerful machines; marvelling at the sight of leather-clad warriors dicing with death; spectacular

Another glory night for Ole Olsen at Coventry – this time after heading home Bees team-mate Alan Molyneux and Swindon's Jan Andersson in the 1978 Midland Riders' Championship.

crashes and winners pulling victory wheelies at the chequered flag.

Stephen Williams: What made speedway special to me between 1975 and 1983 was the happy memories of making the journeys, whilst watching out for like-minded people with their car stickers on show. Then there was the excitement of the meeting itself and the fish and chip supper from a chippy in Stourbridge on the way home to Stourport-on-Severn on a Saturday night, especially if Ole Olsen had been riding and had done us proud.

Richard Parsons: I still go to speedway, though not as much nowadays, but I do go to Cardiff every year and the odd meeting at Lakeside and Rye House. I love speedway because it has everything: you can hit the highest of highs when you win and nothing beats winning the league, but you hit the lowest of lows when one of your heroes is injured, or even worse.

Keith Wiggins: The basic product of four guys all trying to win a race in a confined space is great entertainment. I cannot put it into words but I'm always happy at a speedway meeting. The friendly welcome at tracks up and down the country and the races are superb, no matter how the promoters try to spoil things.

Rob Scrutton: After 40 odd years, speedway has become a big part of my life and I have followed my club, Ipswich, through the good years and those not quite so good. Win or lose, as long as I've seen some good racing, I'm reasonably happy but I also like to see them win of course. I'm pleased that I have followed one of my father's interests and that my daughter has similarly followed one of mine. I'm also lucky that my team are still going, whereas so many other fans no longer have that privilege.

Peter Lush: The skill and courage involved. Unlike some other forms of motorsport, the riders are paramount, not the machines. And for courage, that incident at Poole in the play-off final a couple of years ago, when Chris Harris was run over, brushed himself down, and went out for the rerun, was incredible. So different from some sports where players collapse at the slightest knock. I think, generally, the riders respect each other as well.

I do find there is a big difference between watching on television, which is what I mainly do now, and being there live. I went to the Pairs meeting at Somerset in 2013 and standing 15 yards from the track, seeing the riders within inches of each other at high speed and dodging occasional bits of shale coming off the track, was terrific. But on the other hand, on television, I learn a lot about the tactics from the commentators.

Alan Thompsett: It's been a part of my life every day since 1976. Silly little things like 'leaning into a bend' and 'broad-siding' when going round a curve – as a passenger in a car; the beauty of programme covers and race-jacket designs; re-staging meetings with Britains Model Speedway Riders, then on push bikes down the park or in the street; a session at Olle Nygren's training school; a perfectly completed, error-free racecard.

Gary Moore: Because it's so different and in the minority. I was always proud of the fact that when I was at primary and secondary school, I was the only speedway fan I knew of and it was like my little secret.

Arnie Gibbons: Let's try the build-up of excitement as a meeting climaxes in a last heat decider, the sudden rush of adrenalin as your favourite executes a stylish passing manoeuvre, the noise and the smell on entering the stadium, reminiscing about the days when stadiums were packed, journeying to new tracks in distant places, and gossiping with friends old and new on the terraces about the latest happenings in our beloved sport.

Paul Rickett: Speedway is one big happy family. It's a bit like being in a sporting Freemasons – you make friends for life and have a good old moan and groan with them every week. On the

Fans could 'replay' a meeting using Britains' model riders.

other side of the safety fence, having flirted with what it takes to ride a bike (I was rubbish), I still look at the four riders hurtling around and marvel at what they do. Speedway riders are the bravest, most bonkers, sportsmen on the planet. I've told the wife that my ashes are going on the first turn and I mean it . . .

Andy Povey: The sport is unique, albeit strange at times, but despite all its problems, it's still a brilliant product. Four men risking their lives by throwing themselves around an oval track. Riders and management are generally approachable, which makes it attractive to kids. You would never get that in football. The social side in speedway has always been good.

England team manager John Berry with Kenny Carter and Kelvin Tatum in 1985. Many regarded former Ipswich boss JB as the best choice to spearhead a new independent body to run domestic speedway in Britain.

Stephen Roberts: The fans. You could mingle with people of all ages, irrespective of what team they supported. I used to stand on the third bend at Cowley and got to know everyone. I was never an advocate for getting a meeting over with quickly because we liked to discuss the sport and the meeting in general. I no longer go to speedway, having moved away from Oxford and have lost interest due to the present state of the sport and lack of leadership from the top. How we could have done with John Berry at the helm.

Paul Minns: The noise as that first bike fires up when they begin warming up the bikes in the pits. A trip to the track shop for the essential programme, a necessity for any speedway fan. The anticipation as the parade time nears, the bikes being wheeled out to the centre green awaiting their riders. The air horns of the supporters as the home team are introduced, followed by the boos that greet the villain of the visiting team. Tension at the start as the riders slowly settle, line up and wait for the tapes to rise. Engines reach a crescendo, the green light is on and they're away. Four riders race vying for the best line, they throw their machines into the first bend. They hang off their machines as they round the bend, then flat out down the back straight. From your position, you can see all the action right from the start, the jousting over the four laps right through to the last, desperate corner and dive as the rider tries to catch the one in front. Fourteen more heats of elbows flying, handfuls of throttle and riders delicately balanced, racing wheel-to-wheel. A close finish and it's off home discussing the incidents and action as you go. Same time, next week!

Debbie Howland: I have friends in speedway from 34 years ago to some I met this year at Cardiff. Everywhere you go, people talk to you. That doesn't happen in the world these days. It doesn't matter who you support, we're all speedway people, speedway friends.

Rob Glover: You get regular, local, top class motorsport, with top quality riders, and where you can speak to them in person. Speedway has great atmosphere with the noise of the bikes and supporters.

John Murphy: For the past 40 years, speedway really has been 'family'. I met my future wife there and many friends who keep in touch, although some are far away. The social networking revolution has been wonderful to keep speedway alive and kicking. The sport has always had ups and downs and this will never change. The challenge is keeping the sport going, but there is so much potential. With much nurturing, it will survive. I have been optimistic for the past 40 years and see no reason to change.

Clive Read: Having stopped going to speedway for the best part of 20 years, I have recently started going again. Speedway is special in that it pits riders against each other in an intense setting – going sideways, without brakes, accelerating to 70mph quicker than any other sporting machine, wheel against wheel, rider against rider, where the best ones have such dexterity and

Always spectacular and great to watch, that's Shawn Moran.

control they can turn on a sixpence and change the course of a race in a matter of seconds. Kelly and Shawn Moran had that in abundance, and plenty of others have inherited their mantle, including Emil Sayfutdinov, Darcy Ward and Tai Woffinden. Few other sports can match the excitement of seeing top riders doing battle in such a way.

Mark Sawbridge: A friend of mine attended speedway for the first time and it happened to be the night that the annual St John's Ambulance collection was being made. At the interval, the riders came into the crowd to collect the money from the fans. My friend was astonished: "Imagine Wayne Rooney doing this at half-time at Old Trafford."

In many ways, this hit the nail on the head for me as to why speedway is special. There is a bond between the riders and fans that still holds the sport together. In one of his books, Jeff Scott makes the point that speedway stadiums are among the last places that you can go to be yourself. At football matches, there is pressure to be one of the 'pack'. Have you ever tried applauding an opposing player?

In a speedway stadium, no-one cares too much what you look like, how old you are, whether you are male or female, what team you support and so on. I've often been fascinated by the demographics of a speedway meeting, as its crowd transcends any defined boundaries concerning gender, age and so on. There have been attempts to move speedway towards the young, trendy mob so beloved of marketing folk. These have all ended in failure and we are much the better for it.

Gary Miles: Speedway has always been part of my life. For all my 40-plus years, I've been a supporter, a marshal, a track grader, a pusher, a mechanic and a very amateur rider on an old Weslake at Lydd and at Iwade. Now my eight-year-old son has got the bug and he is the fourth generation of my family (my granddad, my dad, myself and my son) to throw his leg over a speedway bike. It shows that speedway people are born, they're not made!

Martin Smith: I'm still full of admiration for the riders who continue to thrill and entertain us with their daring deeds but it is team racing that makes speedway special for me. Team history, iconic race-jackets, a legacy of wonderful riders and the ever-hopeful pursuit of new and further honours. Team racing is at the very core of the magic of speedway.

Kevin Ashcroft: Speedway is like an addiction, with the smell of the bikes and the intensity of the racing. In the winter months, you miss it and can't wait for March when the season starts again. It's special for many reasons, including the family atmosphere where fans from all clubs and countries mix together.

Craig Saul: From a personal perspective, it's a combination of things.

Its uniqueness as a team motorcycle sport. The friendliness of the crowd. Speedway is still a true family sport and, while bigger alternatives like football are now claiming to be family-friendly, they are still chasing speedway's shadows in that regard. The action. And, yes, the

Chris Harris has been one of the most exciting riders to watch in recent years.

build-up to a race is just as important as the 60 seconds that follow. The explosiveness of excitement and emotion that it can still generate. Anyone who was at Cardiff for Chris Harris' last bend against Greg Hancock will appreciate that, on its day, speedway can still be the very best sport in the world.

Chris Rowsell: It's a special evening (much better under lights) and the excitement that it can engender is greater than other sports. You find in a sport such as football, it tends to be partisan and people don't enjoy watching other teams anywhere near as much as watching their own, but the speedway supporter, although just as partisan about following their own team, gets just as much pleasure watching any form of racing, be it other teams racing, individual events or international meetings. Many people are quick to write off speedway as boring – first out the gate wins and all that – but we have to educate them to 'take a mate' or get them to watch some speedway with you on the TV, so that you can explain the finer points. If we do not, then, sadly, the way things are going, speedway will struggle to survive and it is too good a sport for that to happen.

Andrew Gallon: It used to be – not so much now – a great all-round experience: the spectacle of the racing (I've never taken a first-timer who wasn't impressed), the friendliness of the spectators, the openness of the riders (even to journalists) and, of course, the noise and the smell. Under lights, early or late in the season, it's compelling drama. A sport without pretensions but with plenty to recommend it.

Steve Ridgway: It was a milestone, if you like, of 'growing up', something we could relate to, that gave each week a purpose, that could feed youthful enthusiasm at a time before other, more pressing, matters took over. I suppose that smell, that atmosphere, all those things were distinctive, hypnotic and addictive at a time when we were so much more responsive to stimuli like that, living as we did in a world that wasn't governed by 24-hour TV, computers and associated gadgetry. But time's moved on, hasn't it.

Rob Peasley: It's the fact that everyone can go a meeting and stand (or sit, if they insist) wherever they like. No segregation, with both sets of fans on the terraces next to each other. There's nothing more fun when engaging in a bit of banter with the supporters from the other side. Plus, there's the fact the riders and the fans are not mutually exclusive to each other. They actually mix and I don't think that happens in many professional sports. A prime example was Oxford junior Phil Roberts, who crashed and broke his back at Cowley in 1989. The following year, my brother was knocked down by a car and broke both his legs. While he was stuck at home, Phil visited us to cheer up my brother. I think that's pretty unique to speedway.

Richard Simmons: What makes speedway so special is that you can mingle with the riders. They always have time for the fans and you can talk to them as normal people, unlike overpaid footballers. Speedway riders earn their money because if they don't race, they don't earn. Footballers take note! I have made many friends through speedway, met some fantastic riders, and can also say I am friends with an Ipswich legend in Mark Loram, who came to my wedding reception in 2006. That turned a few heads, I can tell you!

Nick Nicklin: With two evenly-matched opponents on a well-prepared track, speedway can be the most exciting and exhilarating sport,

Mark Loram turned heads as a surprise wedding guest.

generating a terrific atmosphere. In my mind, I can easily transport myself back to the World Final of 1981 or, more recently, the British Grand Prix of 2007, and still feel the excitement and tension generated by those great occasions and the action and drama unfolding on track.

Despite the tension and highly charged atmosphere, there was, and still is, never any trouble at a speedway meeting and it has a deserved reputation of being a safe family sport.

Martin Neal: At its best, it's such an exhilarating sport to watch. You're right up close to the action and it takes something pretty out of the ordinary to do what those guys do. There have been times when, for one reason or another, I haven't been a regular speedway watcher but I've never lost touch and always come back.

Mark Simms: That 60-second burst of pure excitement and the high you feel when the result goes your way, especially if done in spectacular fashion, as was often the case with some of the great Aces over the years. I'd say I'm addicted as I'm always looking to relive that feeling again every time a race starts.

Dean Felton: Simply, it's just my life. I hate to see the way it's run these days. Sometimes, I wish I could turn my back on the sport like many have done but I can't.

David Golley: Work means I missed far too much of the 2013 season, but I still follow the sport on a daily basis, hope that Mildenhall keep winning and still enjoy the magic of the noise, the thrills and spills and the excitement – or is it madness? – of four guys racing in an enclosed space at high speed with no brakes. Add the passion of the fans and there really isn't another sport like it.

Derek Barclay: Speedway is much more than 'motorsport' – it's really a gladiatorial sport, man and machine together against man and machine. At its stripped down best, it's about pure skill and bravery and none of that has been lost. It's been a great year (2013) at Central Park, Kent as we've seen new people come to the sport and get hooked, just like I got hooked at Canterbury over 40 years earlier. That's why speedway is so special.

Graham Goodwin: Speedway is the perfect sport in that it has the adrenaline-fuelled element of pure competitive racing, but also has all the attractions of a team sport, like football

Fans gathered on the first bend at Central Park, Sittingbourne, where Kent Kings became the newest track to open on May 6, 2013

or rugby, where you are fiercely loyal to your club. Yet we don't suffer with any kind of hooliganism. Fans of rival teams can still mingle together even if they are fanatically supporting different riders or teams.

Chris Young: It's man and machine, skill and courage. It can love you (winning in the last heat) and it can break your heart (losing in the last heat) but can make me smile like no other sport. I watch a football match and once it's finished, I never watch it again, yet when I watch a speedway meeting, I will watch again and again, poring over it to see what riders do in certain situations, how they adapt to the track.

Glenn Collins: Speedway has provided me with so many happy memories of meetings I went to and all the time I got to spend with my dad, who died when I was 13. It's a unique sport in the sense that people who aren't fans of the two teams racing will still go along and watch because they love the sport. And fans of rival teams all get along and have a chat. There is never any real malice between people, unlike fans of other sports.

Chris Camp: The Groveway is now a housing development and all traces of the original Milton Keynes track and stadium are long gone. However, if you listen hard enough, you can still hear the roar of the engines as they race from the start heading into turn one and still hear the cheers of the crowd hailing another 5-1, gained the hard way. Although the sights and sounds are now lost to us in MK, the memories remain and thankfully so do a number of the friendships. Friendships forged in the cauldron of the cut and thrust of a sport which, at its best, is just that. The best.

Alan Robertson: You may ask how someone can just stop attending speedway when it had filled up so much time? I suppose my feelings began to erode about 10 years ago. Gradually I began no longer enjoying my nights on the terraces at Belle Vue but remained a regular up until about six years ago.

For a period of several years I attended speedway simply out of routine. I suppose there are a variety of reasons, but I simply wasn't enjoying standing on the terraces – it was becoming a chore. I still watch whenever it's on television but haven't been to a live meeting since 2006.

At home you don't have to sit through 10-15 minutes before the next race, not if you have recorded it for later viewing. You can scoot through the two hours by whizzing through the needless gaps and just concentrate on the racing.

Matches became irritatingly predictable when they abolished the old tac-sub rule. At least, before that, if the racing was a little off, supporters had the chance at being a terrace team manager between heats, strategically trying to pre-empt the legit manager's move. We've all done it.

The Golden Double, its replacement, I will never take seriously. It should be confined to less imperative events, perhaps testimonials or winter indoor meetings.

I was growing disillusioned with riders racing for so many different clubs throughout Europe. It was surely having an affect on their loyalty to my team. How far up the list of priorities were the globetrotters putting Belle Vue?

My formative years spoilt me. Men were committed to the one team for more than a season and built an identity with that club, which is practically unheard of nowadays.

Riders today are more like agency workers and appear to accept offers depending on priorities. It is a waste of time even trying to build up some sort of kinship because this time next year, my money's on them being elsewhere.

Having written articles in the Belle Vue programme from 1990 right until my last season, 2006, very rarely did I pay to attend a meeting at Kirkmanshulme Lane. It cost me nothing – zilch, free of charge. The realism, I suppose, which is a slur on current day league racing, its rules and regulations, is despite this, I no longer wanted to attend.

It was in stark contrast to my youth, when I scrubbed a car to warrant my place in the stands.

Early Knights: Cliff Anderson is the home rider battling with Red Star Prague duo Jiri Stancl (1) and Milan Spinka (2) in one of the first meetings staged at The Groveway after Milton Keynes opened there in 1978.

Now interest had gone. I didn't even want to attend despite not having to pay to get in.

Unlike my youth, when close seasons were an eternity, now (and I'm not exaggerating) I was sick in the stomach when March arrived. For a couple of years I was going to speedway purely out of habit, becoming gradually disillusioned, a drip-drip loss of appetite that grew into disrepair. I didn't want to go anymore and wasn't strong enough to make that choice. It had been my life, and even now I won't walk away completely.

The play-offs, I tend to agree, have introduced a grand climax to the season. But they come at the expense of the season-long league programme preceding them. It encourages teams to fine-tune their line-ups as the season progresses, as long as sufficient time is left to make the play-off assault.

There are too many opportunities for teams to drop points and still make it into the last four. The whole league programme is just a series of qualifying matches. Although there may be bumper crowds at the play-offs, especially the final, at what cost is that to the league programme? For example, top against second in the league during June isn't as attractive as it is in the play-offs. Whereas the Play-Off Final and its aggregate method devalued the KO Cup, I do also feel they have shaved a fraction of the crowd from the round-robin fixtures which precede them.

Reading were chasing Elite League glory when they arrived in Manchester for a mid-September match in 2006. They needed just the aggregate bonus point to clinch top spot in the table. But it was irrelevant to them. When the Bulldogs unloaded their machines that night,

Lee Richardson in action for Lakeside Hammers. His death following a crash in Wroclaw, Poland on May 13, 2012 shook speedway.

their main intention was steering as far away as possible from the aggregate bonus point, giving them second place in the table . . . and an easier semi-final passage. I had seen stunts like this before – Bruce Penhall, 1982 Overseas Final, for one. But the latest one came when I was at the end of my tether with the sport. Reading had a cosmopolitan and attractive line-up, and I had honestly looked forward to a keenly-fought encounter, hopefully good speedway with the best side winning.

Events of that night left a lousy taste. Reading folded like a cheap Christmas card. I couldn't be bothered anymore, standing for hours on often-chilly terraces when stunts like that were happening.

Perhaps I'm wrong and maybe my cynicism really does call for medical attention, but the damage of that night is irreparable. Reading – and who could blame them? – had no stomach for the fight. The lackadaisical attitude was all too evident from the off. Their intentions reeked. Imagine how others felt, people who paid good money. I wasn't one of them but I was still disappointed. Speedway had turned into something resembling professional wrestling.

It was the final straw. My days on the terraces were nearing a conclusion.

You could say, with hindsight, justice was done in the Play-Off Final weeks later, when the Bulldogs were robbed against Peterborough, who played perfectly the Golden Double rule and overhauled Reading's lead at the death. Reading were much the better team over two legs but, unlike the Belle Vue fiasco, their mistake this time was that they were deadly serious about amassing as many points as possible . . . and it rebounded on them.

Peterborough sufficiently went enough behind to play a couple of Golden Doubles and overhaul Reading right at the death of the second leg. Great TV, even for the neutral, but for me it was a cheap method of providing some for-the-moment thrill-factor and wasn't in the best interests of the sport's credibility.

The World Cup a few years ago, when Crump and Pedersen slowed going over the line so that both Australia and Denmark could make a tactical move, I really thought the sport's authorities would finally ditch Golden Double and Jokers. But what do I know? There were a

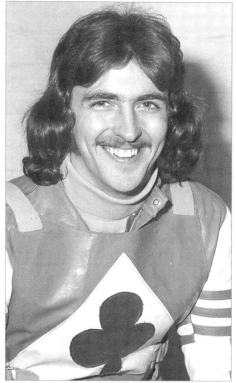

Paul Tyrer at Belle Vue in 1974.

few instances of play-acting in the 2013 World Cup, and moves like this make me question just what races are or aren't real.

I'm regularly questioned on the Internet about why I continue to post on speedway forums, especially as my words for modern-day speedway aren't always positive. I haven't an answer; just that speedway isn't allowing me to drift right now. Not fully away, at least. I'm still there, in front of the TV, whether for the weekly live match on Sky or for the GPs. You can't cut off completely, and at least the GPs provide some decent, honest racing.

My hoard of speedway memorabilia has long gone, bit by bit, which would have been unthinkable five years ago. Bizarrely as this may sound, I continue to purchase memorabilia on one of the Internet auction sites and recently added Ivan Mauger's 1977 World Pairs racejacket to the collection. I maintain getting *Speedway Star* every week, more to continue my collection (I have every copy from 1952) than anything else, but I never read one. Like an old pop record, or a scent of perfume from the past, there is something evocative about flicking through an old speedway publication. I have many DVDs of old speedway – the golden days, my era, of the 70s and 80s. I still adore the old stuff.

I suppose, in a way, speedway to me nowadays is like my taste in music – I preferred it from the 70s and 80s compared to now, but every now and again there's a current tune I may enjoy.

Witnessing Peter Collins at his peak, taking a keen interest in another Belle Vue man, Paul Tyrer, who I took to out of sympathy towards the end of my first season after Belle Vue fans began going hard on him. Indeed, a memorable moment I'll carry to the grave is actually meeting Tyrer – a few times, about six years ago – and enjoyed a glass or two of beer in his company. I acquired his race jackets, and, unlike most of my collection, they're going nowhere.

Speedway helped fashion me during my time watching it. I offered full support to my heroes and I was happy with the effort they gave back. It can also whack you in the face unexpectedly – discovering riders often pay the ultimate price for their heroics.

My first experience of a speedway death was a genuine shock, coming hours before the 1975 BLRC when I caught the headline in the morning paper about a speedway fatality. It was Gary Peterson, Wolverhampton's New Zealand rider. The news sent a spooky feeling through my young bones. It was a chilling moment I can vividly remember.

Weeks before I had used an old cover of *Speedway Star* with Gary's picture on it to act as a dust-jacket on one particular school exercise book. Opening my briefcase and pulling out the book the following Monday was weird. I couldn't grasp he was no longer with us.

The loss of Lee Richardson affected me similarly on what should have been a truly memorable day of Manchester City winning the title. Now I'll remember it with contrasting emotions having heard of his death only hours later.

You have to take the rough with the smooth. Nobody can deny me my speedway memories, good or bad. Last heat 5-1s by Wilkinson and Morton at Leicester and Hackney in 1976 to snatch 40-38 Belle Vue wins; grabbing the title at Wolves with the last kick of '93; taking my first overseas trip for the 1980 World Final in Sweden.

Speedway never gets any better than your initial years. For me, my diet as a teenager was Sheffield (Thursday), Ellesmere Port (Friday) and Belle Vue (Saturday). That was over 30 years ago, 1980 seeing a six-month diet and proving my most prolific year for attending matches, just a few short of the 100 mark. I was speedway-bloated in the end!

The sport was a major part of my life, and I wouldn't exchange part of it. The occasions I have the need to grab a box of old *Speedway Stars* out from under the stairs, the time-stained issues from the 70s, 80s and even 90s, it dawns on me why I loved the sport. The feelings are still there, if only buried in a mist of memories.

I suppose, while they are, I can't cut completely away from speedway. Nor do I want to, if I'm honest.

CONTRIBUTORS

We wish to thank the following people who responded to our questionnaire.
There simply isn't enough space to include every single response submitted
by each contributor (which would have led to repetition in many cases)
but you all played your part in this book.

Paul Ackroyd
Tim Allan
Eddie Andrews
Kevin Ashcroft
Dave Banks
Derek Barclay
Tony Barnard
Keith Barraclough
John Baxter
Chris Beard
David Beresford
Mick Bird
Roy Blanchflower
Chris Birtles
Mrs Pamela Birtles
Richard Bott
David Brassington
Mick Brown
John Brownhill
Brian Burford
Mrs Lucy Burton
Ken Burnett
Pete Butler
Ron Byford
Chris Camp
Ken Carpenter
Steve Casey
Derek Chalmers
John Chaplin
Oliver Chapman
Phil Chard
Richard Clark
Roly Clarke
Roy Crissford
Glenn Collins
Jez Coupland
John Cross
Philip Dalling
John Davidson
Jeff Davies
James Easter
Dave Ede
Andrew Edwards
Tony Emmott
Kevin Fall
John Farr
Dean Felton
Chris Fenn
Karl Fiala

Nicholas Foote
Vitek Formanek
Andrew Gallon
Eddie Garvey
Colin Gear
Arnie Gibbons
Richard Gilson
Ian Glover
Rob Glover
David Golley
Bill Goodswen
Graham Goodwin
Paul Goodwin
David Gordon
Chris Gosling
Robert Gray
Robert Griffin
Ray Griffiths
Bill Halliwell
Bert Harkins
Stanley Harris
Stephen Hawthorne
Rod Haynes
Terry Heath
Paul Hiscock
Dexter Hockley
David Hoggart
Michael Hook
Dennis Hoppe
Eric Howard
Debbie Howland
Garry Hutson
John Hyam
Clive Inwood
Martin Jackson
Peter Jackson
Malcolm Jealous
Paul Jeffries
Edward Jinkerson
Stephen Jinkerson
Alan Johns
Jenna Johnston
Steve Johnston
Alan Jones
Steve Jones
Mike Keir
Paul Kerry
Mike King
Richard Lambert

H. Langham
Matthew Lawrence
Gordon Lea
Tony Lethbridge
Dennis Lindo
Bert Loader
Brian Longman
David Latham
Wally Loak
Alex Mackenzie
Eric Marchment
Tracy Marrows
Ian Martin
Richard Mason
Michael Mayo
Rob McColl
Gary Miles
Gary Moore
Howard Murphy
John Murphy
Martin Neal
Bryan Newbold
Nick Nicklin
Doug Nicolson
Glen Norton
Peter Oakes
Richard Parsons
Dick Partridge
Rob Peasley
Mrs Paula Peirce
John Perry
John Pharaoh
Maurice Plowright
Andy Povey
Stephen Quinsey
Bob Radford
Cedric Read
Clive Read
Phil Rice
Paul Rickett
Steve Ridgway
Mark Simms
Stephen Roberts
Alan Robertson
Dave Robinson
Garry Robinson
Cecil Rockey
Martin Rogers
Robert Rogers

Pete Rout
Chris Rowsell
Malcolm Salter
Craig Saul
Mark Sawbridge
Barry Scowen
Rob Scrutton
Glynn Shailes
Ian Shelton
Andrew Skeels
John Skinner
Barry Simmonds
Richard Simmons
Martin Smith
Steve Smith
John Somerville
Dave Stallworthy
Carol Stock
Adrian Stockwell
Paul Tadman
Ken Taylor
Tim Templeton
Geoff Theobald
Alan Thompsett
Geoff Tillotson
Mike Turner
Richard Tyrrell
Greg Unwin
John Vine
David Walker
Kay Walker
Keith Walker
Ray Walters
Harry Ward
Paul Watson
Tony Webb
Christian Weber
Keith Wiggins
Robert Wiles
Andy Wilkinson
Mark Wilkinson
Steve Wilkes
Steve Wilks
Stephen Williams
Mrs Julia Wilson
Ken Wrench
Doug Wyer
Chris Young

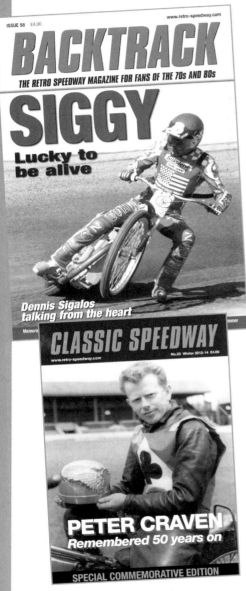

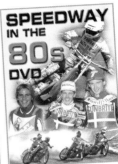
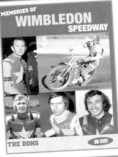
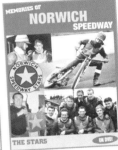